# Sight Unseen

# Sight Unseen

## Beckett, Pinter, Stoppard, and Other Contemporary Dramatists on Radio

### Elissa S. Guralnick

Ohio University Press • Athens

Ohio University Press, Athens, Ohio 45701
© 1996 by Elissa S. Guralnick
Printed in the United States of America
All rights reserved

Ohio University Press books are printed on acid-free paper

01 00 99 98 97 96 5 4 3 2 1

Library of Congress Cataloging-in-Publication Data
Guralnick, Elissa S.
Sight Unseen : Beckett, Pinter, Stoppard, and other contemporary
dramatists on radio / Elissa S. Guralnick
p. cm.
Includes bibliographical references and index.
ISBN 0-8214-1128-4 (alk. paper)
1. Radio plays, English—History and criticism. 2. English drama—
20th century—History and criticism. I. Title.
PN1991.65.G87 1995
822'.02209—dc20 95-23093
CIP

DESIGNED BY LAURY A. EGAN

IN MEMORY OF MY MOTHER

*Eva Bogdnoff Schagrin*

(1911–1994)

# Contents

# Preface

THE DISTINGUISHING FEATURE of plays conceived for radio, that we do not see them, is true not only literally, but also metaphorically. Unlikely to be noticed in reviews or in scholarship, even less likely to be published—at least post-1950 (earlier is different); and at least in English-speaking countries (Germany is different)—radio plays ghost away on the airwaves, leaving behind not a trace of their existence.

To be sure, there are exceptions. But they only prove the rule. When a play produced in Britain on BBC Radio wins, for example, a Giles Cooper Award, it is assured of publication in the Methuen/BBC series Best Radio Plays of the year. Some five or six plays are thus annually honored, from the five or six *hundred* that the BBC broadcasts. The rest, overwhelmingly, never see their way to print—an astonishing decay rate, given that stage plays, by contrast, are nearly always published once professionally produced. As for playwrights with major reputations in the theater, if they choose to write for radio, as many of them do, newspapers carry advance notice of the broadcasts; reviews, however brief, are sure to follow; and the playwrights' standard publishers bring out the scripts. Usually, however, the volumes sell poorly, so that first printings often turn out to be the last. Thus it happens that, no matter their author or publisher, radio plays tend to languish in libraries, principally gathering dust. Aside from the occasional radio enthusiast, nobody reads them. Not even most scholars. Only those who embark on a full-scale assessment of a playwright's whole career will address the plays for radio, and then just in passing, from a sense of obligation toward the so-called minor work. In effect, there is one way and one way alone for radio plays to attain a high profile: they must transfer to the stage, a move that legitimates them, but at the cost of estranging them from their medium of origin. In going theatrical, such plays lose their past, to be reborn through revision as bona fide stage plays. As radio plays, they remain sight unseen.

Now regarded optimistically, this state of affairs may be said to impose on the chaos of literature the salutary rigors of natural selection. By this argument radio, where production costs are low, becomes a spawning ground for plays that for various reasons—say, an untried writer, or a controversial theme, or an experimental format—would not be otherwise produced. Any plays that show promise proceed to a theater, while those that disappoint disappear, all unnoticed. Survival, then, naturally falls to the fittest. Or so we may choose to believe, if we wish. But believing commits us to some curious assumptions. First, that the blindness inherent in radio has no aesthetic value, and further no import, with the consequence that any play written for the medium can move to a stage without suffering loss. Second, that radio plays of distinction are so sure of discovery by theater producers that those left behind can be safely ignored.

Well, possibly. Yet if similar assumptions were applied to chamber music in relation to symphonies, howls of derision would be the response. Might not radio plays, at least some proportion of them, be akin to chamber music in achieving, at their best, a profound expressivity, not *despite* limitations in scale, but *because* of them? There is circumstantial evidence suggesting it is so. Consider, for example, the high-profile playwrights alluded to above—Harold Pinter, Tom Stoppard, Caryl Churchill, David Mamet, to name but a few—who choose on occasion to write for the radio, when they likely could command a stage at will. Their choice of an ostensibly inferior medium would appear to bespeak their impression that radio offers unique opportunities. In this vein, it bears mention that Beckett himself wrote radio plays at the height of his fame and, even more telling, refused to give permission for any of these plays to be performed on a stage. This, although one of them—namely, *All That Fall*, that rarest of rarities, a radio play that has entered the canon—is more visually seductive than most of his stage plays. What is it that Beckett found attractive in radio? What purposes has radio fulfilled for other playwrights? And can plays that are specially crafted for the medium be intrinsically superb, the equal in merit of plays for the theater? It was largely in pursuit of answers to such questions that this book was conceived; and from the nature of the inquiry, the manuscript took shape.

Accordingly, *Sight Unseen* offers neither a history of radio drama nor a broadly inclusive survey of its highlights. Rather the book is intended to complement those histories and surveys that already exist, most of them British—notably, Ian Rodger's *Radio Drama*, Kate Whitehead's *The Third Programme*, John Drakakis's *British Radio Drama*, and Peter Lewis's *Radio Drama*. Such overviews implicitly extend an invitation to scholars and critics to critique a genre's major texts and assess their authenticity as literature. In my own scale of values, authenticity arises when a literary work sustains and rewards explication. So it is, in what follows, that I engage in close reading of radio plays that are widely admired among the cognoscenti, but that yet are little known (unless in their stage versions) among the general community of readers and scholars. If my selections are all of them contemporary, it is so by design: I am seeking to dispel the misguided idea, prevalent especially in the United

States, that radio drama is outdated, obsolete. Similarly, if most of the selections are by prominent playwrights identified as highbrow, that too is by design: I am seeking to emphasize that radio drama is not déclassé, though the medium is prominent in popular culture. What alone reflects chance are the playwrights' nationalities: all are British except one (Arthur Kopit is American)—or two, if Beckett counts as Continental. The British bias, as I see it, is virtually inevitable, given the preeminence of BBC Radio in the production of English-language radio plays. But whether inevitable or eccentric, the bias does not mean that I am seeking to discover what is British in the character of radio drama. On the contrary, I am seeking to disclose what is general: namely, the genre's expressive potential, both through and beyond its medium of broadcast.

Why beyond, when the book owes its being to radio? Because the principal sources of power in drama, irrespective of venue, are what a play says, in itself, in its script, and how well the statement is crafted. Only where dialogue arrests our attention are we likely to care how its medium of broadcast contributes to its message. Moreover, only where the writer's art commands our respect are we likely to think of a play as significant. For these reasons, in the chapters that follow I have analyzed the plays for whatever is significant, not just what is radiophonic. As for particular productions, I have cited them but rarely and have made little mention of so-called production values—sound effects, background music, electronic filters for noises and voices, and the like. In adopting this approach, I hazard the objection that radio plays must be heard to be known, a scruple true enough for plays that exploit the sound of language in defiance of semantics. Conceived as a species of electronic music, in which phonemes take the place of notes, such drama can neither be written nor scored: it exists, by definition, solely in performance. Yet in this, it is anomalous. For with radio as with theater, the vast majority of plays fare quite comfortably in print, taking meaning first and foremost from their dialogue. And wherever words are paramount, they constitute the crux to which appraisals must appeal. The BBC itself concedes as much in its method of selecting Giles Cooper Award winners for the best radio plays of the year. As indicated annually in every published volume of these plays since the award's inception in 1978: "Selection was made on the strength of the script rather than of the production, since it was felt that the awards were primarily for writing and that production could unduly enhance or detract from the merits of the original script."[1] Surely, to follow the BBC's lead in this matter can hardly be to err by much if, in fact, it is to err at all. Despite the clear danger—that in reading without listening, we may overlook the radio in radio drama—the demands of *close* reading should protect against the risk. For radio effects, when authentic, arise not as ornaments added in production, but as elements integral to the conceptual and aesthetic demands of the work. Every play that is intelligently crafted to the medium is laden with tacit assumptions about the nature and operation of an invisible stage: assumptions that attention to the script should disclose. Does a given play for radio invite the mind's eye to envision what the ear has heard; or does it seek to trick our inner eye, for the most part so secure in its sightings? Does a play take the ear essentially for granted; or does it challenge our sense of what language entails? Does it mirror the mind: solipsistic, impressionistic, elliptical in thought? Or does it reproduce the world, as in sound documentaries? Or—perhaps the most audacious of possible alternatives—does it gamely presume to mimic the stage, thereby making of radio a viable, if not quite an ordinary, theater? Through such choices as these do radio plays take the measure of their medium. And such choices as they make can be inferred from the page no less readily than from prerecorded broadcasts.

The eye, the ear, the mind, the world, the stage. These being the fixed points in radio's compass, I have made them the leitmotifs of the chapters that follow. Thus, in choosing individual plays for discussion, I have sought those that foreground particular motifs, in order to sample the genre's full range. Each of the plays, then, is radiophonic—and inalienably so, in part or in whole. And each of them is challenging, aesthetically and intellectually, in every dimension, not just those allied to radio. What is more, as an entirely practical matter, most of the plays are in print from major publishers. The exceptions are David Rudkin's *Cries from Casement* and John Arden's *The Bagman*, both published in the 1970s and now out of print, though of course they are available in libraries. For the reader's convenience, I might have done well to replace these two plays with other selections. But since work of this caliber should never have been pulped or remaindered in the first place (and *Cries from Casement* by BBC publications no less!), I could hardly have justified excluding the plays on the grounds that their publishers forsook them.

At issue in the opening chapters of the book is the near universal preconception about radio, that despite its blank screen, it is powerfully visual. Chapter One invokes a play that takes unusual pains to confirm this preconception: Howard Barker's *Scenes from an Execution*, which treats the eye of the mind as the equal, or more likely the master, of the eyes in our head. Chapter Two, by comparison, investigates a play that mocks the mind's eye in the process of engaging it: Tom Stoppard's *Artist Descending a Staircase*, a pretty piece of paradox that makes us see, as truth, that the truth cannot be seen. Underlying both plays is an exercise in portraiture. *Scenes from an Execution* would have us imagine a painting that is committed to canvas in the course of the play: a portrayal of the Battle of Lepanto, Venice's stunning naval victory over the Turks in 1571. Decried on its unveiling as unpatriotic because pacifistic, the painting is ultimately lauded as a masterpiece. *Artist Descending a Staircase*, for its part, would have us imagine a portrait of Marcel Duchamp, who is nowhere in the script (at least explicitly), and yet everywhere (at least by implication). Though the one play, *Scenes*, is principally an inquiry into the vexatious relationship between politics and art, and though the other play, *Artist*, is principally an appraisal of modern art's virtues and defects, each is secondarily—and not inconsequentially—an affirmation of radio's visual authority, improbable but nonetheless distinct.

Of course, radio speaks to the ear as to the eye. And insofar as the ear on occasion prevails, particular plays may have affinities to music. Chapter Three, then, addresses the musical dimension in radio drama, as it emerges in Robert Ferguson's *Transfigured Night*, a monologue (or is it an aria in prose?) in which a speaker who has loved and lost expresses pain so acute, yet so obscure in its causes, as to leave us uninformed though deeply moved. Such a naked appeal to emotion—that is, emotion divorced from understanding—may, in and of itself, mark the monologue as musical, since music is said to stir passion, not thought. But to Ferguson, music engages more than feelings, as comes clear from the monologue's title, which is borrowed from Schoenberg. A formidable innovator in contemporary music, the creator of both atonality and serialism, Arnold Schoenberg took music, conceptually and structurally, in directions where writers could follow. To read Ferguson's script in connection with Schoenberg is therefore to ponder the formal similarities between music and language, as well as to recognize this fundamental difference: that whereas music is essentially about itself alone, words refer perforce to both objects and ideas, about which they contrive to tell stories.

Can the gulf between language and music be closed? In particular, can language be made to make sense—either emotional or aesthetic—without producing narration and thereby becoming inimical to music? These questions, as it happens, pertain not just to Ferguson, but also to a writer whom Ferguson cites, in fact echoes: the redoubtable Samuel Beckett, author of six plays for radio ("pieces," as he called them), all of which the chapter proceeds to discuss. Considered in the context of Ferguson's play, these pieces can be heard as dramatic experiments in which Beckett endeavors to silence narration so that language might sing. His efforts, however, succeed only partially, because stories persist in arising, no matter how artfully he tries to suppress them. One way of interpreting Beckett on radio, the chapter thus argues, is to see how his plays seek to circumvent narration, then to look for the stories that emerge none-theless. For an example of language quite divorced from story-telling—or indeed from any semblance of rational discourse—the chapter turns at the last to John Cage's *Roaratorio; an Irish Circus on* Finnegans Wake. Designed and produced as a radio happening, *Roaratorio* submits Joyce's prose to chance operations in the interests of heightening its "poetrewed music." The resulting (and incomprehensible) script, which is chanted in performance against a cacophonous background of prerecorded noises, transmutes language into something new—not to mention, passing strange—though whether musical or not may be disputed.

It is relatively rare, of course, for radio drama to perform a transmu-tation so profound. The usual procedure is for a radio play to transmute raw experience—what the mind perceives, what the world portends—into dramatic situations that the radio accommodates. Thus does radio become, metaphorically, a mind at play, a world in action: a mind, insofar as the characters' dialogue mirrors their thought, ranging free of all temporal and spatial constraints; a world, insofar as the characters' dialogue mirrors their condition, invoking both the time and space that hem them in. Chapter Four addresses plays in which the mind is what predominates. In the first of them, Arthur Kopit's *Wings*, a woman who has suffered a disorienting stroke attempts to make sense of the world as it is, while finding that what *is* can be no more than what she thinks. The play's special daring, aside from its theme, derives from Kopit's choice of an elderly speaker whose stroke has diminished her verbal lucidity, ostensibly a *sine qua non* on the radio. In the second of the plays, Harold Pinter's *A Slight Ache*, a husband and wife try to make what they think be the measure of what is—try to make the world become as they would have it. Although the play ends inconclusively, Pinter warns that such behavior is the psychic equivalent of playing with fire. Or so we can conclude from the figure of the matchseller, who, while sparking no flames, yet gives Edward a fever, the equivalent of fire in a play that transpires in an inner, psychological landscape.

Such a landscape figures, too, in David Rudkin's *Cries from Casement*, the sole play to be discussed in Chapter Five. But in *Cries*, the mind's narrow and perilous terrain is traversed by broad boulevards leading outward to the world. It could hardly be otherwise, given the play's central figure, Roger Casement, diplomat, humanitarian, and Irishman, executed by the British in the midst of World War I: executed nominally for treason (he negotiated with Germany at the height of the war in an effort to secure independence for Ireland), but arguably for homosexu-ality (he kept a diary, to his sorrow, of his secret encounters at home and abroad). Clearly, this Casement was a deeply private man with a highly public profile. Thus, to render him on radio, Rudkin was obliged to represent not just the world of Casement's mind, but also the world of his world: namely, Africa, America, and Europe, in whose affairs of state Casement participated; and particularly Ireland, in whose disputatious history Casement constitutes a chapter. The play, as a consequence, compresses the globe into radio's span, no larger than a tiny talking box. What is more, it proposes to alter that globe by reconceiving Casement's place in the world's collective memory. For where the world remembers Casement as a southern Irish martyr, *Cries* portrays him rather as a voice for all of Ireland, urging North and South at last to make their peace. How, then, should we classify this revisionist play? As history, or politics, or literature? That the question should even arise is a fair indication of how deeply immersed in the world *Cries from Casement* must be. So much so, in fact, that Casement's principal biographers have treated it as history, though its approach and technique are unmistakably literary.

The eye, the ear, the mind, the world. Radio drama engages all four with an ease and assurance that make them its own. But all four are as nothing, unless the genre can also lay claim to the stage. For the usual charge against radio—that it is merely a crippled form of theater—seems intuitively valid, no matter how striking the genre's achievements. Can the charge, then, be refuted and intuition laid to rest? John Arden gives us reason to think so in *The Bagman* and *Pearl*, two radio plays that bring the book to its close in Chapter Six. Singularly unapologetic about their medium of broadcast, these plays take the bold and unorthodox approach of making radio vie with the stage by subsuming it: that is, they incorporate theatrical performances into their soundscapes. Thus, *The Bagman*, a Bunyanesque fable, stages puppet shows on radio (not Punch-and-Judy antics, but serious satire), while *Pearl*, set in 1640s England, opens with a full-dress production of Shakespeare's *Julius Caesar* and ends with still another stage play—a dramatization of the biblical story of Esther. Since the purpose of these plays-within-plays, in their fictional context, is to stir up republican sentiment against monarchy on the one hand and Charles I on the other, *The Bagman* and *Pearl* must be understood chiefly as efforts to promote (and assess) the value of activist drama. But they must also be seen as assessing (and promoting) the value of radio drama. For by integrating radio with theater—in particular, the classical theater of England, France, and Germany—they attest to the medium's cultural significance and vindicate its claim to be an alternate stage.

So much, then, for radio's apparent deficiencies in relation to theater. If the medium offers a dramatist less, in a material sense, than a conventional stage, that less is yet as much as the dramatist makes of it. On occasion, as happens in the plays addressed here, the old adage applies: less is actually more. In most other instances (though who would have guessed it?), less is more than enough, if only for the reason that radio charms us by indulging our passion to "see for ourselves." However improbably, nothing is missing when we listen to radio, because all of us are expert at seeing what we hear. The ability to do so is part of our psychology; instinctively, we visualize sounds in terms of images. By contrast, we tend not to hear what we see, if our response to silent films is any measure: without music, they are lifeless; without titles, obscure. Thus it is that the talkies put an end to silent pictures, which were hobbled, not helped, by their muteness. If radio drama has survived in spite of movies, not to mention the television and video industries, there is just one explanation: radio plays are well served by the dark from which they issue. How that darkness contributes to their meaning and effect is at issue in what follows, analyses of plays that do radio proud.

# Acknowledgments

CKNOWLEDGMENTS provide an opportunity to give offense. There are those who, on being forgotten, will wish that they had been remembered. Conversely, there are those who, on being remembered and on thinking their advice ill-employed, will wish that they could sue. To both I apologize, no less for my memory slips than for my incorrigibility, which has left my book no better than one finds it.

Chief among the institutions to which I am indebted is The George A. and Eliza Gardner Howard Foundation of Brown University. In awarding me a year's fellowship, the Foundation gave me time for uninterrupted reflection, during which a third of the book was written, a third revised, and a third conceived, though not executed. Every page of what follows thus reflects the Foundation's support in some substantial part. Supplemental support was provided by the University of Colorado at Boulder, including a Dean's Summer Stipend, awarded by Dean Charles R. Middleton.

While the project was still in embryo, the Modern Language Association published a version of the chapter on Stoppard: "*Artist Descending a Staircase*: Stoppard Captures the Radio Station—and Duchamp," *PMLA* 105.2 (1990): 286–300. Revised and expanded, the article is here reprinted by permission of the Association. For encouraging me to consider submitting my work to *PMLA*, I am grateful to Leo Damrosch and John W. Kronik. And for what can only be called inspired editing, I owe both thanks and admiration to Claire Cook. Besides confirming my impression that radio drama has a huge potential audience among literary scholars, the essay on Stoppard had the happy effect of introducing me to Everett C. Frost and Oscar Mandel, both of whom have since assisted me by fulfilling time-consuming requests with daunting speed and exemplary thoroughness.

In the United States, my research for *Sight Unseen* was largely conducted at The New York Public Library for the Performing Arts, where I was able to study Cage's *Roaratorio* (not easily come by) and to search through clipping files that constitute a trove of information on innumerable playwrights and on drama in general. In Great Britain, I worked principally at BBC Broadcasting House, where administrators, directors, and actors alike extended me their patience and their courtesy. Special thanks are due to John Tydeman, then Head of BBC Radio Drama, who engagingly discussed his experiences as director of *Artist Descending a Staircase, Transfigured Night*, and *Cries from Casement*. Thanks, too, are due to Gerry Jones, then a BBC director, who is himself an award-winning playwright. Though his drama would have suited the chapter on The Mind, I hesitated to presume on our friendship, which has afforded me privileged glimpses into the semi-autobiographical sources of his richly dramatic conceits. Finally, there is Martin Jenkins, Senior Director of BBC Radio Drama, whom I inconvenienced so considerably and so frequently in the course of my work that he can only be relieved to see me finished at last.

Others to whom I am obliged for all manner of favors and attention include: Nigel Anthony, William Ash, Howard Barker, Erik Bauersfeld, Kate Binchy, Jane K. Brown, Marshall Brown, Steven M. Bruns, Wayne Dodd, Ernst A. Fredricksmeyer, Julia Frey, Hardy Long Frank, Eugene S. Gollin, Philip F. Gura, William K. Kearns, Bernard Krichefski, Richard A. Lanham, Judith Lee, Michael McLachlan, Shaun MacLoughlin, Siegfried Mandel, Nancy D. Mann, Elizabeth Mansfield, Richard Marius, Julia Marsh, Rolf P. Norgaard, Elaine Oppenheim, Neale Reinitz, J. E. Rivers, Adele Ronson, David Rudkin, Richard Shirk, David Simpson, Gary H. Stahl, Steve Trafford, Mark W. Wait, Billie Whitelaw, Faith Wilding, and Katharine Worth. I am also pleased to acknowledge the unfailing graciousness of Nancy Basmajian, Helen Gawthrop, and Holly Panich at Ohio University Press.

Of all my debts, the most extensive and enduring is to Paul M. Levitt, who set me an example of clear and graceful prose in the days when I imagined that genius lay in jargon; who enticed me to study modern drama in the 70s, when I shocked him with my ignorance of Dürrenmatt's yellow shoes; who introduced me to radio when his own plays for the medium were produced by the BBC; who read every chapter of *Sight Unseen* in draft; and who bore the brunt of my defections, for the manuscript's sake, from our joint responsibilities in CU Boulder's University Writing Program, which together we direct.

Familiar, too, with my defections—these from family life—are Stanley, Joanna, and Daniel, who have accepted my inattentions over the past four years with admirable grace. Now, as ever, I am grateful for their indulgence, as well as for their facility in diverting me from my work whenever they saw fit. I would not have wished to miss either the demands or the pleasure of their company, even for plays as companionable as these.

# Sight Unseen

# Chapter One

## THE VISUAL CHALLENGE
### Howard Barker's *Scenes from an Execution*

•

IMAGINE, if you will, a man with a crossbow bolt in his head. He "got this disability in the service of [his] nation," fighting the Turks at the Battle of Lepanto, where Venice was triumphant in "sweeping the atheistic power from the sea" (88).[1] Imagine, too, that his "hand is cleft to the wrist" and that he bears "an open wound through which the movement of [his] bowels may be observed" (49). So grotesquely is he vivisected that this man can only be, in fact, imagined. The stage cannot do justice to his acts of exhibitionism (for he earns his daily bread by exposing himself to paying customers). When he lifts his hat to show the bolt whose "tip is buried in the centre of his brain" or to reveal how the shaft begins to "twitch . . . at times of mental exertion" (49), the effect on stage must be contrived, hence unconvincing. So, too, when he lowers his belt to show "the passage of undigested material along the alimentary canal" (50, pto). But on radio? On radio, we take the man exactly as we find him. For the mind's eye, in seeing him, authenticates him. On radio this wonder is the genuine article—and genuine proof of the contention that there is "a radio equivalent of spectacle" (Dunn, "Interview," 34).

The phrase is Howard Barker's; and if the play in question, *Scenes from an Execution*, is visually extravagant, we should not be surprised. Barker indicates as much in his title, which insists upon the scene, and thus the seen. In fact the play, at least in part, is an extended exploration of the central paradox of radio drama: that, exhibiting no images whatever, it is nonetheless profoundly visual. So it is that *Scenes from an Execution* requires us to visualize virtually the whole of a Renaissance costume drama: a Venetian doge, a cardinal, an admiral, a group of drunken sailors, a bevy of painters, a funeral in a Catholic church, a barracks fitted out to serve an artist as a studio, a room in a palace and, across the Bridge of Sighs, a jail cell in the state's official prison. All of this plus Prodo, the Man with the Crossbow Bolt in his Head.

Yet all of this is not yet all that we are meant to see. For what Barker has attempted in writing the play is "to actually use the act of painting as a radio technique—the practice of visual representation as it occurs in an artist's mind" (Barker quoted in Dunn, "Interview," 34). To this end, he follows the painter Galactia as she fulfills a state commission from the Republic of Venice for a painting of the Battle of Lepanto. (Prodo models for this painting at the start of the play and solicits customers by means of it at the end.) How the painting emerges out of dialogue, and how dialogue thereafter both destroys and recreates it when the state takes offense at Galactia's conception of the battle as inglorious massacre—this is the play's essential action. We visualize the painting, ever varying and various, at the same time that we visualize the scenes in which Galactia paints it, glories in it, suffers for it and, eventually, ascends to social prominence because of it.

To hear *Scenes from an Execution*, then, is to see events unfold and a canvas take shape. But "see" in what sense? Certainly not like a camera: not, that is, by selecting an angle of vision on what is already there to be observed. In a radio play, "there" is formless and void; and darkness resides on the face of the deep, until the listener says, "let there be light." Hence if *Scenes from an Execution* is to be visible, it is we who must summon up the spectacle, we alone who execute the scenes.

A heady privilege. And an awesome task. For how are we to know if what we see is good: if the playwright would approve our private vision? An execution, after all, may as easily be an act of destruction as an act of creation. It may, in fact, be both simultaneously. We might therefore do well to allow that in envisioning the play, we both conceive and misconceive it—just as Galactia, in painting the Battle of Lepanto, both judges and misjudges the glory of Venice. It could hardly be otherwise, when at the heart of all endeavor—not only artistic, but also political and sexual—Barker discovers this dagger: that every doing is equally an undoing, that every gain equally implies a loss.

How people behave, and contrive to prevail, under such equivocal circumstances is the principal concern of *Scenes from an Execution*. And precisely for this reason, Barker has done well to write the play for radio. For in recommending sight where nothing is visible, radio drama embodies the equivocality that the play addresses. By provoking us to conjure visions that are real and at the same time insubstantial, that are impossible (think of Prodo) and at the same time believable, that are singularly ours and at the same time the playwright's, radio drama attunes us to a world of ceaseless permutations—the world that *Scenes from an Execution* engages.

IF THE BATTLE OF LEPANTO (1571) was a stirring naval victory for Venice, it was also, for both sides, a vast human tragedy. Twenty thousand Turks and eight thousand Christians fell in combat before the holy league prevailed. And to what end? As much to protect trade as to control Turkish aggression in the Eastern Mediterranean. As Urgentino, the Doge of Venice in *Scenes from an Execution*, puts it, blood was liberally spilled on the oceans so that Venetians could eat grapes from Crete: "We left two thousand soldiers dead there, but we have the grapes. Little bit of sand. Little bit of history" (53). And little bit of cynicism, wholly unsuited for public consumption. However mixed the motives and results of the battle, Venice must represent Lepanto to the public as a triumph, unequivocally. What better way to do so than through art?

Enter Galactia (fictitious, like all the other characters in the play, although the battle itself is historical fact). Ferociously talented, Galactia is also a consummate realist: her paintings, says Urgentino, "sweat" (53). And because they do, he chooses her, over the objection of the cardinals on the fine arts committee, to produce a one-hundred-foot-long canvas depicting Lepanto—that is, celebrating it. Alas, on two accounts, he errs. For one thing, Galactia regards the battle as a massacre and willfully intends to represent it as such. For another, whatever her intentions, her realism disables her from celebrating war unequivocally. What E. H. Gombrich says of the ancient Greek mosaic depicting the Battle of Alexander and Darius must equally apply to realistic depictions of any other battle: "We need not doubt that the artist and his patron intended to celebrate Alexander's triumph. But it is not only the triumph of victory we are made to share but also the tragedy of defeat" (136). Because to see the vanquished is to pity them, a narrative painting of a battle necessarily equivocates, pleading for the fallen while rejoicing with the victors. Yet equivocation, not to mention outright criticism of the sort that Galactia plans, is just what Venice will not, cannot, countenance.

Or can it? The painting, when unveiled, is clearly an affront to church and state. Neither will abide it. Galactia is imprisoned and the painting stashed away . . . until the Doge has been instructed in how the state can even yet turn the painting to its glory. "In art," suggests the critic Gina Rivera, "nothing is what it seems to be, but everything can be claimed. The painting is not independent, even if the artist is. The picture is retrievable, even when the painter is lost . . ." (84). All that is required is for the state to "absorb" the painting; for "in absorbing it," as

Urgentino learns, "we show our greater majesty" (86, pto). The painting, in short, is co-opted—and ultimately Galactia, too. By a single deft political maneuver, criticism is transmuted into praise.

An equivocal result, if ever there was one—though a rather tame play, if this were all it had to say. For a playwright to accuse a politician of duplicitous behavior toward an artist is par for the course, even when, as here, the state's duplicity is cleverly accomplished.[2] But what if the artist, in her own way, is also duplicitous, or at least double-natured? What if she rails at men's impulse to slaughter, even while herself waging war through her art, not to mention through her fierce sexuality? What if she chooses, for her lover, a man whose simplicity she scorns, and yet covets? What if she strives for simplicity in art, yet produces complexity in spite of herself? What if, again in spite of herself, she actually consents when the state seeks to silence her? And what if, at the end of all, she reforms the state in any case, though not quite in the way she had intended? Under such circumstances—and these are, in fact, the circumstances to be explored below—we would (and do) have the quintessential Barker play: one in which every character and every action is reflected in the play's "internal mirrors" (Donesky, 342), so that each can be seen as itself and in reverse, the better to be known.

What such mirroring suggests is that all things embody their opposites. In Barker's own words, "It has always seemed to me in a rather disturbing way that every argument has its counter-argument, and one arrives at conviction not always out of logic at all" (Donesky, 338). Provocatively, Barker thinks the same of personalities. Thus, in a 1988 interview for the London Observer, he suggests that "both the will to revolt and the will to submit are contained within the same psyche" (Marks, 24). If so, self-definition must be a long heroic struggle, endlessly repeated, never done; for closure is impossible when personalities are constitutionally divided within themselves, as they prove to be in Scenes. Galactia and Urgentino vie with one another, to be sure; but their principal struggles are nonetheless internal. Like virtually every other character of substance in the play, they are metaphorically what Prodo is in fact: irreparably "split up the middle" (51).

The phrase is Galactia's, though she uses it wrongheadedly, to differentiate herself from Prodo. "I am a woman who has lived a little," she tells him; "nothing much, I have not been split up the middle like you have, but I have picked up a thing or two and I tell you I have never been at peace with life, I would not be at peace with life, there is no such thing . . ." (51). Indeed, there is not; nor can there be, so long as people are radically divided in character and purpose. That they are, in fact, divided is the burden of the play from the very first scene, which itself is "split up the middle" to reflect the divisions it addresses. Half the scene depicts Galactia at odds with her lover, Carpeta; half depicts her struggle to pry out of Prodo a truth that, in the telling, will wreck his peace with life. Through it all, Galactia asserts herself—her singular, but not so clearly single, self—with the compulsive energy of one who suspects that her "mind is breaking up and drifting in all directions. . . . I cannot let myself be splintered like this, can I? I cannot!" (49).[3]

The fundamental division in Galactia is between the woman and the painter. The woman would possess Carpeta utterly, and be possessed in turn, while the painter thinks of love as an obsession that intrudes upon her art. Because she cannot reconcile her need to be full of Carpeta with her need to be free of him, she carps at him (he is well named) incessantly. He does not give himself enough: that is, he will not leave his wife. He tries to take too much of her: that is, he fondles her when she is bent on thinking. "No, let go of me, you always start to touch me when I think. . . . Can't you just crush me in the night? I am very happy to be crushed in bed but I am a painter and you can't have that off me" (56–57).[4] In accusing him of threatening her very creativity, she knows whereof she speaks. By his own testimony, *she* has robbed *him* of all his resources: "I am exhausted by you," he tells her; "I HAVE DONE NO WORK!" (47). With her arrogance, her vanity, her contempt, and her passion, she has wholly undone her lover's capacity to function as a fellow artist. Thus, his posture at the outset of the play—he models, stark naked, for Galactia's representation of "dead men float[ing] with their arses in the air" (47)—captures his predicament neatly. Figuratively, he is dead by her hand.

Doubtless, Carpeta's "murder" is not what Galactia intends. She can profit nothing from it; indeed, she does not even try, refusing to concede that Carpeta "is spent" (53), when Urgentino urges her (he, too, deserves his name) to say so. Nonetheless, Carpeta calls her "ambitious and ruthless" (48); and her behavior with Prodo, who enters as Carpeta exits from scene 1, suggests that he is right. For the sake of her art, Galactia badgers Prodo and insults him, all to make him talk about the battle. Where he "spill[s his] guts" (50) literally, she would have him do so metaphorically as well—and against his will—merely so that she can "paint [his] pain for [him]" (50). She would sooner be an artist than humane.

"WHAT SORT OF WOMAN ARE YOU?" (50), Prodo asks of her in anguish. The question is profound. For Galactia has denied she is a woman at all. "Try not to think of me as a woman," she has told him, when he hesitates to drop his pants and show his bowel to her; "Think of me as a painter" (49). Yet in response to Prodo's reticence, she represents a

painter as a special kind of woman: "A midwife for your labour. Help
you bring the truth to birth" (50). A noble goal. But is her answer honest?
We will come to see, as the play proceeds, how art relates to truth.
Meanwhile, we need only ask what truth it is that Galactia in particular
is after. Prodo's? She says so and no doubt believes so. The battle's? That,
too, although she has not been to war herself.

> SECOND SAILOR: Is death like that? In battle, is it? (*Pause*)
> GALACTIA:          Yes. I have never seen it, but I think so.
>
>                                                               (69)

A troubling admission, this. For if Galactia's painting is grounded not in
her experience, but in her imagination, then the truth that she creates
may be the truth about herself and little else.

Galactia says as much unwittingly: "I am painting the battle, Prodo.
Me" (50)—a statement that fairly resonates with irony. If, as the syntax
suggests, what Galactia paints is "me," then her painting is an act of
self-definition; and the self that she defines is the battle she abhors. And
rightly so. After all, she resides in a barracks: "If you are painting soldiers,
you should live among soldiers" (54). She causes suffering, not only for
Carpeta and Prodo, but also for her daughters, who dislike the bar-
racks/studio for its cold and stink and dark. And like the Admiral in her
painting, she abjures mercy: she spurns Carpeta and Prodo, who want
her to be kind; her daughters, who would have her be maternal; and
above all Urgentino and Rivera, who beg her to represent Lepanto as
"the greatest triumph of Venetian history" (67). They beg in vain. For
Galactia is essentially at war with them. When she sends her painting
out, she intends it to be "like some great bomb snuggled under tarpaulins,
and they will unload it and carry it into the palaces of power, and it will
tear their minds apart and explode the wind in their deep cavities . . ."
(75). The artist thus plays out a dream of violence.

Now, a painting is a far cry from a bomb. And yet, in Galactia's case,
not quite so very far as one might like to suppose. Indeed, once Cardinal
Ostensible has pronounced a battle to be merely "a furtherance of political ends by violent means" (78), it is tempting to consider Galactia's
painting as the merest step away: a furtherance of violent ends by artistic
means. Of course, the bomb that Galactia proposes to deliver is strictly
metaphoric. What she seeks to tear apart are minds, not bodies; and in
this respect, her painting is morally superior to conventional warfare.
Nonetheless, in the play's internal mirrors, Galactia's painting proves to
be a form of battle.[5] And Galactia herself resembles no one so much as
Suffici, admiral of the Venetian fleet. The index to their likeness can be
found in their mutual preoccupation with image. "Do you like my face?"

(60), Suffici asks of Galactia. And in doing so, he echoes her own question of Prodo: "What sort of face do I have? Look at it, is it a good face?" (51). Good or bad, it is at any rate the same face that Suffici exhibits to the public; for Galactia has the Admiral's authority and his remorselessness, as well as what she calls his "great, swaggering sensitivity" (62)—although, as it happens, she is neither "so gentle" nor "so subtle" as she is "furious to find [him]" (60) in private.

Why furious? Because he will not conform to her uncomplicated idea of him. Her Sketchbook, which speaks for her, describes Suffici as the "Admiral of the Atlantic, the Admiral of the Two Seas, the General of the Home and Distant Waters" (60)—a military man, in short, to the core. Yet the "Real You" of Suffici is a "homosexual gardener" with "the most compassionate face" (60) that Galactia has ever seen. His double nature takes her by surprise, though it should not. Galactia herself, after all, is "full of contradiction" (60, pto), and so is nearly everyone around her. Think of poor torn Prodo. Having suffered a "half-murder, [a] half-death" (50), he nonetheless parades as whole: "a walking manifestation of the organic solidarity and the resilience of the Christian state" (49, pto). Think, too, of Urgentino, who exemplifies "good taste" (53) in dress and art, yet is somehow detestably vulgar: "He loves artists, and the harder he loves them, the more vulgar he becomes . . ." (66). Although a "devotee" of art (53), Urgentino finds himself dissatisfied with artists whether they defy him, like Galactia, or succumb to him, like Carpeta. Hence he nurtures them and bullies them by turns.[6] As for Rivera, she readily acknowledges that she is two-in-one and actually takes pleasure in the fact: "How beautiful my clothes are, and my whiteness, most impeccable woman, drifting through galleries. But it is very violent, criticism. . . . I try to look nice, though it's murder I do for my cause" (67).[7]

Of all the major characters, only Carpeta is uncomplicated. In art, his ambition is narrow and uncontroversial: he "long[s] to be the finest Christ painter in Italy" (48). In love, he appears to want nothing more taxing than a peaceable relationship with each of two women, Galactia and his wife. Galactia, however, will have none of it. Bent upon creating conflict, she goads Carpeta to leave home and mocks his work: "you have painted Christ among the flocks eight times now, you must allow the public some relief" (47). Thus set upon, Carpeta retaliates—but feebly. No sooner, in fact, does he light upon an insult that hits home than he retracts it.

CARPETA:  And you will never make a decent job of anything be-
          cause you are a sensualist, you are a woman and a

sensualist and you only get these staggering commissions
from the state because you—
GALACTIA:  What?
CARPETA:  You—
GALACTIA:  What?
CARPETA:  Thrust yourself!
GALACTIA:  I what?
CARPETA:  Oh, let's not insult each other.
GALACTIA:  Thrust myself?
CARPETA:  Descend to low abuse—
GALACTIA:  It's you who—
CARPETA:  I am tired and I refuse to argue with you—

(48)

Unlike Galactia, Carpeta does not thrive on turbulence, does not regard
the bedroom as a battlefield, does not imagine art to be a weapon striking
out against injustice. Where Galactia is aggressive, Carpeta is passive.
Where she is arrogant, he is self-effacing. Where she is capacious enough
to embrace a multiplicity of contradictions, he is just a "little man" (73),
so simple that, in truth, he is hardly there at all.

Witness how he starts and ends the play: in the first instance, as a model
for a drowned sailor; in the second, as a "little bag in the doorway" (88)
of Galactia's studio, less a person than an object. To be sure, Carpeta's
inanition may be understood as Galactia's fault. Already at the start of
the play, she has so overwhelmed him that he blames her for his inability
to paint. By the end, she "do[es] not need [him] anymore" (88). Hence
he simply disappears. Yet if Galactia can be said to *execute* Carpeta in
the sense that she destroys him, she may also be said to *execute* him in
the sense of creating (or trying to create) him. For in her efforts to leaven
his simplicity, Galactia galvanizes Carpeta, even if only temporarily.

When Carpeta poses as dead, for example, Galactia insults him into
life by accusing him of showing "KINDNESS WITHOUT INTEGRITY" (47)—a
near, if not a patent, contradiction that neatly captures the moral com-
plications of a gentle man's adultery. Carpeta rises to defend himself but,
true to his character, sidesteps the moral dilemma: "I shall leave my wife,
I have every intention of leaving my—" (47). His impulse, as always, is
to simplify. Later, when he sinks into dejection, complaining that Galactia
makes him "utterly childish," a "clinging . . . rag" (56), she rouses him
with the vexing proposal that his "sensitivity" is actually "brutality"
(57). Carpeta repudiates the charge. And well he should, for he embodies
no opposites. Turn him inside out and he is just the same as ever. In fact,
Galactia proves as much by subjecting his signal emotion, pity, to the
test of inversion. Whether she calls it "the surrender of passion" or "the

passion of surrender," pity turns out to be always the same: "It is capitulating to what is" (57, pto); it is "endur[ing] everything" (57); it is Christ's wounds and crucifixion; it is Carpeta's private death-in-life, from which Galactia tries to rescue him.

The state attempts a rescue, too. For life—eternal life in "the pantheon of Venetian masters" (72)—is what Urgentino and Cardinal Ostensible offer Carpeta when they invite him to assume the Lepanto commission once Galactia forfeits it. The price, though, is high. Carpeta must cut himself off from Galactia emotionally and physically; and he must reconcile his sense of "what—the circumstances—require" (72) with his "own requirements as a painter" (73). He must, in short, split himself up the middle. He cannot. The best that Carpeta can manage to do is to efface himself entirely, so that nothing unique to him remains to be in conflict with the state. Thus, he betrays his love for Galactia in order to report what the Doge and the Cardinal want to hear of her: that she is both mad and immoral, and that his relationship with her is "rather casual" (71). As for the painting, he consents to be governed in producing it.

OSTENSIBLE:   The way you do Christ—the nobility of Christ—transmit that feeling to the officers.
CARPETA:      Yes . . .
OSTENSIBLE:   The battle is not—unwholesome—it is, rather, the highest moment of self-sacrifice. It is as divine—in essence—as the crucifixion—
CARPETA:      Yes . . .
OSTENSIBLE:   And the soldiers are—not victims of a sacrifice but—a fraternity on Christian crusade, do you follow?
CARPETA:      Yes.
[URGENTINO]:  But you must paint it for yourself! It is your painting![8]
OSTENSIBLE:   It is his painting, yes!

(72)

It is his painting, no—because in the event, he does not exist to claim it. Carpeta cannot assert himself even to the modest extent of elaborating upon the vision that the Cardinal articulates. He merely acquiesces. The commission that should have aggrandized Carpeta erases him.

Only his need for Galactia endures. But she, on her release from imprisonment, no longer needs him in return. Urgentino is bemused to think she ever did: "She loves him . . . the great woman . . . dotes on . . . the little man" (73). Even Carpeta is incredulous: "How can you love someone you despise?" (48). "I don't know," says Galactia, "it's peculiar" (48). The explanation offered in the dialogue is that she lusts for him. As she exults to her daughter, "I had twelve lovers by my fifteenth

birthday. . . . For all that I knew nothing until I met Carpeta, nothing!"
(55). By this interpretation, animal magnetism draws them together, in
spite of their differences in temperament and in defiance of the social
conditions (Carpeta's marriage, Galactia's commission) that conspire to
divide them.[9] If so, it is puzzling that desire should fail at the end of the
play, precisely when the sources of discord between them have at last
been resolved: when Carpeta has tried the Lepanto commission and found
himself wanting; when he has tacitly acknowledged that Galactia is the
better painter; when he has finally left his wife. But, then, as Galactia
has resolved never to "be at peace with life" (51), Carpeta presumably
loses his allure because he yields to her.

There may, however, be another explanation for Carpeta's initial success with Galactia: namely, that she is drawn to him because she needs
the very qualities she scorns in him. To be sure, she does not seem
deficient, this prodigious woman who radiates brilliance. Nonetheless,
she is Carpeta's inferior in one regard at least. She cannot match him for
compassion. "You've always painted pity, and I never have," she concedes
to him. "Tell me how to do it" (57). Indeed, in painting her battle,
Galactia could measurably profit from this talent of Carpeta's, as well
as from his simplicity of purpose and even his instinct for capitulation.
Perhaps she knows as much intuitively. In any case, until the painting is
complete and accepted by the state, she keeps Carpeta in her compass
as if to conjure with those features of his art and personality that she
might wish to emulate.

Take Carpeta's way with pity. For want of it, Galactia's portrayal of
Suffici suffers twice: it is untrue; and it is needlessly offensive. Although
Suffici has "the most compassionate face [that Galactia has] ever seen"
(60), she represents him with a "fixed and callous stare" (69). To make
a point about the cruelty of war? Imagining so would be generous. For
by her own testimony, it is "with *one* figure" that Galactia "transform[s]
the enemy from beast to victim, and ma[kes] victory unclean" (58, my
emphasis)—the figure of the Turk who begs Suffici for his life. The
contempt with which Suffici's face is painted is thus entirely superfluous
to Galactia's point. In fact, it is arguably counterproductive since pity,
in capturing the Admiral's own pain, would augment Galactia's indictment of war, even while pleasing Suffici and being accurate to boot. But
Galactia cannot paint compassion. And when she turns to Carpeta for
assistance, he fails her. He cannot tell her how to do it.

In Carpeta's opinion, Galactia's deficiency issues from a personal failure: she does not "have pity, so [she] can't paint it" (57). "You are
violent," he says, "so you can paint violence. You are furious, so you
can paint fury. And contempt, you can paint that. Oh, yes, you can paint

contempt. But you aren't great enough for pity" (57). Greatness, however, is quite immaterial: Carpeta, who excels at portraying the emotion, is by all accounts a minor artist. As for the notion that a painter has to be what he paints, Carpeta is overly simplistic. Art, to be sure, is self-expression. Thus, Carpeta's "Christ paintings" strike Galactia as "self-portraits" (65); and Galactia's great canvas, as we have seen, represents herself as much as anything ("I am painting the battle, Prodo. Me"). But Galactia also paints what she is not. She is not, for example, in the least inclined to beg, as she proves when Urgentino and Ostensible call her to trial. Nevertheless, she can paint a Turk begging for mercy—paint him powerfully, as she believes, by transmuting an emotion that she does understand (ardor for sex) into something analogous (ardor for life). So it is that she encourages her model for the Turk, an Albanian pineapple seller, to ogle her daughter Dementia, over Dementia's objections. And so it is, too, that she turns to Carpeta for advice on painting pity. What she apparently wants is a trick of the trade. What she gets is an assessment of her character.

If Carpeta's response enrages her, it should. He means it to offend. But its actual significance lies elsewhere. By creating contention about the appropriate standard for judging truth in art, his statement reminds us that a painting need not tell the truth about its artist. It may rather tell the truth about experience. This is the standard to which Galactia appeals in her realism: "I am painting [the battle] in such a way that anyone who looks at it will feel he is there, and wince in case an arrow should fly out of the canvas and catch him in the eye—" (53–54). A painting of this kind ordinarily requires that an artist "describe the world" (59) exactly as he sees it. But Galactia, having never been to battle, cannot simply describe; she must also invent. To sight she must add insight; or, as she puts it, "to observation [she] must lend imagination" (56). In the process, she becomes a creator, "compet[ing] with nature . . . , challeng[ing] God" (59). Her conception of art, then, is far more complex and ambitious than Carpeta's, extending beyond self-expression to the outright "arrogance" (59) of forging truths as well as apprehending them.

And yet what Galactia wants in art is, still in all, simplicity—not won as Carpeta wins his, by limiting artistic range, but simplicity nevertheless. In particular, she wants observation and imagination to yield the same result. When they do not, as in the case of Suffici, whom she wrongly imagines to be "bereft of mercy" (59), she objects: "Silly me, I should know the world is full of contradiction, but it's thrown me. See first, and look after. I saw you, and then I looked, and the two don't tally. Never mind, *it must be that I'm not looking deep enough*" (60, pto, my emphasis). Her conclusion is most curious. Given all her contrariety,

Galactia would hardly seem likely to believe that at bottom all opposites are reconcilable: that there is one truth in the Admiral, one truth in Lepanto. Yet so she does. And she insists that her art should reflect this belief, this simplicity. Hence she denies Suffici his compassion, representing him as heartless, with the result that he rejects her painting as "untrue . . . a lie" (76). And she denies the "nobility of the struggle" (78), representing Lepanto as a slaughter, with the result that Urgentino thinks her mad. That others agree with Urgentino's assessment, including Galactia's own daughter Supporta[10]—and, parenthetically, that a second daughter should be named Dementia—may give us pause.

Galactia's so-called madness raises two related issues: one moral, one aesthetic. We must ask, at the outset, if Galactia is mistaken (mad) in her indictment of the battle. If she is not, we must further consider whether a painting is a proper—and effective—vehicle for provoking reform in a modern state. As it happens, the moral issue is more easily resolved than the aesthetic. The whole weight of the play rests behind Galactia in her hatred of the violence done to Prodo and his like at Lepanto. Prodo may repeat "old catechisms" about "Freedom . . . Glory . . . The Honour of the Great Republic and the Humiliation of the Pagan Turk!" (51–52). Suffici may allude to "the Necessary War" (61). But these abstractions are never developed or particularized. We cannot give them credit in the face of Prodo's wounds and the "shoal of dying figures sliding out [of Galactia's] canvas" (69). Rhetorically, it is Galactia who prevails with her ringing denunciation of "capitulating to what is" (57, pto) when "what is" is homicidal: "Rather than pity the dead man I would say—there—there is the man who did it, blame him, identify. Locate responsibility. Or else the world is just a pool, a great pool of dirty tears through which vile men in boots run splashing" (57). Nothing in the play countermands this call to action. It is unequivocal— perhaps the only thing in all the play that is.[11] But how an artist should respond to such a charge is far from certain.

Galactia, for her own part, thinks she knows. She must tell the truth about the battle: paint the pain of it, the anger, and the grief. To do less would be aesthetically, as well as morally, contemptible. But her painting is not only, or even primarily, an aesthetic event; it is also a "public event" (53) and, as such, a political statement with potential political consequences. It can, as Rivera points out, humiliate and hence unseat the Doge. And if it does, all art must suffer, since none of Urgentino's rivals shares his enthusiasm for creating in Venice "a climate very favourable to painting" (66). Galactia professes to lack interest in the Doge's fate. As she has told Suffici, she is "not political," because the "moment you go in for politics, you cavil, you split up the truth—" (61, pto). Yet simply by accepting a commission from the state for a painting of Lepanto, Galactia has gone in for politics. To think otherwise, as Urgentino understands, is madness. Whether she will or no, Galactia is implicated in what Rivera calls a "DIRTY MESS OF TRUTHS, SIGNORA, CLINGING TO THE MOUTH" (67). She cannot have her one truth only.

Indeed, it is doubtful if artists ever can. For however singular the truth a painting tells, there is no assurance that its spectators will understand, or accept, what was intended. In this regard, the range of dramatized responses to Galactia's painting is instructive. To judge from the drunken sailors who surprise her at her work and proceed to stab the canvas, Galactia has, in fact, imparted the noise and stench of battle. Hence her painting should provoke, as she wishes, universal terror and loathing of war. Yet for the most part, it does not. Rather the responses that it generates are various and idiosyncratic.

Consider, for instance, Carpeta. If he cries when the painting is unveiled to him, it is surely not from pity for the dying, but from guilt (because he has supplanted Galactia in the commission) and from shame (because his own work is radically inferior to hers). Suffici, for his part, is wild with indignation, not at Galactia's contempt for the republic's militarism, but at her evident contempt for him personally. As for Supporta, if the canvas provokes her to break with her mother, the reason is not that she sees war as noble, but that she cannot condone Galactia's indifference to the feminist imperative.[12] Where Galactia has used her state commission to wage war against battle, Supporta would prefer that she had used it to advance the esteem of female painters throughout Venice. A hopeless goal, as it happens, even had Galactia chosen to espouse it. For see how her gender interferes with her fellow painters' sense of what her fervent canvas means: "If it had been painted by a man it would have been an indictment of the war, but as it is, painted by the most promiscuous female within a hundred miles of the Lagoon, I think we are entitled to a different speculation" (87, pto). Namely, that it is "THE SLAG'S RE-VENGE" against those lovers who, in leaving Galactia, have assured that she "has never kept a man" (86). Clearly, we have come a dismal distance from the truth that the painting was meant to display.

Yet we have farther still to go. For Prodo, "grotesque celebrity" (50), inverts the painting's meaning altogether. Where the canvas portrays him as "fathoming the shock of what's befallen him and inviting us to share his passionate desire to be somewhere else" (69), Prodo in real life is drawn to the painting and hence to the battle depicted there. Far from wanting to be elsewhere, he chooses to perch by the canvas, exploiting it for donations and for business. He regards it as "a godsend, what with winter coming on" (88). And because he does, the painting in no way apprises him of "the shock of what's befallen him," but rather confirms him in his pathetic conviction that "God steered the bolt, and in his mercy turned my maiming to my benefit" (50). So much for Galactia's truth.

Only the church and the state understand her point precisely—not so much because they are objective as because they are exquisitely sensitive to the threat that the painting may pose to their power. Thus, each is determined to silence her. The church would have the painting burned or hidden, and would even seek to torture Galactia into confessing a sympathy for Muslims. The state, being gentler, is satisfied merely to vitiate the painting's point by transforming its criticism of war into praise of the state's greater glory. A brilliant move. For by differentiating between "the surface of [a] painting" and "the back of it" (79)—that is, by granting to the artist "the brush strokes, the colour, the anatomy" (79) while retaining authority over the meaning that the work imparts—the state co-opts all artists utterly. In essence, it compels capitulation (Carpeta's great failing in Galactia's eyes) from everyone who paints, capitulators and rebels alike.

So it is that Galactia is finally schooled in the one quality of Carpeta's that repels her, while finding that she cannot have those qualities she wants of him: his talent at portraying pity and his presumed success at endowing paintings with a simple truth. No wonder she dismisses him at the close of the play. Having acquired what she distrusts in him while forfeiting the rest, she is right to contend, "I do not need you . . . anymore" (88). And right, too, to suggest that this result is "terrible" (88). For what Galactia faces is not just the death of love, but possibly her death in art as well.

The central question at the end of the play is whether Galactia has become—like Farini, the artist whose funeral she attends in scene 7—a "dead painter, claimed" (65). Certainly, her behavior has been different from Farini's in fundamental ways. Whereas Farini recanted when the church had him put in a madhouse for mocking the Pope, Galactia does not recant in prison. Indeed, she is so loath to leave, except on her own terms, that when the state releases her at the price of co-opting her painting, she reimprisons herself in her studio, which she fashions into "my black hole . . . my gaol" (87, pto). Moreover, Galactia is not a "frightful liar" (65) in her art. At least she does not lie deliberately, as Farini chose to do in secular matters, with his sentimental portraits of "the happy poor, the laughing rags of tramps" (65). Yet once she is co-opted, Galactia does lie, even if despite herself. And in the last scene of the play, she perfectly fits her own description of Farini, acclaimed as he lies in his coffin: the "dissenting voice, drowned in compliments" (65, pto). What, then, has all her struggle been about, if a form of death is her reward?

It is the existential question. And Barker does not shirk it. In particular, he explores the condition of two characters who choose radical alternatives to struggle and dissent: the Man in the Next Cell, who has no incentive to struggle because he affirms no truths whatever; and Suffici, who has no cause to dissent because he accepts all opinions as truths. Both choices, though inversions of each other, yield essentially the same result. They undermine each character's basic identity as human.

Suffici says so explicitly, if uncomprehendingly, when he pronounces the terms of his relativism. "There is no such thing as what happened, surely? Only views of what happened," he says; "*Just as there is no such thing as a man. Only images of him*" (63, my emphasis). This cynical philosophy may well relieve Suffici of moral accountability for his actions, whether he is wielding a sword at Lepanto or caressing men's "buttocks in the garden" (62). But it equally relieves him of the right to dispute Galactia's portrait of him as false. If "there is no such thing as a man. Only images of him," then Suffici must accept what Galactia has portrayed: must accept that she has "winkled out his truth" (89, pto)—as if he had but one—even though he is outraged at her image of his face as calculating and his hands as vulturous, like "talons out of . . . some ornithological atlas!" (76). So long as "there is no such thing as a man," Suffici can justly be reduced to the status of a hulking carnivorous bird.

Likewise with the Man in the Next Cell. Unlike Suffici, he is evidently harmless. But his innocence, such as it is, does not humanize him. By choice, he is "an animal in the straw . . . the toad" (81). And why? Because, as he says, "Only the quiet ones live. The noisy ones, they've carried [past] my door" (81). Better, then, to be "still, and preserve yourself" rather than protest (81); better to "hibernate the long winter of your offence" (81). But what do his seven years of absolute passivity profit him? He cannot describe his own face;[13] nor can he characterize his own mind, except by negation: "WHO SAYS I'M NOT AN INTELLECTUAL? WHO SAYS I'M NOT?" (80). He has no name and, for that matter, no offense. He is incarcerated for "nothing. I did nothing. And that is why I shall never be released" (86). The observation is exquisitely painful, and psychologically acute. For the Man is imprisoned not only by the state, but also (and more profoundly) by his own dehumanizing inertia. Whether or not the state ever frees him, he will remain in jail for life. And when he dies, what will die will be an animal, since the man in him will never have been realized. Such are the wages of his conscious decision, framed as advice, not to "scream and struggle [lest] you . . . wear down what you have" (81).[14]

To be human, then, requires a commitment. In particular, one must be willing to affirm what one values, to deny what one distrusts, and to vie on behalf of one's choices. So it is that Urgentino has his state; Rivera, her art; Carpeta, his pity; and Galactia, the truth that she embodies in her painting. Their endeavors make them all of them human—even Carpeta, whose compliant behavior must not be mistaken for the passivity practiced by the Man in the Next Cell. Admittedly, Carpeta endures and capitulates. But not without a struggle. He strives in his love affair, as well as in his art, however modest the result.[15] And that is his amazing grace, as small as it may seem. His essential dignity is captured in his comment to Sordo, "If you do not wish to paint seriously, you should not paint at all" (70). Although Sordo may laugh and call him a hack, Carpeta's commitment is no laughing matter. It is his assurance that he acquires a human form, a human face, before he dies.

If Carpeta is dignified by struggle, how much more so Galactia, whose efforts are far more substantial than her lover's, and also more productive. To be sure, Galactia does not gain her goal. But, then, her ambition—to tell the truth through art and have that truth be understood—is demonstrably unrealizable. Partly, Galactia fails because the truth is multivalent. Partly, because her version of the truth, as we have seen, is misinterpreted by people bent on understanding what they will, rather than what she has chosen to express. And partly, she founders because any interpretation, even a correct one, finally constitutes defeat. As Galactia says to Rivera, it is "death to be understood" (88). In its immediate context, the remark has a narrow significance: it is Galactia's protest against Rivera for having "SMOTHERED [the] DANGER [of her painting]" on the assumption that Galactia "wanted the picture to be seen" (88) at any price. But the remark has several wider applications. It encompasses the initial willingness of the church and the state to destroy Galactia's painting once they comprehend it—and to ruin Galactia, too. Moreover, and more important, it points to Urgentino's crushing observation at the close of the play: that in "a hundred years," when Galactia's painting is understood and accepted as a masterpiece, "no one will weep for [it], only respect it. Cold, dull respect" (89)—a living form of death. Who can gainsay him? The whole history of art proves him right. Thus, the "peculiar authority" (89) that Galactia exerts through her painting is transient. Like everything else, it must die.

Even so, the painting has its day. It succeeds in drawing tears from Carpeta, no matter why, as well as from the throngs who visit and revisit it when it is hung at exhibition. What is more, it disconcerts the Cardinal and the Doge—conquers them, in fact, however gamely they recover from the blow. For though Urgentino may arrange for the painting to redound to the credit of the state, he can do so only by acknowledging, and acceding to, the criticisms that the painting levels at Lepanto. Whether Venice comes to profit from this considerable concession is well beyond the scope of the play to depict. But as history informs us that Lepanto was not the republic's last conflict at arms, we may conclude that Galactia's painting does not reform the state as she intended.[16]

It does, however, somewhat reform Urgentino. That this cultured and elegant Doge has a mean streak is evident from the sexually sadistic enjoyment he takes in sending Galactia to prison. As he crassly informs her, "I cannot tell you how it excites me to think of your bare breasts against the wall [of your cell], and my buttocks on this brocade" (78). Not for nothing is Urgentino the half-brother of Suffici. Although he may have been "the Great Naval Disaster" (63) during his three years in uniform, Urgentino retains this much in common with the "bawling pack[s] of squaddies" who, in going to war, are "yelling male love" (67): he is titillated by the prospect of inflicting pain. Yet in the course of defending the painting, Urgentino modifies his passion for cruelty. Thus, after Ostensible has proposed "torturing [Galactia] and bribing witnesses" (82) to testify against her, Urgentino complains to Carpeta about Ostensible's "exaggerated sense of mission": "I do think that is vile," he says, "extremely ghastly" (82). More significantly, when Ostensible takes exception to Urgentino's ultimate decision to exhibit the painting, Urgentino answers him so firmly as to silence him completely for the rest of the play: "Cardinal, your single-mindedness is a credit to your jesuit professors, but you must stop hacking. The blunt, dull hack of Christian persecution, the urge to bonfire. Hate it. With all respect, hate it . . ." (86, pto). To take the proper measure of this moment, we must recall that at Galactia's interrogation, though Urgentino may launch the assault, he is summarily displaced by Ostensible, who alone poses questions with Pastaccio. If Galactia's painting serves no other purpose, at least it impels Urgentino to rein in the church—less momentous a result than Galactia had hoped for, but appreciable nevertheless.

In essence, by playing rough with Urgentino, Galactia and her painting smooth the Doge's rough edges and thereby contrive to improve him. We may conclude that, for art to breed change, it must first be prepared to breed controversy. But that, as Galactia knows, is a rather tricky business. Only consider what she says to Suffici early in the play when he accuses her of being, "for an artist, rather coarse" (61). "Coarse for an artist?" she shoots back at him; "It's an artist's job to be coarse. Preserving coarseness, that's the problem" (61). And so it is, though just how much of a problem even she does not anticipate. How can she know that Urgentino will devise a resolution—"There will be no art outside.

Only art inside" (86)—perfectly designed to tame the artist who would seek to raise a ruckus? Hard as she has labored to produce "a noisy painting" (54), Galactia finds her discord made harmonious by Urgentino's cunning.

Still, she has had her brief moment of coarseness, even if she fails to preserve it. Moreover, she has learned to accept what is coarse and contradictory in her own character and predicament. As we have seen, she has spoken her mind most compellingly; yet she has been deviously, expertly, gagged. She has effected a modicum of change in the state; yet she has confirmed the status quo against her deepest convictions. She has resisted the Doge's command, "Celebrate, Celebrate" (54); yet she has somehow in her own right become "a celebrity" (89). It is all intensely vexing and equivocal. And to all of it Galactia says, "Yes." Yes, to the Doge's invitation to dinner; yes, to the way events have splintered her; yes, to the very disappointments and betrayals in which her efforts have implicated her. Yes. It is the last word of the play, and performs the same function as Mcphee's "I! I! I!" at the end of Barker's earlier play, *That Good Between Us*:[17] it expresses a willing and knowledgeable affirmation of life, despite its imperfections.


IN AN INTERVIEW published the same year that *Scenes* was first broadcast on BBC Radio, Barker said of his work: "I think I am supremely optimistic about people compared with, say, Beckett, or Pinter. My world is passionate, after all. People live, suffer, but they affirm something, even if it's only a will to get through" (Dunn, "Interview," 42). Clearly, Galactia affirms such a will, and something more besides: namely, a passion to extend the range of her experience (thus her attraction to battle, and even to Carpeta), as well as a wish to improve the conditions of the world that she inhabits. In a figurative sense, *Scenes from an Execution* exhibits similar ambitions itself. In particular, it seeks to expand the range of expression available to radio drama. Thus the play proposes to depict—literally, to make visible—not only a dramatic action (a common enough goal among radio plays), but also a painting, and an epic one at that (an aspiration at once uncommon and uncommonly audacious). Insofar as it succeeds, *Scenes* may be said to improve, even to perfect, the medium of radio. For if words can conjure up an elaborate canvas done in oil, then radio hardly need apologize for the absence of a visual field. The images missing from a radio performance may be regarded as expendable if words can do the job of paint, as *Scenes* suggests they can. Ultimately, the play appears to speculate upon the possibility that perhaps there are no pictures except that words create them.

Such speculation is not as far-fetched as at first it may seem. Not, at any rate, when considered in light of the Chinese admonition: idea present, brush may be spared performance. Cited almost as a touchstone in E. H. Gombrich's seminal study on *Art and Illusion* (209, 331), this elegant epigram neatly characterizes the phenomenon of abbreviation in visual art, western as well as eastern. As Gombrich has observed, "Any picture, by its very nature, remains an appeal to the visual imagination; it must be supplemented in order to be understood" (242–43). Necessarily so, if only because drawings seek to render a three-dimensional world in a two-dimensional space. By definition, depth in a painting is not really there. The human figures depicted on a canvas are not literally round; nor do the vistas recede into the distance. They merely seem to do so when, under guidance from the artist, a viewer familiar with artistic conventions adds perspective to a surface that is actually flat.

In much the same way do viewers supplement those drawings in which the objects represented are not so much depicted as implied. By way of example, Gombrich contrasts two paintings by Rembrandt: one that renders gold braid on a jacket in painstaking detail; and one that denotes a gold braid by suggestion. In the second instance, loose brushwork hints at the braiding rather than defines it. The viewer is thereby invited to half-create the image that he sees—an invitation that becomes a considerable challenge in the work of later painters, like Turner and the French impressionists, who so stretch the technique of incompletion that their art becomes almost abstract. Almost, but not quite; for their paintings remain representational even when the brushstrokes appear to be chaotic, bearing little if any structural relationship to the forms they conjure up.

At once cunning and subtle, such brushwork proceeds by a kind of understatement that Gombrich characterizes as "magic." What may interest us here is the gloss he provides on that term. "We would not call it magic, though, if it did not work better than the laborious method. There is less paint there to explain and disturb. We remember the Chinese formula: 'Ideas present, brush may be spared performance'—and the idea is more truly present the less there is to contradict our projection" (331). Less, then, is more—a proposition that, taken to its logical conclusion, all but forecasts Barker's experiment in *Scenes*, where Galactia's painting is made to materialize out of thin air. For here is a picture that exists entirely as the viewer's own projection, a fluid creation contradicted by no immutable lines, colors, shapes, or contours. With no artist to act as an intermediary between the viewer and the idea on display, the idea—to extrapolate from Gombrich—is ostensibly free to acquire an immediacy that no conventional painting can rival.

But in the absence of a canvas to provoke a response, what inducement does the so-called viewer have to embark upon the enterprise of projecting any painting whatsoever, least of all one that would suit Galactia? Projection, after all, does not proceed unassisted. As Gombrich explains, "The incomplete painting can arouse the beholder's imagination and project what is not there. . . . [But] there are obviously two conditions that must be fulfilled if the mechanism of projection is to be set in motion. One is that the beholder must be left in no doubt about the way to close the gap [between what is shown and what is not]; secondly, that he must be given a 'screen,' an empty or ill-defined area onto which he can project the expected image" (208). In the case of *Scenes*, the second of these conditions is met simply by Barker's choice of medium, for radio provides a screen wiped clean of every demarcation, even the symbols that constitute print. Indeed, of all the vehicles for promulgating literary texts, radio is the only one that repudiates vision altogether, by its very nature. Gombrich's second condition, then, is fulfilled without effort. What promises difficulties is the first of the conditions. For the gap between radio's blank screen and the painting that Galactia executes cannot be closed by a casual reference to the drawing of a battle. The mere mention of a painting in the dialogue does not offer assurance that the radio listener will envision one.

In general, the only mental images that a radio play is guaranteed to conjure up are those that depict the broad actions implicit in the dialogue. Thus, when Rivera enters Galactia's studio and says to her, "You squat up there like—skirts pulled up like—perched on your scaffolding" (66), the listener has virtually no choice but to see Galactia at work on her *Battle*, yet is entirely free to be blind to the painting itself. Does Galactia, for example, work at the top or at the bottom of her gigantic canvas? To the left or to the right? On what figure? In what color? It hardly matters to the progress of events; hence the listener is likely to draw no conclusions. And thus could the whole play unfurl, with the painting essentially unrealized. That *Scenes* does not, however, run its course without bringing the painting into focus is largely the result of a narrative device that Barker employs to describe not only the physical appearance of the painting, but also the process by which Galactia invokes it into being. Bearing in the printed text the name of "Sketchbook," but no name at all in performance, this device may be understood as the voice of Galactia's creative energy.

In any other medium but radio, the Sketchbook would no doubt seem wholly artificial and consequently jarring. But in a context where every voice is disembodied, there is nothing either special or peculiar about an articulate abstraction. Thus, the Sketchbook, although lacking any physical source to anchor it in reality, ultimately needs none. Because on radio merely to be heard is proof of presence, the Sketchbook confirms its existence through its speech, which largely addresses Galactia's transformation of private experience into public art. That this is its primary function may be concluded from the utterances with which the Sketchbook frames scene 1. The first, a straightforward assessment of the relationship between Galactia's sexual obsessions and her public commission, tells how Carpeta's anatomy appears everywhere in Galactia's preliminary studies for the Battle.[18] The second, though ostensibly no more than a description of a particular section of the painting itself, also has a personal dimension: "The upper left hand corner shows a parting in the angry sky; the clouds have opened and sun bursts through the aperture, flooding the canvas and highlighting all the subjects that lie under the slanting beams, a dramatic diagonal that draws the eye, pulls the eye down jerky surfaces of battle and through passing horizontals to—" (52).[19] Because the image evoked here follows straight upon Galactia's encounter with Prodo, it must surely arise from that meeting, however tenuously. And so it does. For the sunlight that streams across the canvas, though not specific to Prodo's appearance or disclosures, is nonetheless an emblem of his effect on Galactia, a reification of her enlightenment upon hearing his report of a battle in which bones, oars, and flesh break loose from their pinnings and rain down in a terrible tumult. What the Sketchbook, then, describes, along with the painting itself, is Galactia's state of mind in conceiving it. In this way does Barker capture what he has called "the practice of visual representation as it occurs in an artist's mind" (Dunn, "Interview," 34), even as he initiates the mechanism of projection by means of which radio listeners imagine Galactia's painting into life.

Once underway, projection is fostered mainly by the dialogue, which yields numerous glimpses of the painting as the characters respond to it, each in his turn. The Sketchbook, by contrast, speaks sparingly, falling permanently silent at the close of scene 8—partly perhaps because a narrative element soon grows intrusive, and partly because the painting, once made public, loses the privilege of speaking for itself and must submit to being spoken for by others. Yet, before disappearing, the Sketchbook makes two major statements that rigorously govern how listeners envision the painting. In the first, it specifies that the "dead and dying occupy one third of the entire canvas" and that "by a method of foreshortening, their limbs, attached and unattached, project uncomfortably towards the viewer" (65–66). In the second, it discloses that the painting displays "a triangular configuration" involving The Young Sailor Struck, Suffici, and Prodo, with "a shoal of dying figures sliding out the canvas to the left" (69). However the subsequent dialogue may elaborate the painting, the Sketchbook here assures that the work's basic structure—what may be called its composition—is fixed. In so doing, it virtually forces listeners to imagine the essentials of the painting, whether or not they can see it in detail.

In fact, detail is most likely unachievable, for reasons rooted in the psychology of the human mind. The fruits of the imagination are simply less vivid than those of the organs of perception. Thus, a locale when recollected is none so distinct or particularized as it is when revisited. Nor is a symphony heard in the mind with the brilliance it achieves in performance. Likewise with touch, taste, and smell. Indeed, on those very rare occasions when an imagined phenomenon excites the senses as powerfully as if it were real, we consider ourselves not to be imagining, but hallucinating.[20] In projecting Galactia's painting, then, even a listener adept at envisioning imaginary sights will see a canvas that is far less well delineated than those on the walls of museums. So it is that Clive Merrison, who played Carpeta in the BBC production of *Scenes*, has spoken of Galactia's painting as "an impressionistic wash in your mind's eye" (Dunn, "Massacre," 15)—a comment that at once attests to the success of Barker's enterprise and gives evidence of its necessary short-comings. Even Barker's graphic dialogue cannot endow a mental image with high definition. That being the case, the question arises whether Barker's whole experiment with visual projection is not thereby entirely invalidated.

Rudolf Arnheim no doubt would contend that it is. The author of classic inquiries into the psychology of art, film as well as painting, Arnheim took up the problem of radio in 1936 in a book that remains a standard in the field. Among his principal contentions is that radio is so fundamentally aural that efforts to invest it with a visual dimension, if not fruitless, are at least a violation of the medium's essential character. (That such fundamentalism has found few adherents among either play-wrights or listeners does not reduce its interest as a theory about the intrinsic qualities of a radio broadcast.) Conceding that "the average listener makes supplementary visual images for himself . . . probably to a considerable extent," Arnheim nonetheless maintains that "the urge of the listener to imagine with the inner eye is not worth encouraging, but, on the contrary, is a great hindrance to an appreciation of the real nature of wireless and the particular advantages that it alone can offer" (137).[21] But what if one of those advantages is precisely to provide a critique of the visual experience? Then even Arnheim must give Barker due license and watch where it leads.

Where it leads is directly to the back of Galactia's painting, to the part she gives away when Ostensible and Pastaccio interrogate her. As Galactia puts it, "If the surface of the painting is my territory, the back of it is yours" (79, pto), by which comment she concedes that as an artist she asserts no control over the meaning of the images she paints. People must make of her canvas what they will—an invitation they embrace, as their range of responses to her Battle makes only too plain. But for all that Galactia's concession serves her well when the state is about to imprison her, sparing her from entering an argument whose conclusion is foregone, she is far from content at the prospect of forfeiting responsibility for the conceptual premise of her work. She clearly intends for her Battle to capture the outrage of war and, moreover, to constitute an equivalent outrage in the violence of its attack on a warfaring state. Hence when Rivera domesticates the painting, Galactia vociferously objects: "You PANDERED. You LIED. Got me out [of prison] by LICKING AND LAPPING. One hundred feet of pain and you LICKED IT SMOOTH" (87–88). If only she knew, she would equally object to the interpretation put upon the painting by her fellow artists, Sordo and Lasagna, and possibly even to the meaning extracted by the man who weeps and holds her hands at the end of the play. For what he may actually be thinking is anybody's guess.

What we, by contrast, are thinking is perfectly predictable. Although our image of the canvas must vary from person to person, we all know exactly what the painting expresses. We know, despite Urgentino's protestations, that it does not glorify the state. And we know, despite the ubiquitousness of Carpeta's anatomy, that it is not the Slag's Revenge against her lovers. Rather the painting is a declaration on behalf of the dying: it "speak[s] for dead men, not pain and pity, but abhorrence, fundamental and unqualified, blood down the paintbrush, madness in the gums—" (67). What Barker has accomplished, then, is revolutionary. He has reversed the standard condition of the visual image. In particular, he has made the surface of the painting the viewer's territory and returned the back of it to the artist. This, at the price of reducing both the prominence and the clarity of the visual image. We may conjecture that Galactia would not mind.

She herself appears, in fact, to harbor a suspicion that images are nothing without words. This, at any rate, is the possibility she seems to raise in her initial encounter with Prodo, when she insists that he supplement the exhibition of his wounds with an account of "how [he] got them" (50). Merely to see his deformities is not enough for her. She must hear "WHO DID IT TO YOU, PRODO, AND WHAT FOR?" (51). Although the fact of Prodo's participation in battle may be impressed upon his flesh, the meaning of his experience evidently resides in his commentary, not in his "daft appearance" (51), which wrongly makes him out to be "a monkey" (50). The visual spectacle that Prodo presents is therefore not Prodo at all. To be seen for what he is, he must mediate his image, pass it through a clarifying filter. So it is that Galactia asks him to expatiate upon his wounds. Her goal, to be sure, is to translate his words into images anew—but images that smell of blood and raise a noise, the "noise of men minced" (50). Images, in short, that tell a story. Without words to give voice to the freakish spectacle of his pierced brain and spilled gut, Prodo is essentially invisible.

In Prodo's case, of course, "essentially" means "psychologically," a fact that goes far to explain why images alone are inadequate to capture him. For as a means of specifying the inner workings of the mind, words have long, perhaps always, been recognized as superior to pictures. Thus, the conviction of those who see sound as fulfilling, not diminishing, the potential of film: "The Hollywood sound film operates within an oscillation between two poles of realism: that of the psychological (or the interior) and that of the visible (or the exterior). . . . The truth of the individual, of the *interior* realm of the individual (a truth which is most readily spoken and heard), is the truth validated by the coming of sound" (Doane, 59). But if images depend on words, it is not solely for the expression of emotions. Only consider Urgentino's request that Galactia "show [Suffici] for what he is—a tactical genius" (62–63). As Rivera wants to know, "How does she do that? Show him holding a compass?" (63). A similar question arises when Galactia later asks of Ostensible: "How do you paint the upholding of a principle?" (78). The fact is that visual imagery falters in expressing any number of concepts that language quite readily enables us to see: for example, a thousand-sided figure, or a man *not* scratching his nose. In addition, language can clarify images that are inherently ambiguous: for instance, a stick-figure drawing of "a man climbing a hill with a cane," a picture that cannot, on its own terms, be distinguished from a stick-figure drawing of "a man sliding back down the hill, dragging his cane after him."[22] In these instances—as in trompe l'oeil photography, where a close-up of a naked human body, for example, may look more like a landscape than a torso—the images do not come fully clear unless assisted by a caption. The words, in effect, create the pictures.

But only, of course, in effect. It takes radio to do the job in fact, since radio alone guarantees that the screen of the mind is absolutely blank—a condition so unnatural that the mind is compelled to fill the void with creations of its own. The stage cannot duplicate, or even approximate, this power. Thus, to see *Scenes* on stage is to see a lesser play, even if one that remains indisputably distinguished.[23] For in translation to the theater, *Scenes* sheds its engagement with the visual imagination. Once Galactia's canvas receives a literal treatment, however rudimentary—and some treatment on stage is inevitable, given that the painting is unveiled for Carpeta and displayed before Suffici, as well as the public—the impulse for the audience to imagine the painting for itself all but vanishes. Why imagine what is already physically present, particularly when a purely mental image cannot possibly compete with a spectacle at hand and alive? In the theater, Galactia's painting ceases to offer a visual challenge to the audience and becomes, instead, a visual problem for the director—a problem, moreover, to be solved not by means of attention to words that invoke mental images, but through the use of theatrical effects, which, virtually by definition, are inimical to the exercise of imagination on the part of individual spectators.

Two examples may suffice: one, from a minimalist production of *Scenes* at the Almeida Theatre in Islington, London, in early 1990; the other, from a more elaborate presentation at the Colorado College, Colorado Springs, Colorado, in the fall of 1986. At the Almeida, where Glenda Jackson recreated her radio role as Galactia on a nearly bare stage, the painting was shown only once (when revealed to Carpeta) and was then represented by a great white cloth stretched above the actors' heads and suffused with light. Given the simplicity of this treatment of the painting, the theater came as close as it arguably could to inviting projection of the sort described by Gombrich. But who in that audience attended to the cloth in an effort to fill it with phantasmal shapes and figures, when standing beneath it, competing for attention, were Galactia and Carpeta? Very likely, no one—a fact that the director, Ian McDiarmid, may have anticipated when he eliminated the Sketchbook from the script. No need for the voice of a painting-in-process, if the painting-as-complete is never to be.

Under the circumstances, a fuller theatrical illusion need not come amiss. Such, then, was the choice of the director Joanne Klein in an estimable student production of *Scenes* at the Colorado College. Here, the painting was represented by the writhing contortions of dancers positioned on scaffolding that served as a background to much of the action. Nonetheless, when the canvas was exhibited for Suffici's perusal, Urgentino and Suffici turned their backs to the audience and faced not the scaffolding, but a new and different proxy for the painting: a stark black curtain, fully closed. Thus did Klein achieve an ingenious compromise between defining the painting for the spectators and leaving them free to envision it themselves. In fact, by arranging for the curtain to compete with the actors' backs, rather than their faces, Klein actually halted the action on stage, however briefly, as if to encourage the audience to pause for a moment and fabricate a painting of the mind. Even so, Urgentino's red cape of office, displayed against the black, created a visual spectacle so striking that projection may well have been compromised in any case.

Both of these productions, in their separate ways, served the play honestly and well. But at the end of all, *Scenes* is fundamentally a radio play and surely fares best in that medium. Prodo and the Sketchbook seem natural on radio, whereas on stage they can only be strained, unconvincing, or, worst of all, silly. The prison scene, too, which is set in utter darkness, can proceed on the radio without disadvantage, whereas on stage it is noticeably awkward. (In London, it was played by actors stationed in the wings, while the stage remained empty and dimmed. At the Colorado College, the same scaffolding that at other times simulated the painting was used as the set for the prison.) But primarily what disqualifies *Scenes* from a fully satisfactory production in the theater is Galactia's painting itself. For by a fine aesthetic irony, her Battle of Lepanto can never be as eloquent when visible on stage as when seen, though invisible, on radio.

Early in *Scenes*, Galactia announces her desire to produce "a noisy painting" (54). Such a wish to overcome the silence of the visual image apparently has ancient origins. Thus, Gombrich relates that the classical "painter Theon revealed his painting of a soldier to the accompaniment of a blast of trumpets, and we are assured that the illusion was greatly increased" (207). As for Galactia's painting, it may not raise a fanfare; but, far more than Theon's, it is realized through sound. So it is that Galactia earns the truth of her contention that "painters make too much of light. I can work by a candle" (55). Indeed, by the time she has undergone imprisonment, she can actually work in total darkness. "Have you ever painted blind?" she asks. "Actually it isn't dark. We make so much of light, but light's relative. I now think daylight is terribly CRUDE" (84). Better than anyone else, the radio listener may apprehend her meaning. For through Barker's intercession, the listener can claim, like Galactia, to have discovered in the void "whole biographies, and sexual miseries, and me the first to make a picture!" (84, pto). It is the special achievement of radio to make painters of us all, in the innermost reaches of the mind.

# Chapter Two

## THE IMPERFECT EYE
### Tom Stoppard's *Artist Descending a Staircase*

•

**N**OW YOU SEE IT, now you don't. Such is the nature of an image on radio. Present though absent, seen though unseen, a radio image by rights should alert us to be on our guard: to proceed with fair caution, if not outright distrust. Do we dare believe our eyes when what they see is empirically not there? Most assuredly we do, if only because we are highly suggestible. The same impulse that leads us to conjure a monster when something goes bump in the night makes us eagerly receptive to the multitude of phantasms conjured by radio playwrights. For their part, the playwrights—illusionists all—take pains to assure that the spectacles they raise are compelling and wholly unambiguous. As a fundamental article of craftsmanship, radio playwrights make sights emerge from sounds so straightforwardly that the connection between what we hear and what we see must appear unimpeachable. And yet nothing could be further from the truth. We need only consider that the role of a child in a radio play can be carried off convincingly—in fact, undetectably—by a woman who pitches her voice bright and high,[1] and the moral comes clear: radio is ready-made to make us doubt the things we know, or think we know. All that is needed is a playwright with a mind to be ironical. A playwright, that is, like Tom Stoppard in *Artist Descending a Staircase*.

In a plot that puts radio smartly to the test, *Artist* offers two mysteries that admit of solutions only if hearing is synonymous with seeing. Take mystery number one: The elderly artist Donner is dead, sprawled at the foot of a staircase. Presumably, somebody pushed him. But who? A tape that, by happenstance, captured the sounds of Donner's descent provides irrefutable evidence. Yet the tape can support at least four interpretations, all of them plausible, one of them persuasive, but none of them definitive, since the play circles back on itself in such a way that the mystery persists, even once it is solved. So much for the proposition, advanced in the play,

that "the tape recorder"—twin sister to the radio—"speaks for itself"(18).[2] It speaks, to be sure, but in double-entendres that invite us to
question the visions they provoke. As for mystery number two, it is
similarly vexed, arising from Donner's misfortune in love. As a youth,
Donner idolized a blind girl named Sophie. But Sophie loved Beauchamp.
Or did she? So it seemed at the time, since Sophie's ardor was predicated
on her memory of a painting that, to judge from her description, could
only have been Beauchamp's. Unless, as now seems, it was Donner's.
Though Sophie's words speak the truth, they generate images one of
which evidently lies. To see *Artist* in the eye of the mind is thus to gaze
upon the face of certitude shot through with doubt.

It is also to gaze, however improbably, upon the gnomish face of Marcel
Duchamp. Not that Duchamp is a character in the play, or even the object
of anyone's discussion. He is rather invoked through a network of allusions, beginning with the title, that obliquely recapitulate his life and his
work. As for the controversy that even now attaches to Duchamp because
of his avant-garde aesthetics, the play re-enacts the terms of the debate
by pitting Sophie, who champions traditional art, against Donner,
Martello and Beauchamp, who defend the outré. *Artist* thereby produces,
entirely through sound, an optical illusion: a portrait of Duchamp that
arises out of dialogue, though no one so much as pronounces his name.
Look once, and the play explores Sophie's affections and Donner's demise.
Look again, and it describes a profoundly unorthodox artist who intended
his art to appeal to the mind as much as the eye, if not more so.

Where better to encounter such an artist than on radio, a medium that
makes the mind become, in fact, an eye? And how better to perceive him
than in the context of a play that depreciates sight in favor of insight?
It is insight, after all, that alerts us to beware of simple solutions to
*Artist*'s two mysteries: Who killed Donner? and Whom did Sophie love?
And it is insight, as well, that enables us to "see" Duchamp, invisible,
inaudible, and unnamed though he may be. If *Artist*, then, taunts us with
our blindness on radio, even to the extent of employing numerous trompe
l'oeil—really, "trompe l'oreille"—effects, it does so to good end: to
remind us that our senses, by their nature, are imperfect guides to truth.
Being subject to both oversight and error, they mislead us without warning, so that truth, insofar as we know it at all, must emerge from intuition
and from inference no less than observation. Thus does radio in *Artist*
epitomize the human condition: in our blindness, we see; in our sight,
we are blind; and the truth remains open to question.

To all appearances, *Artist Descending a Staircase* fulfills the established requirements of the classic mystery story. There has been a death:

Donner, an elderly artist, has plunged down the stairs that lead from the attic where he has resided to the landing below. The clues point to murder. A tape recorder running at the time of Donner's death has recorded a sequence of sounds that his roommates and fellow artists, Martello and Beauchamp, interpret, according to the headnotes, as follows:

(a) DONNER *dozing: an irregular droning noise.*
(b) *Careful footsteps approach. The effect is stealthy. A board creaks.*
(c) *This wakes* DONNER, *i.e. the droning stops in mid-beat.*
(d) *The footsteps freeze.*
(e) DONNER's *voice, unalarmed: "Ah! There you are . . ."*
(f) *Two more quick steps, and then Thump!*
(g) DONNER *cries out.*
(h) *Wood cracks as he falls through a balustrade.*
(i) *He falls heavily down the stairs, with a final sickening thump when he hits the bottom. Silence.*

(15)

Each of the roommates suspects the other; yet each is apparently wrong in his suspicions, for each has misconstrued the tape. When, at the end of the play, Beauchamp lunges for a fly that is driving him mad, he exactly reproduces the sounds that preceded Donner's plunge:

(a) *Fly droning.*
(b) *Careful footsteps approach. A board creaks.*
(c) *The fly settles.*
(d) BEAUCHAMP *halts.*
(e) BEAUCHAMP: *"Ah! there you are."*
(f) *Two more quick steps and then: Thump!*

(58)

The mystery, at this moment, is solved—for the audience, if not for Martello and Beauchamp, who may (or may not) be aware of what the clues now suggest: namely, that Donner has died in an accident, having lost his footing while swatting a fly.

All very neat, and entirely plausible. Nonetheless, there is a joke at the heart of this inquest. For neither by means of the plot nor by any other means can we, as listeners, know this fly to be, in fact, a fly. Since the drone, as it is called, must sound equally like buzzing and like snoring, it can presumably be rendered, in a radio studio, either by a humming insect or by an actor feigning sleep.[3] And if the droning that we hear was created by an actor, and if the actor was, perchance, the very one who played Donner, then Martello and Beauchamp have rightly understood the tape, or nearly so, and we have been in error—a predicament that leaves the mystery still unsolved. In fact, once we allow that what we hear at the end of the play might be, literally speaking, not a fly droning, but rather Donner dozing (or an actor who pretends to be Donner pretending to doze), we are virtually obliged to regard the final sound effects as vaulting us back to the start of the play, in which case the first line of dialogue, spoken by Martello ("I think this is where I came in"), points humorously to the actor who assumes Martello's part and is now, for the second time, making his entrance. The mystery of the play thus becomes not Who killed Donner? but How do we ever escape from this circular plot?

Such a mix-up over just what question needs addressing would appear to be in keeping with Stoppard's other forays into mystery at about this time. In *After Magritte* (1970), the crime that Inspector Foote attempts to solve is a figment of his own imagination, while the actual mystery demanding a solution is the seemingly inexplicable tableau with which the play begins—a tableau "after Magritte," in which a woman wearing a ballgown sniffs about the stage on her hands and knees, while a second woman draped in a towel lies on an ironing board with a bowler hat reposed on her stomach, a man in rubber waders over evening dress trousers stands on a chair with his torso unclothed, and a constable gazes through the window, unable to enter since a barricade of furniture is blocking off the door. Yes, the whole bizarre scene can be logically explained, as can the equally ludicrous spectacle that draws us into *Jumpers* (1972), where the murder of a philosopher-gymnast is committed (but by whom?) before our very eyes. The culprit, as it happens, is never revealed—a circumstance that highlights Stoppard's interest in the question of how we know the things we know, or think we know. But only in *Artist Descending a Staircase*, and only by means of the radio format, does Stoppard succeed in creating what he seems to be after: namely, a play in which a mystery is equally solved and unsolved. His point? Presumably, that what we take for truth is merely paradox.

Certainly *Artist* is nothing if not paradoxical. Consider, for example, how frequently the dialogue misfires, and with what effect. We fool ourselves if we imagine that the comic exchanges among the three artists constitute merely the romp that Stoppard often favors. Rather they are evidence that talk is inconclusive, creating dilemmas, not solving them. Sometimes confusion arises because the speakers cannot rearrange their minds to fit each other's train of thought, as when Martello misconstrues the point of Beauchamp's cry of innocence:

MARTELLO:    Mental acrobatics, Beauchamp—I have achieved
             nothing but mental acrobatics—*nothing!*—whereas

you, however, wrongly and for whatever reason, came to grips with life at least this once, and killed Donner.

BEAUCHAMP: It's not true, Martello!

MARTELLO: Yes, yes, I tell you, *nothing!*—Niente! Nada! Nichts!

(18)

Sometimes the source of confusion is a speaker's failing memory, which inclines to take its life from puns, instead of recollections.

DONNER: You never danced with Edith Sitwell.

BEAUCHAMP: Oh yes I did.

DONNER: You're thinking of that American woman who sang negro spirituals at Nancy Cunard's coming-out ball.

BEAUCHAMP: It was Queen Mary's wedding, as a matter of fact.

DONNER: You're mad.

BEAUCHAMP: I don't mean wedding, I mean launching.

DONNER: I can understand your confusion but it was Nancy Cunard's coming-out.

BEAUCHAMP: Down at the docks?

DONNER: British boats are not launched to the sound of minstrel favourites.

BEAUCHAMP: I don't mean launching, I mean maiden voyage.

DONNER: I refuse to discuss it.

(23)

And sometimes a muddle is the calculated message of dialogue that hits the mark by missing it.

DONNER: I think, in a way, edible art is what we've all been looking for.

MARTELLO: Who?

DONNER: All of us!—Breton!—Ernst!—Marcel—Max—you—me—Remember how Pablo used to shout that the war had made art irrelevant?—well—

MARTELLO: Which Pablo?

DONNER: What do you mean, which Pablo?—*Pablo!*

MARTELLO: What, that one-armed waiter at the Café Suisse?

DONNER: Yes—the Café Russe—the proprietor, lost a leg at Verdun—

MARTELLO: God, he was slow, that Pablo. But it's amazing how you remember all the people who gave you credit . . .

DONNER: He gave you credit because you had been at Verdun.

MARTELLO: That's true.

DONNER:     It was a lie.
MARTELLO:   Wasn't I? It must have been pretty close to Verdun . . .

(29)

Taking "Pablo" for Picasso and "credit" for esteem, we mistake what we are hearing, and yet hear it aright, since our error leads us straight to the puns that the playwright intends. Depending on how we interpret what we hear, wrong is right and right is wrong; thus, what to Donner is a lie is, with justice, a truth to Martello. Heard like this, the whole play is a conundrum.

From such a welter of misunderstandings, the truth—about Donner's demise, about the value of edible art or, for that matter, any art—seems likely to emerge, if at all, by indirection. Especially so, since language is shown to be sometimes intentionally evasive. Nothing in Pinter, for instance, is more Pinteresque—more indicative of speech as "a constant stratagem to cover nakedness" (Pinter, 579)—than Donner's poignant efforts to conceal his ancient jealousy of Beauchamp:

BEAUCHAMP:  At our age, *anything* we do is faintly ludicrous. Our best hope as artists is to transcend our limitations and become *utterly* ludicrous. Which you are proceeding to do with your portrait of Sophie, for surely you can see that a post-Pop pre-Raphaelite is pure dada brought up to date—
            (*Smack!*)
DONNER:     Shut up, damn you!—how dare you talk of her?!—how dare you—
            (*And weeps—*)
            —*and would you stop cleaning the bath with my face flannel!!!*
            (*Pause.*) I'm sorry—please accept my apology—
BEAUCHAMP:  I'm sorry, Donner . . . I had no idea you felt so strongly about it.
DONNER:     (*Sniffle.*) Well, I have to wash my face with it.
BEAUCHAMP:  No, no, I mean about your new . . .

(24–25)

What Donner is expressing is not only the pain that his unrequited love for Sophie still arouses but also his suspicion that Beauchamp won her wrongly, through a misunderstanding. And yet we, no less than Beauchamp, miss the point of the exchange; for not until later, in a flashback (and see how time itself becomes a paradox), does Martello suggest that it was Donner whom Sophie really loved. If only Sophie had not gone entirely blind before meeting the artists, or if only her sight had been clear enough, before, to have allowed her to distinguish between Beauchamp's snow scene and Donner's white fence, then no one would question whose face beside what painting drove Sophie to love at first sight.

Of course, "sight" is a misnomer, since Sophie cannot see; and "love," too, is dubious, by Sophie's own admission: "It was quick: one moment the sick apprehension of something irrevocable which I had not chosen, and then he was the secret in the deep centre of my life. I wouldn't have called it love myself, but it seems to be the word that people use for it" (36). But if not love, what is it? Surely not affinity, since from the outset Sophie is skeptical at best, contemptuous at worst, of what passes for art among Beauchamp and the others. Nor can she be drawn for long by prospects of affection, given Beauchamp's neglect and possible disloyalty. Yet her need for him persists, a minor mystery in itself, made tragic if Martello is correct in deducing that it was Donner, not Beauchamp, with whom Sophie fell in love.

Somehow, we accept Martello's theory: the plot demands a painful turn, if only because we take pleasure (paradoxically) in irony, in sentiment, in poignancy. But is Martello really right? After all, as Donner reasons, he might have been "lying, just getting his own back—you see, I damaged his figure, slightly" (27). And indeed, the truth and Martello are not close companions. Martello is willing, for example, to propose that it "must have been Donner" (20) who stole Beauchamp's marmalade, when he himself seems implicated, having made it a point to discover from Donner that the marmalade was hidden in the pickle jar. To lie about Sophie, then, would probably not daunt him, whether his reason was nasty, as Donner conjectures, or generous, as one might conclude from the context in which he makes his revelation.

MARTELLO: Is it still important, Donner? Would it comfort you if you thought, even now, that Sophie loved you?
DONNER: I can never think that, but I wish I could be sure that she had some similar feeling for me.
MARTELLO: Did you ever wonder whether it was you she loved?

(55)

The only thing sure is that nothing is certain—neither the object of Sophie's affection, nor the cause of Donner's death, nor the identity of either the marmalade thief or the roommate who washes the tub with Donner's face cloth. And yet we feel we know the answers to these questions, so cogent are the probabilities.

Figuratively, Stoppard has us running in circles. Literally, too. The very shape of the play is circular, beginning in the here and now (point A in

the following diagram), receding through flashbacks to 1914 (point F),
then recapitulating all the steps in flashes forward to the here and now

again. As Stoppard explains "the play is set temporally in six parts, in
the sequence ABCDEFEDCBA" (13)—a movement that suggests the form
of a circle even before the final action has driven us back to the start of
the play, where Martello's opening line, "I think this is where I came
in," strongly suggests a second time around. Lest we still miss the point,
Beauchamp underscores the theme of circularity with his penchant for
making recordings on continuous tapes that go round and round in
endless repetition.

"I know that in this loop of tape," says Beauchamp, "there is some
truth about how we live" (56). If so, that truth is metaphorical, residing
in the similarity between the circular course of Beauchamp's tape and
the equally circular course of the characters' lives. Judging from the ways
in which the characters repeat themselves and one another, we might
take the play as evidence that everything that goes around will come
around again. Or, in a variation on Santayana's epigram, those who have
a past are condemned to repeat it.

Take Donner, for example. His past, insofar as he has one, is Sophie,
and hers is the past he repeats at the end of his life. On discovering that
Sophie in fact may have loved him, Donner takes on her outworn artistic
opinions and sets about to paint a "real Academy picture" (25), replete
with Sophie's vision of a "unicorn in the garden" (44). In thus circling
back to Sophie, Donner rejects the avant-garde and "return[s] to traditional values" (24)—a move that punningly accords with Sophie's surname, Farthingale, which suggests both circularity and antiquarianism.
Unfortunately for Donner, his return to the past seems to prompt a cosmic
irony: he reiterates not only Sophie's taste in art but also, roughly speaking, her fall to her death. And because of his own sad descent in pursuit
of a fly, he ends by fulfilling the fate he had feared in his youth at the
outbreak of war: "I don't want to die *ridiculously*" (50). The past, which
has haunted poor Donner for decades, has finally caught up with him;
or, rather, he has caught up with it, having all but contrived to meet (and
repeat) it by circling back.

In the action of the play, other circles, other repetitions, are described by all the other characters as well. Beauchamp, for example, repeats his own past when Martello accuses him of pushing Donner down the stairs: "You didn't mean to *kill* him. It was manslaughter" (19). Although Beauchamp apparently neither meant to kill Donner nor did so, at least not on this occasion, he can easily be said to have committed figurative manslaughter years earlier, when he innocently cheated Donner out of Sophie—if, of course, Martello's deduction is right. But in drawing the wrong conclusion about Donner's fall down the stairs, is Martello just repeating a tendency to err, thus revealing that he probably also is wrong about Beauchamp's displacement of Donner in Sophie's affection? Perhaps. At any rate, in his current project—a metaphorical bust of Sophie with ripe corn for hair, pearls for teeth, and fruit for breasts—Martello is baldly repeating the concept of art he pronounced in 1914, when he determined to make literal the figures used in the Song of Solomon to describe a beautiful woman ("I shall paint her navel as a round goblet . . ." [51]). As for Sophie, whose name and aesthetic convictions suggest a return to what was, even her future is a replay of her past, as we learn from her sense of what awaits her in her never-to-be-realized move from Lambeth to Chelsea: "Perhaps there will be another accordionist waiting for us across the river. And no doubt the smell will be much the same on the left bank" (33). Sophie is so rooted in the past that she remains there, circling back, in a sense, by never moving on.

Interestingly, the circular movement that is featured in the action of the play is also featured in its language and structure. At the start of the play, for example, Beauchamp turns off his recording of Donner's last moments at the very point when Donner would be saying, "There you are"—the words that Beauchamp says himself at just that instant. Beauchamp thus repeats Donner and displaces him much as he may have displaced him years before in the love affair with Sophie. Another verbal repetition, this time with Beauchamp repeating himself, involves Beauchamp's descriptions of his method of recording:

I record in loops, lassoing my material—no, like trawling—no, like— no matter.

(15)

Layer upon layer of what passes for silence, trapped from an empty room—no, trawled—no, like—no matter!

(56)

Possibly Beauchamp repeats himself from habit—possibly, as "no matter" would seem to imply, from a lack of the very creativity and substance his art is supposed to reflect. But whatever we may make of this echo and others, they clearly form part of the pattern in which the play itself repeats itself.

When Sophie and Martello, for example, describe how they met (and note that this meeting is their second encounter, as the circular motif would seem to demand), she finds herself "telling everything back to front" (40), just like the play, which reverses chronological order by telling about the present first, than gradually returning to 1914. Her telling, in other words, mirrors the play's, just as her two signal scenes are so constructed that one mirrors the other. In each of these scenes—those labeled "D" in Stoppard's alphabetical scheme—Sophie delivers what is essentially a monologue on her move away from Lambeth. The first of these monologues is spoken to Beauchamp, who is physically present but absent emotionally, while the second is delivered to Donner, who is surely there in spirit, although not, despite what Sophie thinks, in fact. The scenes, then, repeat each other—admittedly with significant differences—as do the opening lines of the play's first three scenes, all of which involve misunderstandings. (Scene A displays Beauchamp and Martello misconstruing Beauchamp's tape. Scene B displays Beauchamp wilfully misconstruing Donner's opinion of his recordings. And Scene C invites the audience—at least those who have forgotten that Donner is sculpting a Venus de Milo from sugar—to misconstrue the manner in which Martello is attempting to sweeten his tea.) Here is a play that is determined to repeat itself, though in ways that Beauchamp, with his own repeating loop of tape, has evidently never imagined.

Despite Beauchamp's belief that his recordings contain "some truth about how we live," it is not his tape but Stoppard's that wrestles with the truth—concluding that wherever we may search for it, our efforts just return us to the place where we began. The truth is thus elusive, perhaps even illusory, not the least when we are sure that we have found it. What, for example, is the truth about Sophie's affections if, while making love to Beauchamp, she envisioned him as Donner? Surely Beauchamp was no less beloved for having been, had Sophie known, the wrong man; nor was Donner forsaken, though he never had the joy of a single embrace. And yet love misdirected, misconstrued as it were, is hardly what we mean by love. So if Sophie loved both men, she also loved neither, though she may, after all, have loved Beauchamp quite singularly, in her mind as in his flesh. All these several possibilities pertain, complicating (muddling) our understanding of Sophie, just as the meaning of the play's ending is complicated (made multifarious) by our inability to distinguish the sound of a buzzing fly from the sound of a dozing Donner or, rather, the sound of an actor pretending to doze.

Such a wealth of ambiguity leaves the characters, no less than the audience, embarrassed by their riches. When each interpretation of events implies an equal and opposite reinterpretation, the simplest decision grows vexed. That the police should be notified of Donner's demise, that his lifeless body should not be left to molder in the stairwell, would seem to be entirely self-evident; yet the characters recognize only the problem, not the solution:

MARTELLO:   Which reminds me, you can't leave Donner lying there
            at the bottom of the stairs for very long in this weather,
            and that is only the practical argument; how long can
            you *ethically* leave him?
BEAUCHAMP:  It is nothing to do with me.

(17)

How much more difficult, then, they must find it to know what makes sense in more ambiguous circumstances: how, for example, to behave in matters of friendship and love, how to choose between the relative merits of artistic endeavor and social responsibility, how to determine what constitutes art, as opposed on the one hand to craftsmanship and on the other to charlatanism. No wonder Martello falls captive to irony: "God forgive my *brain*!—it is so attuned to the ironic tone it has become ironical in repose; I have to whip sincerity out of it as one whips responses from a mule!" (18). Sincerity is laughable (witness Donner in his zealous moods) when the world contrives to contradict our every notion.

In a contradictory world, even art grows ironic. For Beauchamp, Martello, and (in his youth) Donner, succumbing to irony means creating works that represent absurdity by being in themselves absurd. For Stoppard, it means subjecting absurd behavior or conditions to rational scrutiny. So it is that all of Stoppard's early plays grapple with the problem of making senselessness make sense. And so it is that one of them, *After Magritte*, even touches on *Artist*'s particular concern: namely, how art domesticates nonsense. But in design and conception *After Magritte* is less ambitious than *Artist*, just as Magritte is himself less provocative than the artist whom *Artist* most closely observes: neither Beauchamp, nor Martello, nor Donner, those poignantly inconsequential fellows, but the formidable Marcel Duchamp, the controversial exponent of the modern sensibility in twentieth-century art.

ADMIRED in America long before the Europeans paid him any heed, Duchamp toward the end of his life was discovered at last by the British. In the summer of 1966, the Arts Council of Great Britain sponsored at the Tate Gallery a major Duchamp exhibition—the first in Europe—en-

titled The Almost Complete Works of Marcel Duchamp. And when the
great man himself arrived for the opening in June, the BBC took the
opportunity to interview him, as it had at least twice before, in March
and September 1961. During the month-long exhibition, BBC television
aired a film about Duchamp, *Rebel Readymade*; and the Arts Council
issued a catalog including 242 items, which indeed comprised nearly all
Duchamp had ever done. Necessarily omitted, since it remained a secret
until the artist's death in 1968, was the shockingly naturalistic *Etant
donnés*—a massive sort of diorama, impossible to move or even photo-
graph in its entirety, given that it occupies a small enclosed room at the
Philadelphia Museum of Art, where it was posthumously constructed
according to Duchamp's detailed plans. Both the catalog and gallery did,
however, feature a painstaking replica of *The Bride Stripped Bare by Her
Bachelors, Even*, Duchamp's enigmatic masterpiece, a painting on glass,
once accidentally shattered, then reconstructed by the artist, but nonetheless so fragile that it could not be transported from its home in
Philadelphia.

The Whether Stoppard, who that summer was preparing *Rosencrantz and
Guildenstern* for its premiere at the "fringe" of the Edinburgh Festival,
had the time or inclination to attend to all the fuss, he must certainly
have noticed some tremor in the art world. Duchamp was in the air,
breathing irreverence and sucking the wind out of overblown conceptions
of the dignity of art. This genius (or, as some would have it, fraud), who
in 1917 had "chosen" a urinal, signed it R. Mutt, upended it and titled
it *Fountain*, then sought to display it at an exhibition of the Indépendants,
only to be straightway rejected, had never lost his edge or his capacity
for raising a furor. One imagines Stoppard warming to the spectacle. For
as *Artist Descending a Staircase* betrays, Stoppard at some point acquired
an extensive knowledge of Duchamp—or, at any rate, developed so
preternatural an affinity with him that even the play's least assuming
details have demonstrable connections to the artist.

The title of the play, then, is not an idle joke. Duchamp's *Nude
Descending a Staircase*, a *succès de scandale* at the 1913 Armory Show
in New York City, is arguably still the most famous painting of the
twentieth century, and the allusion to it calls attention to Duchamp's real
achievement, however his detractors may defame his work. For the
painting stands as evidence that Duchamp was experimenting with motion while the cubists were still having none of it; that he was reconceiving
and revitalizing paintings of the nude when every other modern painter
had abandoned the subject; that he had sensed, before most others, the
contemporary fascination with machinery; and that for nearly all his life
he was so intensely modern that much of his work eluded and outraged

even the avant-garde. (Note that the cubists persuaded him to withdraw *Nude Descending a Staircase* from the 1912 exhibition of the Salon des Indépendants.) Duchamp, as Stoppard's title would seem to imply, is the giant who casts in the shadow those pygmies Beauchamp, Martello, and Donner. Yet the pygmies, in keeping with the play's sense of paradox, are nothing themselves if not versions of Duchamp, cubistically fragmented. Indeed, the whole play is in essence a translation of Duchamp's famous painting. For just as the painting is a portrait of a nude who emerges, if at all, only from the interplay of geometric shapes that attempt to evoke her (or is it him?), so the play is a portrait of an artist, Duchamp, who emerges, if at all, only from the interplay of innumerable teasing allusions to his life and to his work.

The very names of the characters suggest as much. Martello is transparently Marcel. Beauchamp (that is, Beecham, as the British would say) needs only a French pronunciation to approximate Duchamp. And Donner, in French, not only sounds like the significant word in the title of Duchamp's last great work, *Etant donnés*, but also, being an infinitive, recalls *A l'infinitif*, the collection of previously unpublished notes that Duchamp issued in facsimile in 1967. Small surprise, then, that each of the artists, to different degrees, can be seen to embody Duchamp.[4]

Beauchamp, in particular, resembles Duchamp in his guise as the lapsed painter. Having left off work in 1923 on his never-to-be-finished *Bride Stripped Bare by Her Bachelors, Even*, Duchamp devoted himself for decades thereafter to such eccentric projects as motorized optical experiments, facsimile editions of his notes for *The Bride Stripped Bare*, and miniaturized reproductions of his major works, neatly packed into a carrying case entitled *Box in a Valise*. In addition, he turned his attention to chess, eventually publishing a book on the subject and competing in international tournaments. Painting, Duchamp contended, bored him: he had never liked the paints and the brushes and the canvas. Moreover, he was wary of art that appealed to the eye instead of the mind. How very like Beauchamp, with his curious defense of his recordings: "I'm trying to liberate the visual *image* from the limitations of visual *art*. The idea is to create images—pictures—which are purely *mental* . . . I think I'm the first artist to work in this field" (38–39). The statement could well have been Duchamp's, so expressive is it of his practice and philosophy.[5]

As for the recordings themselves, they are broadly allusive to Duchamp in his relations with the avant-garde. Beauchamp's ludicrous tapes of Ping-Pong games, chess matches, and even silences can be taken, for example, to reify André Breton's conception of the artist as "nothing but a recording apparatus, [whose] role in the mechanism of inspiration is entirely passive" (Haftmann, 188). Though Duchamp was equivocal about Breton and the surrealists, he is nonetheless regarded as a father of surrealism. Thus, the tapes, with their apparent allusion to Breton, can be seen to encompass Duchamp, particularly if we take into account the "musical work" Duchamp produced with John Cage in Toronto in 1968. That work, to the consternation of the audience, consisted of a chess game played on a board that had been wired for sound, each square having been connected to amplifiers and speakers. The result was vintage Beauchamp, only bettered; for whereas Beauchamp's recordings of chess games—"Lenin versus Jack Dempsey," for example (44)—are a pretense, this one (recorded by Columbia) was real. Even Beauchamp's recordings of silence evoke Cage and Duchamp, as is evident from one of Duchamp's more provoking pronouncements: "Happenings have introduced into art an element no one had put there: boredom. To do a thing in order to bore people is something I never imagined! And that's too bad, because it's a beautiful idea. Fundamentally, it's the same idea as John Cage's silence in music; no one had thought of that" (Cabanne, *Dialogues*, 99). Moreover, the silences layered on silences that Beauchamp seeks to capture are allied to Duchamp's peculiar principle of the *infra-mince* or, in English, "infrathin," a category of barely measurable phenomena exemplified by "the faint sound made by velvet trouser legs brushing together, the difference between the space occupied by a clean, pressed shirt and the same shirt, dirty" (d'Harnoncourt, 37).

In other ways, too, Beauchamp resembles Duchamp. Beauchamp's cavalier treatment of Sophie, for instance, reflects not just the spirit of Duchamp's lengthy bachelorhood in the company of women whom he did not encourage yet equally did not put off, but also his curious marriage in June 1927 to Jeanne Lydie Marie Sarazin, who filed for divorce after only six months on the grounds that all she had had from Duchamp was his total indifference. In their peculiar combination of aloofness and gallantry toward women, Beauchamp and Duchamp could be each other's double, as well as in their penchant for making "indefensible statements about art" (45). There are shades of Duchamp, too, in Beauchamp's candid reflection that the "artist is a lucky dog. That is all there is to say about him. In any community of a thousand souls there will be nine hundred doing the work, ninety doing well, nine doing good, and one lucky dog painting or writing about the other nine hundred and ninety-nine" (46). It was, after all, Duchamp who contended that "one is a painter because one wants so-called freedom; one doesn't want to go to the office every morning" (Cabanne, *Dialogues*, 25).

And then there is Beauchamp's tenth horse, a figure fairly rife with allusions to Duchamp and modern art. It may be a coincidence that in French the child's word for hobbyhorse is *dada*, the name of the movement (surrealism's forerunner) that Donner remembers from the Café Voltaire (actually the Cabaret Voltaire) in Zurich (26). Perhaps it is also a coincidence that Beauchamp rides his horse across France in 1914, the same year that Raymond Duchamp-Villon, Duchamp's brother, completed his powerful sculpture of a horse half-become a machine, as if in illustration of the modern conception of horsepower (Cabanne, *Brothers*, 110, 136). But there is nothing accidental in Beauchamp's evocation of his marvelous steed: "He's not physical!—He's not metaphysical!—He's pataphysical!" (49). The science of imaginary solutions, pataphysics was formulated by Alfred Jarry in his scandalous play *Ubu Roi*, a work of such interest to Duchamp that he designed a quirky bookbinding for the 1935 edition. Moreover, in 1959, apparently as a joke, Duchamp entered "the Collège de 'Pataphysique in France . . . with the rank of Transcendent Satrap (the highest in this life) and the supplemental honor of being Maître de l'Ordre de la Grande Gidouille" (d'Harnoncourt and McShine, 28). Whether Duchamp actually subscribed to the pataphysical rejection of "all scientific explanations of any kind" seems doubtful; but he must have been drawn, not to mention entertained, by the pataphysical argument that "everything could just as well be its opposite" (Tomkins et al., 32)—a position that would appeal equally to Beauchamp, and clearly to Stoppard as well.

The correspondences between Beauchamp and Duchamp, then, are intricate, in fact seemingly exhaustive. Yet equally striking, though less extensive, correspondences link Duchamp with each of the other two artists, Martello and Donner. Martello's art, to be sure, may seem less like Duchamp's than like Salvador Dali's, at least in the bust of Sophie, which resembles nothing so much as Dali's *Ruby Lips*, a work that "takes literally the romantic cliché of 'lips like rubies and teeth like pearls'" (Tomkins et al., 128). But in his ambition to create "a wooden man with a real leg" (34), Martello quite wittily mirrors Duchamp, who proposed in *A l'infinitif* a number of projects that earned the name of art purely by being impossible to create. Similarly, in his ironic outburst at the start of the play—"Mental acrobatics, Beauchamp—I have achieved nothing but mental acrobatics—*nothing!*" (18)—Martello echoes not only the opinion of those "generations of art critics" (17) who consider Duchamp overrated, but also the good-natured cynicism of Duchamp himself, who refrained from taking his own endeavors—or anyone else's, for that matter—too seriously.

Even Donner, whose ardency sets him apart from Duchamp, bears an otherwise arresting resemblance to the artist, much of which is captured in Donner's riotous proposal to make art edible by sculpting a Venus de Milo in sugar or a Thinker in salt (27–28). His "sugar art" works as a wry inverted reference to Duchamp's wooden birdcage filled with sugar cubes sculpted from marble—an artwork that functions rather like a trompe l'oeil in its effort to amaze us by its unexpected weight. As for *Le penseur* in salt, it recalls Duchamp's spoonerism on his own name: Marchand du Sel (translated as Salt Seller). Moreover, "edible art" can be heard as a pun on "oedipal art"—and Duchamp, in fact, was quite wild about puns[6]—thereby raising the ghost of those oedipal theories that critics have used to explain both Duchamp's major works and his passion for chess. Finally, Donner's interest in "justify[ing] a work of art to a man with an empty belly" (28) roguishly recalls Apollinaire's prediction that "it will be the task of an artist as detached from esthetic preoccupations, and as intent on the energetic as Marcel Duchamp, to reconcile art and the people" (Apollinaire, 26)—a statement that Duchamp, by the way, considered ridiculous (Tomkins et al., 33).

In a more somber vein, it is Donner who makes the play's only explicit reference to Duchamp when he purportedly quotes him: "That was Marcel . . . I think he had talent under all those jokes. He said to me, 'There are two ways of becoming an artist. The first way is to do things by which is meant art. The second way is to make art mean the things you do'" (26–27). No fairer distillation of Duchamp can be imagined. Moreover, even Donner's interest in the nude recalls Duchamp, who, as an art student at the Académie Julian, "tried entering the Ecole des Beaux-Arts competition, which was a 'flop' as you say in English. The first test was to do a nude in charcoal—I flunked" (Cabanne, *Dialogues*, 21). Nonetheless, the nude remained for Duchamp a "fundamental preoccupation": he produced not only a figurative rendering of the subject in *Nude Descending a Staircase* but also, in his drawings and studies for *Etant donnés* during 1944 and 1948–49, "the first literal treatments of a nude (if one excepts the borrowed nude of *In the Manner of Delvaux*, 1942) since 1912" (d'Harnoncourt and Hopps, 21). In short, after a lifetime of embracing almost every kind of abstract art, Duchamp, like Donner, returned to realism with a vengeance. Admittedly, Duchamp retained his sense of humor in the process, as Donner did not; Duchamp even produced in *Etant donnés* a work whose very realism seems radical. But despite these disjunctions, the likeness is telling.

Only what does it say? Nothing unambiguous, we may be sure, if the play is to speak for either Stoppard or Duchamp. The openendedness of the mystery that *Artist* presents is itself a clear suggestion that Stoppard will not introduce simplicity to questions still more vexing—questions about the value of modern art and the virtues of one of its principal renegades. Stoppard's taste for ambiguity, moreover, is well reflected in his comment to Mel Gussow in 1972 (the very year that *Artist Descend-*

*ing a Staircase* was broadcast): "I write plays because dialogue is the most respectable way of contradicting yourself" (Whitaker, 4). Had Duchamp been a playwright, the statement might well have been his. In fact, he made a similar remark about the practice of his art: "I have forced myself to contradict myself in order to avoid conforming to my own taste" (d'Harnoncourt, 35). Not surprisingly, then, each of Duchamp's major works has been shown to assault us with mutually inconsistent meanings: "In [Duchamp's] capricious meta-reality . . . everything can be read at least two ways at once. If there is a law informing the whole, it is Paradox, the resonance of apparently contradicting alternatives" (d'Harnoncourt and Hopps, 16).

Given Duchamp's meta-reality coupled with Stoppard's own tendency toward paradox, it follows quite naturally that *Artist Descending a Staircase* should promote Duchamp even while mocking him.[7] It is Duchamp, after all, who is skewered when Donner proposes that an "artist is someone who is gifted in some way which enables him to do something more or less well which can only be done badly or not at all by someone who is not thus gifted. To speak of an art which requires no gift is a contradiction employed by people like yourself who have an artistic bent but no particular skill" (23–24). Duchamp's very biographer begs the question of skill in asserting that Duchamp "had solved his own inner doubt about his technical competence as an artist, by focusing on ideas rather than technique, and by moving art itself from the easel to the brain" (Marquis, 115). So when Donner announces that "skill without imagination is craftsmanship and gives us many useful objects such as wickerwork picnic baskets. Imagination without skill gives us modern art" (24), we find ourselves forced to devalue Duchamp by consenting to Beauchamp's reply, "A perfectly reasonable summary."

But devalue Duchamp as we may, we must also concede that the whole of modern history accords with Martello's observation to Donner about the way that World War I rearranged our sensibilities:

DONNER:      [The war is] what killed it for me. After that, being
             an artist made no sense. I should have stopped then.
             Art made no sense.
BEAUCHAMP:   Except for nonsense art.[8]

                                                                    (30)

We know, too, that Martello, in debating with Sophie, is right about the relative merits of technique and creativity: "Anybody could do it—yes, I insist: painting nature, one way or another, is a technique and can be learned, like playing the piano. But how can you teach someone to *think* in a certain way?—to paint an utterly simple shape in order to ambush the mind with something quite unexpected about that shape by hanging it in a frame and forcing you to see it, as it were, for the first time—"(42). When Sophie reflects that Turner could have painted like Martello had he wanted, Martello's response is unimpeachable: "It would not have occurred to him to do so; I think that's really the point" (34).

Thus, however Sophie (read: the audience) may scoff at modern art, Beauchamp, Martello, and Donner (read: Duchamp) emerge triumphant, since they perceive the need for art to change and grow. While Sophie may have better taste than her companions do, as well as better sense and possibly more love, she lacks their creativity and insight, as her blindness would seem to suggest. And, insofar as the play can be read as an allegory, the wages of blindness appear to be death. A solemn reading, perhaps, for a play far more jovial than not. But the poignancy implicit in the depiction of Sophie encourages solemnity. Moreover, the only two characters who die in the play are those who turn aside from innovation.[9]

Is Stoppard, then, an apologist for modern art? For Duchamp? It would seem so—until we reflect on the antics of the artists by whom Duchamp is represented. How these ineffectual, although endearing, clowns can glorify Duchamp remains a mystery as resistant to solution as the mystery that constitutes the plot. We are caught in a conundrum from which escape seems impossible—unless Duchamp himself has shown a way with his teasing observation about the meaning of his own conundrum, *The Bride Stripped Bare by Her Bachelors, Even*: "There is no solution because there is no problem" (Tomkins, 57). Perhaps, instead of seeking problems and solutions, we should look to Stoppard's play simply for representations of a riddling reality. Thus do likely solutions to the play's central mystery prove at last to be inadequate. And thus, too, do the many details that create the portrait of Duchamp defeat our best attempts to assess his achievement. We are simply left bemused by a host of contradictions, which serve to embody Duchamp and to evoke him. Indeed the play is so designed as to evoke Duchamp at almost every turn.

All the joking and quick-wittedness that animate the dialogue, for instance, recall Duchamp's legendary badinage, in youth, with Francis Picabia and Guillaume Apollinaire. The sense of paradox underpinning the play is, as we have seen, so quintessentially Duchamp that examples could be endlessly multiplied, though no single instance better illustrates the point than Duchamp's famous door, constructed as a space-saving device in his tiny apartment in Paris. Built to serve two doorways alternately (the one, between the studio and the bedroom; the other, between the studio and the bathroom), the door had the remarkable property of being "open and shut at the same time" (Tomkins, 54)—much as

Stoppard's mystery is solved and unsolved simultaneously. As for the circles in the play—the circular movement of time, for example, and the looping of Beauchamp's continuous tape—they might be viewed as roughly related to Duchamp's experiments with circularity: his *Rotary Demisphere*, or his *Rotoreliefs*, which were "round cardboard disks that fitted on a phonograph turntable and whose printed abstract designs, when revolved at 33 r.p.m., produced the illusion of recognizable objects in three dimensions" (Tomkins, 59). As Duchamp once explained in an interview, "Always there has been a necessity for circles in my life, for, how do you say, rotation" (Adcock, 190). Moreover, the frequent repetitions in the play—that is, the way in which the characters repeat each other's actions, though with differences—would seem to reflect Duchamp's artistic practice. Though Duchamp was almost fanatical about never repeating his successes, never grinding out a host of variations in a style that he felt he had conquered, he compulsively "rehearse[d] his career forever [like] the criminal forever returning to the scene of the crime" (Antin, 114). In fact, the themes in his work remained so much the same over sixty-odd years that even his radical *Etant donnés* has been said not only to "bristle with cross-references, visual and conceptual, to many other [of his] objects and verbal constructs" but also to be, in particular, "an alternative vision of the same elements" as those present in *The Bride Stripped Bare by Her Bachelors, Even* (d'Harnoncourt and Hopps, 13, 24).

If such subtle correspondences between the structure of the play and the nature of Duchamp bedazzle us, more dazzling still is the way that Duchamp and his art inform even the plot of the play—at least the part involving Sophie. The source of Sophie's unhappiness in love was her possibly having confused, in her gathering blindness, the foreground and the background of a painting. What Sophie believed to be a snow scene (by Beauchamp) might have easily been, as Martello proposes, a white fence (by Donner): "Thick white posts, top to bottom across the whole canvas, in inch or two apart, black in the gaps—. . . Well, one might be wrong, but her sight was not good even then" (56). And if it had been? As several of Duchamp's works establish, depth is an equivocal illusion in art. In his *Passage from the Virgin to the Bride*, for example, the foreground and the background seem to vibrate. Similar vibrations are readily apparent in his superimposition of blue on red hearts (or is it red hearts on blue?) entitled *Coeurs volants*. Stereoscopy apparently attracted Duchamp, as did the captivating property of a painting on glass—namely, that the background (what is seen through the unpainted part of the glass) is constantly changing and, if the audience chooses, constantly likely to come to the fore as the focus of attention.

As the audience for *Artist Descending a Staircase*, we might ask what would happen if Sophie, who constitutes the background of the play, were likewise to come to the foreground—that is, to displace Donner's death as our focus of attention. The result would, in fact, be revolutionary. For the play would then translate into language, not the painting that provides its name, but rather another work: *The Bride Stripped Bare by Her Bachelors, Even*. Sophie, after all, is a bride surrounded by bachelors, and one, moreover, stripped bare both literally and figuratively—literally in Beauchamp's bed, figuratively in Martello's bust and in Donner's unicorn painting, as well as in her devastation over Beauchamp's desertion. Further, Sophie's story embodies the pun implicit in the work's original title: *La mariée mis à nu par ses célibataires, même*. As critics never tire of noting, *même* is a homonym of *m'aime*, so that the title can be translated "The Bride Stripped Bare by Her Bachelors Loves Me"—a statement variously interpreted with reference to Duchamp but singularly applicable to Donner. His anguished cry, "Oh my God! Oh my God!" when Martello reveals Sophie's probable mistake (56) is, after all, just shorthand for "Then Sophie stripped bare by Beauchamp loved me."

Was there ever a play so elusive as this one? or so successful at conjuring an artist in another medium? In speaking with the Italian art collector Arturo Schwarz, Duchamp once said: "The content or the value of a painting cannot be evaluated in words. You cannot find any language to speak about painting. Painting is a language of its own. You cannot interpret one form of expression with another form of expression. To say the least, you will distort the original message, whatever you say about it" (Schwarz, 562). Perhaps. Yet Stoppard, as we have seen, does not evaluate Duchamp or the paintings; nor does he interpret them or speak about them. Rather he performs an act of alchemy, translating Duchamp from one form of expression to another, replacing sight with sound.[10] The achievement is stunning, and as full of paradox as this enigmatic play would seem to demand. For in rendering Duchamp on the radio, and in choosing to do so by means of allusion rather than direct presentation, Stoppard contrives to bring vision out of darkness and presence out of absence—a pretty piece of self-contradiction.

To SEE Marcel Duchamp in *Artist Descending a Staircase* is not to perceive him so much as to create him from numerous clues in the dialogue. His phantasmal appearance is thus an extreme example of a general rule in radio: what we see is essentially our own fabrication, wrought through the agency of words. Such a role is decidedly suited to Duchamp, who not only fashioned himself an extremist, but who also relied upon language to mediate visual experience. The puzzling titles that he gave to his work—for instance, *Why Not Sneeze Rrose Sélavy?*, which denominates a birdcage containing marble sugar cubes—are presumably meant to elicit visual images unrelated to the objects on display. Similarly, a single word, "art," creates whatever significance ultimately attaches to his notorious readymades—items that he chose to exhibit precisely for their lack of aesthetic distinction, like a typewriter cover, a snow shovel, and his infamous urinal. Are the readymades put-ons or serious comments on the nature of artistic achievement? The answer must lie with the beholder; we respond with respect or derision according to our bent. Yet, however we respond to them, readymades prove that a label alone is sufficient to transform an object we would otherwise look *past* into one we consent to look *at*.

In radio, the counterparts of readymades are tapes of the sort produced by Beauchamp: namely, unimproved transcriptions of reality. Beauchamp blithely records sounds selected at random, then proposes to introduce artistry by naming the result. In this spirit, he designates a Ping-Pong game "Lloyd George versus Clara Bow" (39), a title that Sophie considers a joke, although Beauchamp regards it as a clever mental image. Either way, Beauchamp's tape gives us cause to reflect upon radio's artistic presumptions. In fact, Stoppard would seem to insist on the matter by having Beauchamp and Donner exchange salient quips about another tape of Beauchamp's: his so-called master-tape, "a bubbling cauldron of squeaks, gurgles, crackles, and other unharmonious noises" (21) whose merits Donner hotly disputes. According to Beauchamp, "If I had one good man placed high up in the BBC my tape would become art for millions, in time" (23). Donner, however, remains unconvinced: "It would not become art. It would become a mildly interesting noise instead of a totally meaningless noise" (23). Whoever is right—and John Cage's efforts to generate, on radio, an avant-garde music made of random words and sounds suggest that Beauchamp is not utterly misguided or, at any rate, not utterly alone[11]—this much is clear: the visual interest of readymade recordings is at best rudimentary. The appeal of tapes like Beauchamp's must primarily be aural, since the pictures they produce are either simplistic (the Ping-Pong game) or confusing (Donner's fall) or altogether unintelligible (the master-tape). They thus offer a warning to radio playwrights that the eye of the mind has substantial limitations, for which writers are required to compensate.

That Stoppard compensates ably in *Artist* is self-evident. Were he less proficient in his craft, we could hardly envision the complicated actions of the two separate mysteries that constitute the play; even less could we visualize an apparition like Duchamp. But for all that Stoppard makes us see in *Artist*, he equally confirms that we are blind—as blind, at times, as Sophie, whose condition we can better appreciate on radio than in any other medium. Consider, for instance, the flashbacks concerning Sophie's aborted move to Lambeth. Because Beauchamp, Martello, and Donner, in the first of these flashbacks, are called by their nicknames, Biscuit, Banjo, and Mouse, we have no means of telling, on radio, which of the men is Sophie's lover. In the printed script, by contrast, their identities are clear, as they must be on film or on stage. The New York stage production, in fact, introduced an interlude between scenes C and D (or 3 and 4) in which the elderly artists came to the front of the stage to be explicitly paired with their youthful counterparts.[12] As for the second of the flashbacks, when we hear it on radio we are no better able than Sophie to determine whether Mouse is regarding her in silence: "Mouse? Are you here? Say something. Now, don't do that, Mouse, it's not fair—please, you are here . . . Did you go out? Now please don't . . . How can I do anything if I can't trust you—I beg you, if you're here, tell me" (53).[13] The pain we feel for Sophie can only be heightened by our sharing her confusion—a confusion emblematic, as it happens, of our lasting inability to know who it was she really loved, even after we have gathered that Biscuit is Beauchamp.

The radio performance thus conspires to instruct us in how Sophie's blindness feels; and in doing so, it underscores the confusions in identity that permeate the play. Beauchamp, Martello, and Donner, for instance, are often indistinguishable in the radio performance—and rightly so, since they are barely individuals in any case, having for decades shared the same room, loved the same woman, and produced the same kind of art. Moreover, they themselves have trouble differentiating among the seemingly innumerable artists and writers they have known. Although they struggle to remember who was who and when and where, their efforts turn out to be largely in vain, as in the following exchange:

BEAUCHAMP: In Zurich in 1915 you told Tarzan he was too con-
           servative.
DONNER:    Tarzan?
BEAUCHAMP: I don't mean Tarzan. Who do I mean? Similar name,
           conservative, 1915 . . .

                                                                    (25)

When Beauchamp finally reconstructs that "Tarzan" is, in fact, Tristan Tzara, he is still off the mark in recalling that Tzara, with his dadaist excesses, was conservative. It is all in the nature of a joke, we can be sure; and yet given the context—a play that presents the truth as difficult to see—we can guess that failing memory is another form of blindness.

So, too, is the perplexity implicit in the play's clever trompe l'oreille effects, which cause us, when *Artist* is broadcast on radio, to misconstrue what we hear and hence to see things amiss. The most audacious example is an inspired pun of sorts—a translation into sound of Sophie's failure to distinguish between the foreground and the background of a painting. At the start of the play, when we hear Donner dozing, then rising and falling, we naturally assume that the accident he suffers is happening "now"—that is, in the foreground of the play—when in fact it happened "then" and is currently serving as the tape-recorded background to Beauchamp and Martello's discussion of Donner's demise. Until we learn that the drones and the footsteps and the awful descent have taken place in the past, we imagine that someone is falling in the present, just as Sophie imagines that Ping-Pong is in progress when she hears Beauchamp's gramophone recording in the background. These twin deceptions, a brilliant stroke on Stoppard's part, expose the touching naïveté of Beauchamp's comment that "the tape recorder speaks for itself. That is, of course, the point about tape recorders" (18). For here is a play in which nothing, but nothing, speaks for itself—least of all tapes that can barely be distinguished from tapes within tapes, which themselves confuse buzzing with snoring, and an accident with murder. If radio spoke for itself, we would have known from the start that Donner fell down the staircase while chasing a fly—or we would soon have supposed so, since Stoppard mentions a fly in the first lines of dialogue, then brings one intermittently into the action in the course of the play. But since the fly is in the background, we fail to take note. So much for the suggestion that we actually hear what we hear.

Clearly, in fashioning *Artist* for radio, Stoppard took pains to reveal our limitations as listeners: to prove that our ears are inattentive and our eyes imperceptive. And yet consistent with the paradoxes rife throughout the play, his very proof presupposes that we recognize our errors and correct for them. How else can we know that our senses have faltered, unless we perceive their mistakes? So it is that we wrongly, then rightly, interpret the comical cut that takes Beauchamp, Martello, and Donner from a walking tour in war-torn France to a room where the three are reciting in unison, "Left! . . . left . . . right . . . left . . . right . . . right . . . turn . . . right a bit . . . left a bit . . . turn . . . left . . . turn . . . stop!" (51). Though the chant sounds at first like a drill undertaken by prisoners of war, we soon gather from the context that this trompe l'oreille maneuver is really a game to assess Sophie's sense of direction. And just as Sophie, though blind, proves eminently able to keep track of her movements, so we, too, prove able to detect and emend our misimpressions.

But what of misimpressions that retain their authority even after they have proven to be false? For instance, Beauchamp's tenth horse. We presume him to exist from the same kind of evidence that always substantiates characters on radio: from sounds that he makes for himself (that is, his hoofbeats) and from comments that others make to and about him ("Whoa—whoa—Try not to startle my mount, Donner" [47]). And yet something is singularly odd about this beast who gives Beauchamp "a magical feeling" (47), who belongs in a "phantom calvary," and who "leaves no footprints," being "not physical," but "metaphysical" (49). Or rather "pataphysical" (49). Or rather absolutely fraudulent, as the following dialogue indicates:

BEAUCHAMP: Steady, steady . . .
DONNER:      For God's sake, Beauchamp, will you get rid of that coconut!
BEAUCHAMP: Coconut!—not a bad name. And yet it lacks a certain something. Would Napoleon have called his horse Coconut? . . . Napoleon . . . not a bad name.
                                                                              (47–48)

On hearing this banter, anyone familiar with radio sound effects is certain to remember how hoofbeats are produced: namely, by clapping together the halves of a hollowed-out coconut shell. And with this simple recollection, Beauchamp's horse dematerializes. We instantly infer that he was never there at all. Although how can that be? For in seeing him, did we not actually create him, so that, by radio magic, he was there when he was not?[14]

Now you see it, now you don't. Such is the burden of this horseplay of Stoppard's, which is premised on the notion that radio images are at bottom pure paradox. Being only imagined, they are all of them false. Being faithful to our fancies, they are all of them true. And being subject to revision as our reason demands, they are powerfully expressive of our need to make meaning from the welter of impressions that we gather through our senses. There is wisdom, then, in Beauchamp's amusing remark that the "first duty of the artist is to capture the radio station" (23). For the goal that the radio sets for the playwright extends to all art: to give substance to shadows and voices to silence, in trust that from make-believe truth will emerge.

# Chapter Three

## THE MUSICAL DIMENSION
### Robert Ferguson's *Transfigured Night* from Three Perspectives: In Itself, In the Orbit of Schoenberg, and In the Shadow of Beckett's Radio Drama . . . with a Coda on Cage's *Roaratorio*

•

"B UT IT ONLY TAKES the end for all to become clear" (43).[1] So says the mesmerizing and, in large part, mesmerized Narrator of Robert Ferguson's *Transfigured Night*, a memory play—really, an elaborated monologue—exquisite in its anguish. Every word that the Narrator speaks is a product of his pain. Yet instinctively he shrinks from the prospect of ending, terrified lest, drawing to a close, he should encounter the silence that would confirm for him his utter isolation. Perversely, then, he rambles on, reciting his humiliations as an aging actor fallen on hard times and as the hopeless suitor, most malapropos, of an ingenue oblivious to his love. Reciting his humiliations? One might almost say, singing them. For the Narrator's monologue, on radio, has the feel of a recitative, even an aria. Existing in performance purely as sound, taking shape not so much from its storyline as from its variations on several basic themes, and validating the truth of the emotions even at the cost of narrative coherence, *Transfigured Night* conforms to Walter Pater's view of art: it "constantly aspires towards the condition of music" (Pater, 135).

That condition is generally regarded as non-referential (though whether wholly so or only largely so is a matter of dispute in the various theories of how music makes meaning). For with very few exceptions, purely instrumental music sets no stage, evokes no scenes, creates no characters, tells no stories. As a consequence, music is by nature anti-thetical to drama, which everywhere copes with its own materiality, even when its stage is bare, its action minimal, and its actors withdrawn or unprepossessing. Everywhere, that is, except on radio. For on radio, plays are presented in a venue that is truly no venue at all. Until (or unless) they are specified, voices on radio emanate from nowhere, and also from no one in particular. Thus, radio drama could—could it not?—be as resistant to paraphrase as music, if only playwrights chose to make it so. And yet, how choose? By depriving words of meaning altogether? But in that case, the sounds that ensue would not really be words, though they well might be music. Perhaps, then, by limiting language to the expression of abstractions? But language so conceived would less likely make music than philosophy. How, then, proceed? This is the question that Ferguson addresses in *Transfigured Night*, not only through a narrator who explicitly hankers after music ("And it came into my head to sing," he says in closing), but also through allusions to Schoenberg and Beckett, whose own work gives focus to Ferguson's.

Schoenberg, in fact, is invoked in the monologue's very title, which is English for *Verklaerte Nacht*, an early string sextet of Schoenberg's, based on a poem of again the same name by Richard Dehmel. The sextet engages language not by setting words to music, as in opera or song, but by seeking to discover a musical voice for what Schoenberg has called the "real content" of words, as opposed to the "mere thoughts" that they express (Schoenberg, 144). Thus, Schoenberg is for Ferguson a sort of kindred spirit, exploring the extent to which music and words are commensurate languages. Or if not commensurate, then radically implicated one with the other, as in those of Schoenberg's works where the boundaries of music are stretched in provocative ways, with words sometimes serving as a structural principle, sometimes assuming a hybrid identity, half-spoken, half-sung. What is more, since Ferguson produces verbal equivalents for a number of Schoenberg's innovations in atonality and serialism, Schoenberg may be said to establish a standard against which the musicality of *Transfigured Night* can be judged.

As for Beckett, he is the *éminence grise* with whom Ferguson must vie in his pursuit of words-as-music. For Beckett's radio plays comprise a radical experiment in pursuit of that same end. Perhaps because Beckett is more widely known on stage than on the radio, Ferguson explicitly alludes only to two familiar stage plays: *Waiting for Godot*, which the Narrator mentions by name in the monologue; and *Krapp's Last Tape*, from which Ferguson silently borrows a scene. But it is Beckett's highly idiosyncratic radio drama that casts its long shadow over *Transfigured Night*—suggesting, on the one hand, that words most mimic music when they are least inclined to narrate; and warning, on the other hand, that as words are reluctant to forfeit narration, so audiences are loath to see narration forgone.

Whether by chance or design, Ferguson essentially heeds Beckett's warning. Thus, *Transfigured Night* imparts a tale of sorts (actually, an unsolved mystery), for all that it seeks to make music. Listeners initially attend to the Narrator's rambling disquisition in the expectation of discovering exactly what offense he gave to his repertory company and the girl he adored. Only when the mystery fails to come clear does the monologue's music emerge. In this respect, *Transfigured Night* is akin to Beckett's *Embers*, itself a radio monologue that draws music out of mystery. And yet, kinship aside, Beckett is far more audacious than Ferguson in his approach to words-as-music. For in all of his radio drama, but especially in *Words and Music* and *Cascando*, what Beckett attempts is essentially to eliminate narrative from language, so that words can make music instead of telling stories. Words, however, balk at the prospect; and though Beckett contrives to subdue them, he never fully masters their resistance. It is rather John Cage (working in Germany and in the German tradition of *Hörspiel*) who routs narrative entirely—a feat that he achieves in his radio work *Roaratorio*, which so utterly dissipates the meaning of words drawn from *Finnegans Wake* that little remains beyond cadence and inflection.

Three different artists—Ferguson, Beckett, and Cage—with three different versions of words-that-make-music. Yet all three alike in this regard: that they take as their premise the musicality of radio, where language lives exclusively as sound.


TRANSFIGURED NIGHT? Not so, alas. Not if the phrase summons visions of rapture, or even affection requited. However little the Narrator, for all his volubility, may willingly disclose about the night that plagues his memory, this much at least he admits: the events that transpired condemned him to abandon all hope of succeeding in love. Condemned him, too, to tell the tale incessantly, although piecemeal and by fits and starts, with every repetition yielding new information and recasting the old until the story is awash with contradiction. No matter. "It only takes the end for all to become clear" (43). And in the end, it is clear that the Narrator is alone.

What appears to have happened (we can only surmise) is that, while playing a bit part opposite an actress with whom he was—and is—infatuated, the Narrator disgraced himself by coming out of character. As he describes the misadventure, he was cast as a policeman in an opera about a gypsy, Maritana, whose lover, Don Sergei, was imprisoned during Holy Week for duelling. Don Sergei escaped from jail and rejoined Maritana. But no sooner was he by her side than he spied a policeman bicycling toward him from afar, presumably to rearrest him. The couple despaired, believing their love to be doomed, and Don Sergei fled into the mountains. Yet the policeman was merely delivering a summons protesting the gypsies' illegal encampment.

Here, according to the Narrator, the script of the opera broke off. For the show to go on, the policeman had to improvise his part, deciding for himself whether to drop off the summons without comment, or to investigate the cause of Maritana's all too evident distress. The Narrator-qua-policeman did neither. Elated by the proximity of the actress whom he loved, ravished by their moment together on stage, he made a fatuous appeal for her attention: "Excuse me, miss. Would you care for a slice of bread?" (54). The actress took no notice of the comment, as inane in the context of desire as in the service of the plot that it failed to advance. She just gazed into the distance, presumably in hopes of glimpsing Don Sergei in flight. Meanwhile, the Narrator, stung by what he took as a personal rejection, "searched for an appropriate response, and finally set my teeth to the bark of the slender birch, biting at it with the abstracted ferocity of . . . (*Pause.*) With all the tenderness of . . . (*Pause.*)" (54). At this moment, with the Narrator giving every evidence of having broken down in full view of the audience, someone turned off the stagelights. Finis for the memory, as well as the performance.

If the Narrator relates this sad debacle haltingly, if he manages a full account only after several failed attempts, and if even then he speaks with something less than perfect candor, we need not wonder why. The wonder, indeed, is that he tells the tale at all. Apparently, he thinks to reshape it, in the telling, by ringing changes on those facts that most discomfit him, or that particularly redound to his discredit. If so, his success is decidedly mixed. He never rightly reinvents his painful story, even in imagination—never manages an intimate encounter with the girl of his dreams, even in his dreams. His cramped and peevish nature appears to be inalienable, fixing his memory on agonies past, while foiling his efforts to remember those agonies as other than they were. In his mind as in his life, the Narrator's propensity for humiliation will out. And yet, no matter how his monologue may thwart him, it rewards him as well, rectifying at least some of his disabling ineptitude. At the end of all, the Narrator talks to good end.

That his speech serves him well is surely something of a miracle, since almost from the start the monologue appears to disappoint him. He opens with the veritable moment of his crisis, intent upon improving it, if not through outright lying, then through selective inclusions and omissions. But the story proves maddeningly intransigent: even retold, it does not satisfy. True, the Narrator succeeds in so editing events at the outset as to obliterate the sources of his pain: "I dismounted, leaning my bicycle against a tree, and stood watching her. She was looking away, in the opposite direction. A mountain rose tall and dark beyond us, and I seem to see her in my mind's eye turning, wandering slowly up its twisting pathway whilst I, casting about for some appropriate response, finally set my teeth to the bark of the slender birch beside me, biting at it with the abstracted ferocity of . . . (*Pause.*) With all the tenderness of . . . (*Pause.*)" (41). We hear nothing, in this version, of the Narrator's ludicrous attempt to win the actress's attention by offering her bread, and nothing, as his story continues, of a performance gone awry. Instead, after a curious digression on his repertory company's practice of using "real" scenery as opposed to mere props, the Narrator implies that the performance (not yet said to be an opera) ended well: "At this point, so close to the end, the script called upon us to improvise—a commonplace now, perhaps, but something of a novelty, in those pioneering days. I bit deep into the flesh of the silver birch, ghost among trees, and stood observing with theatrical intensity the blood, and the marks of the teeth etched in the green whiteness of the wood. The sun set. Earth's long shadow stretched out into space, and back she came, running back down the mountain track, and bowed low to the faces scattered pale across the darkness before us" (41). Thus does the Narrator represent his hysteria as role-playing, an unexceptional instance of improvisation. As for the dimming of the stagelights to halt the performance, that, too, he represents as a part of the play: it is simply the setting of the sun. His mention of blood is no doubt disconcerting, but the reference is so brief as to all but pass notice. In sum, the Narrator appears to have tamed his galling memory. Yet he does so at a cost that he cannot abide: the Girl (as the actress is called in the script) remains utterly out of his reach. His telling of the story has misfired.

As a consequence, he tries again. Twice, in fact, with different, but increasingly deplorable results. In the first instance, the Narrator imagines himself making "a quiet entrance" while the Girl

> waited, herself watching after someone making his exit on the far side of the stage. 'Sergei' she called, 'Sergei'. Then she turned and saw me. She stepped towards me. Took both my hands in hers.
>
> GIRL: (*in the theatre*). You came. Oh I'm so glad you could come. Thank you for coming.
>
> (42)

Here is the response that fulfills his heart's desire. But he evidently cannot exploit it. His memory—actually, his power of invention—fails with the actress's expression of welcome. Instead of thinking to embrace her in this, his waking dream, he returns his attention to the scenery, especially the mountain, which again he says is real, as if the stage could accommodate a genuine geological immensity. Clearly at a loss for what to do, what to say, he stands "waiting for the right moment" (42), as if it had not come; waiting for "the sun to go down" (42), lest the play (as he conceives it in his reverie) escape his control and commit him to climbing the mountain, as apparently he fears to do. "It was not a question of boots," he observes pathetically; "We had boots adequate to the climb. Nor was it the height of the mountain, for as high as it was, it was not overhigh" (42). What was it, then, that held him back? He does not say. He simply cuts to post-performance, when the actors go their "separate ways, as show-people do" (42). Again he is alone. Insupportable.

Time for another retelling. He takes up the tale at the point where the Girl extends her welcome. But instead of pressing forward, he contrives to postpone something happening by lingering over the scene: "The lark spiralling above us. Just ourselves, and the bread, and the trees, and the mountain. There we sat by the grey river, safe in the shadow of the mountain, and there we broke bread, and laughing and mindless scooped the waters of the river to our mouths, lifting the waters of the river to our mouths, and for just a moment the water seemed clear and bright, sparkling as it flashed from the shadow into the light, sparkling like . . . (*Pause*.) like . . ." (42). For want of a simile, the Narrator's idyll is undone. While he searches for the words that inexplicably elude him ("dripping like jewels from her lips" [49], he later says), his fear moves the story along in despite of his wishes. In particular, he imagines the Girl recommending the very action that he dreads: "I know—let's climb that mountain!" (42). True to form, he declines—and, truer still to form, in a manner guaranteed to afford him embarrassment:

> x:      (*patiently*). But dearest, we have not boots for such a climb.
> *There are titters from the audience.*
> GIRL: (*astonished*). I beg your pardon?
>
>                                                                          (42)

Mortifying. For appalling stupidity, the comment quite rivals the offer of bread. Fiction has failed to improve upon truth.

That being the case, truth—or some approximation of it—begins to insist upon a hearing. Twice in what follows, while attempting to defend his improvisational technique, the Narrator remembers and repeats the dismal line that he actually delivered: "Would you care for a slice of bread?" (43, 45). Though he does not acknowledge, on either occasion, that the comment foretold his emotional breakdown, the alternative result that he fashions cannot please him: more tittering from the audience; another withering "I beg your pardon" from the Girl (43, 45). In a similar pattern of admission and denial, he acknowledges the dimming of the stagelights, but represents the event as Don Sergei's habitual manner of ragging him during rehearsals. And the motive for such animosity? According to the Narrator, none other than sexual jealousy—a suggestion that launches him into an impassioned, syntactically tortuous, and ultimately self-incriminating harangue about an ex-lover (nominally, Don Sergei, but really the Narrator himself)

> who makes his exit carrying with him still the memory unrequited, the unrequited memory, the unassuaged memory, the unassuaged memory, the unrequited, inassuagable memory of inexpressible things unlikely if not now then not ever to find expression, the inextinguishable memory of things left unsaid, and all that which must remain unsaid, words, words on words, mouldering, crumbling to the ground, subjected there to unspeakably, inexpressively massive geopsychological pressures over aeons of time until gradually an image crystallises, a mountain, perhaps, something having a purely symbolic existence, of the failures, perhaps, the disappointments, the sorrows, all the intolerable that cries out for the hiding shadow of symbol to fall upon it . . .
>
> (44)

We may note the mountain, in particular. Whereas previously the Narrator maintained that it was real—insisted, in fact, on that implausibility, even while granting the mountain "symbolic significance" (41)—now he strikes straight to the heart of the matter, speaking a truth that he elsewhere pretends not to know: namely, that the mountain reifies his own "massive geopsychological" pain, which he can neither ignore nor surmount. Cannot even obscure, as his speech hurtles on with a logic of its own, confusing memory with pure fabrication, yet all the while exposing brutal facts: the physical evidence that the Narrator is aging ("bald patches visible beneath the spotlights" [45]); his consequent inability to command leading roles ("those heroes I once played myself, in the clear, firm voice of youth" [46]); his lapses in memory, presumably for lines, but also for his personal history (the "accusations of amnesia" [48]); and, most troubling of all, his disengagement from his own sexuality.

Although the fever of sexual longing is the Narrator's only real subject, he explicitly mentions the sexual act only once in the monologue, and then in a dubious context. As he would have us believe, his company

resorted to staging a sex show "to bring the crowds back" (50) when
business fell off.

> That was a hard part, humping the diva in the shadow of a card-
> board birch, pale backs going through the motions for the benefit
> of watchers scattered silent in the darkness before us, humping and
> pumping and puffing up balloons in the shadow of a paper moun-
> tain, going through the motions, as the man said when . . . (*Pause.*)
> But the way she sang that high C was one of the strangest and most
> beautiful things I ever heard in my life. The note left her throat, it
> left her body, it seemed to float out over the audience like a star,
> drifting on up into the infinite.
> *The* GIRL *gives a hacking cough.*
> Then a crumb stuck in her throat, and she began to cough, hacking
> away like an old crow. I must've warned her a hundred times about
> eating on the job.
>
> (50)

Judged as fact, this astonishing statement fairly begs to be dismissed, if
only because the same company that purportedly regarded *Murder in
the Cathedral* and *Waiting for Godot* as "guaranteed crowd-pleasers"
(49) would seem unlikely to have later descended to hard porn. Or is it
Eliot and Beckett who were never produced, existing only as chimeras
in the Narrator's mind? Impossible to say, so tangled is his discourse.
But from his memory or invention, whichever it is, what plainly emerges
is the Narrator's willful and willed rejection of sex, for all that it attracts
him. In this spirit, he depicts sex as sordid ("humping and pumping and
puffing up balloons"), treats it as the stuff of bitter puns ("a hard part"),
and implies that it devalues the landscape (the "cardboard birch," the
"paper mountain," elsewhere asserted to be real). Moreover, when the
moment of orgasm threatens to beguile him by emerging as ethereal (a
"high C" evoked from a diva), he deflates the cry of passion to an
unappealing cough, as if thereby to negate his desire.

Desire, however, persists, irrespective of the Narrator's efforts to disown it. In fact, it has been present all along, although disguised—objec-
tified, really, in a metaphor whose meaning comes clear when the
Narrator, in describing the sex show, talks of "humping and pumping
and puffing up balloons" (50), which can only represent a penis at the
ready. In light of this new information, we may recall that a balloon
came to figure quite abruptly, not to mention rather curiously, in one
version of the Narrator's pastoral scene with the Girl. Altogether unpre-
pared for, it was suddenly revealed to be "stuck in the tree above" the
couple, allegedly placed there to serve as an aid to improvisation: a

potential object of discussion, according to the Narrator, providing a subject "quite remote from bread" (43). Remote, indeed. For here, as we realize in retrospect, is the Narrator's sexual organ made manifest, although camouflaged and rendered ineffectual: no touching allowed. Thus does the Narrator simultaneously display and deny his desire, even while protecting it from harm. But not for long.

Twice in what ensues the Narrator imagines an open assault on the balloon: once by a child who would injure it; and once by the Girl, who would liberate it. In the first instance, the Narrator tells of having played a bit part—"painful memories" (46)—that "called for me forcibly to restrain a small boy, attempting by means of a pin stuck into the end of a stick, to burst a balloon caught fast in the branches of a tree. Quite a struggle the little rascal gave me. My cap fell off, and as I stooped to pick it up I received a sharp prick from the pin in the full of my bottom" (46). Did such an event ever happen in fact? In fact, it does not matter. What matters is the insight here provided into the Narrator's sense of his sexual nature, which he conceives to be infinitely fragile. To protect it, he will risk—indeed, endure—humiliation. But will he ever consent to reclaim it, this part of his person that he transforms into a symbol, not unlike the mountain, in an effort to keep it at a distance? Apparently not, as we learn when the scene is replayed with the Girl in the role of the child.

In this recapitulation, the Girl attends to the balloon (now explicitly red, like the sexual organ it embodies) not in order to destroy it, but instead "to knock it free" (49)—an ambiguous action that might as easily repel it as restore it to its owner. Either way, the Narrator feels threatened: "I watched smiling until I could bear it no longer and jumping up in wild play took hold of her and held her arms against her sides, pleading with her to, suggesting that, . . ." (49). Suggesting what? Presumably that the balloon be left where it is, in perpetual limbo. But instinctively, the Narrator—who is certainly not playing, wildly or otherwise—cuts his sentence short, as if to shield the balloon by changing the subject. Thus, in customary fashion, he diverts his attention to the scenery, "pointing out to [the Girl] the clear spring river running like quicksilver beside us" (49), and so on and so forth, until he must pause. For just as, "God knows, one cannot cough forever" (45), though a cough is a handy diversion in a pinch, so one cannot forever resort to lyric sketches as a means of denying desire. And when lyricism fails, as eventually it must, desire returns—with a vengeance.

So it is that the Narrator's pastoral scene gives way to the squalor of the sex show, and then, without the slightest transition, to a vaudeville routine in which the Narrator's habit of self-mortification reaches singularly staggering proportions. The balloon now makes its last appearance, its carnality quite unmistakable: it is aptly described as a "delicate red membrane." Yet not so delicate, it seems, as to perish from the sort of abuse that the Narrator, like the child before him, practices upon it.

> I opened with the old balloon-and-stick trick, always a favourite, for some reason. With a pin embedded in the end of my wand I jabbed and prodded and stabbed away at a balloon, I beat it and smacked it from one end of the stage to the other. And yet miraculously, miraculously, miraculously, the pin appeared not to penetrate that delicate red membrane, to expose the nothingness within, the nothingness that might have shocked, that might have disappointed, and yet without which there could have been no red balloon. Over and over I performed the trick. But God knows, one cannot perform the same trick forever, whatever the heart's desire. I moved on.
>
> (50–51)

Here is a furious image of compulsive, even frantic, masturbation conceived of as self-punishment. What should gratify the Narrator—his "miraculous" ability to produce and sustain an erection—invites only his fear of "the nothingness within." Thus, he harries the balloon, which he ought to caress. And when he thinks to "move on" (as he does, because he must), his subsequent stunts merely testify further to his boundless insecurity and capacity for cruelty, mainly to himself.

By the time that his routine as the "masked conjuror" (50) has fizzled out, the Narrator's mask is all but off. For in his two concluding jokes, he essentially confesses to his innermost fears. The first of the gags implies his dread that perhaps he is unsexed: "I'll write a TV series about impotent secret agents. Call it 'Emission Impossible'" (53). The second, his dread that he is not there at all.

> LEE: I've just heard the Irish knock-knock joke. Want to hear it?
> X:   Not much.
> LEE: You say 'knock-knock' to me.
> X:   Knock-knock.
> LEE: Who's there?
> *Pause.* LEE *snorts. The audience titters, the laughter swells.*
>
> (53)

Thus is the Narrator cast in a part (the null Irishman) emblematic of every small and "soul-destroying" (46) role that has ever come his way: it disappears into itself. And when it does, the Narrator, who would seem to have no memory of a life outside the theater, loses even that semblance of identity that he has borrowed from the stage. In or out of character, he is ultimately faceless.

This, then, is his condition when he returns to his humiliating tale and finally tells it straight. Straight, that is, from start to finish. Straight from the disclosure that his company's director, "a Mr Hobson," wrote an opera "about a girl called Maritana" (53). Straight from Hobson's revelation that the opera was unfinished and destined to remain so: "you'll have to improvise, X. Veteran like yourself shouldn't have any trouble" (54). Straight from the Narrator's tedious line: "Excuse me, miss. Would you care for a slice of bread?" (54). Straight to the ending where the Narrator encounters, and faithfully reports upon, the Girl's indifference and the darkened stage.

> She did not hear me, as she was never meant to hear me. She stood looking off in the opposite direction, and then wandered slowly away up the twisting mountain track whilst I searched for an appropriate response, and finally set my teeth to the bark of the slender birch, biting at it with the abstracted ferocity of . . . (*Pause.*) With all the tenderness of . . . (*Pause.*)
> *Silence.*
> Some joker turned down the lights and left me standing there, with no lines to say, no one to say them to, with no tree, no river, no mountain, no bird, only the pale faces of the watchers scattered dim across the darkness before me. And the bare boards. And the bare walls trailing bare wires. I stood wondering what to say, wondering what to do. And it came into my head to sing.
>
> (54–55)

If ever the Narrator thought to reinvent his story through the agency of words, this final retelling would appear to be the death of that intention. Hence his impulse to sing: to find an alternate means of expression less likely than words to betray him.

And yet has he, in fact, been betrayed? Maybe so. And maybe not. Or if so, maybe not entirely. For possibly we err in assuming that the Narrator's final version of his story imparts the straight truth, complete and unimproved. Dreadful as it is, this rendition of events may just refine upon some still more grievous history even now obscure. Indeed, there is reason to think so. For if a certain Mr. Hobson did, in fact, compose an opera "in the style of the 1840s" (53) about a gypsy Maritana, only to leave the work unfinished, one has to wonder why. There is, after all, a genuine period piece on the subject: the opera *Maritana* composed by William Wallace and first produced at Drury Lane in 1845. The Maritana who presides over Wallace's improbable and convoluted plot is, like Hobson's, a gypsy. And her lover—Don César, not Don Sergei—is imprisoned like Sergei during Holy Week for duelling. What is more, he makes a neat escape from jail. The signal difference between Wallace's plot and Hobson's is that Don César, once free, does not take flight from a policeman cycling round on "routine business" (53). Nor does Wallace call for anyone to improvise.

Is Hobson, then, a plagiarist caught short with an imperfect score of Wallace's light opera? Or has the Narrator simply forgotten what roles he performed in what productions, so that somehow he confuses *Maritana* with a similar opera involving gypsies and policemen? The Narrator himself admits to being unreliable, contending that it "isn't easy to explain, the way in which an actor can become involved in a part to such an extent that presently a confusion arises between . . . (*Pause.*) To the point where it becomes difficult to . . . (*Pause.*)" (43). And yet his difficulty, as he here describes it, would seem to be in separating not one part from another, but a stage part from real life: the same difficulty, as it happens, that causes him to confuse stage props with "real trees, real mountains" (41). Moreover, one cannot help but wonder, in any case, why the Narrator was appearing in an opera. He was an actor, not a singer—a fact that seems to cross his mind when he confesses that "it came into my head to sing" (55).

Something is surely amiss in the Narrator's story, though what exactly it may be, we can never really know. We cannot be forbidden, however, from supposing. Let us, then, suppose that the Narrator's repertory company staged a production not of Mr. Hobson's *Maritana*, but of William Wallace's, casting the Narrator in no specific role, but only in a crowd scene or two. And let us further suppose that the Narrator, who confesses that he rankled at playing bit parts, resolved to remedy this slight by improvising: in particular, by dressing up as a policeman and bicycling onto the stage with the astonishing intention of interpolating a love scene into the plot. If so, it would not have been the first time he had so misbehaved. By his own admission, he had once refused to leave the stage when he was called upon merely "to sit on a park bench feeding bread to a pigeon while a nanny sat reading beside me" (46). On that occasion, he was to take out a cigarette, ask for a light, and, receiving none, make a timely exit. He "kept to the script throughout rehearsals . . . , gave no hint of [his] plans" (46), then on opening night pursued a dreary conversation with the nanny (played, of course, by the Girl) until her "lover, having with commendable initiative donned a policeman's uniform, entered, and displaying to the full his considerable talent for improvising, escorted me from the stage with my arm twisted behind my back" (48). In view of the Narrator's ineptness at improvising, we may surmise that the impromptu appearance of this lover-qua-policeman could well have given him the idea for his own impromptu appearance in *Maritana* as a policeman-qua-lover. With the opera thus disrupted, it would follow that the stagehands would have turned off the lights—and that the Narrator would have summarily been fired. After all, on the occasion of his dalliance with the nanny, it was "only under the most solemn promise that there would be no repetition [that he was] allowed to remain with the company" (48).

If this supposition is correct, then the Narrator's final version of his story spares him on several accounts. For one thing, it neglects to mention his dismissal from the company. For another, it represents his misconduct on stage as a poor stab at improvisation rather than as something worse: namely, an ignominious intrusion by the Narrator into an action that did not concern him. To improvise badly is one thing; intentionally to subvert a performance is another. And if this was the Narrator's crime, he does well to equivocate—especially given that he may have more to hide. In particular, once on the stage, whatever did the Narrator bite? Although he says it was the tree, he also mentions flesh and blood in his opening version of events: "I bit deep into the flesh of the silver birch, ghost among trees, and stood observing with theatrical intensity the blood" (41). But as trees (whether real ones or props) do not bleed, we may inquire if the Narrator perhaps bit himself—or possibly the Girl, in a grotesque perversion of affection. This, the kiss of Dracula, would likely have won him a slap, maybe even a blow, in response. And such a turn of events would, in turn, then explain the Narrator's otherwise perplexing remark about how "Show-people lead such strange lives—a smile, a kiss, a blow to the side of the head, whatever the script calls for—" (43). But on this possibility, the monologue is silent. It declines to confirm such speculation.

Thus, if the monologue has never quite cooperated with the Narrator—if it has refused to bend his story to his liking and has revealed a great deal more of his disgrace than he intended—it nevertheless may be loyal at the last, concealing the worst of his shame. Despite his own grim prediction that "it only takes the end for all to become clear" (43), "all," in the Narrator's case, is never fully clarified. Indeed, on first or second hearing, the monologue divulges appreciably less of the Narrator's history than is actually there to be discovered. The most that a single performance imparts is a general impression of the Narrator's failures in love and on stage, and a sense of his anguished obsession with some shadowy embarrassment. Insofar as the monologue yields any revelations whatever, it does so with the utmost reluctance. As long as the monologue is heeded but not studied, it guards the very secrets it enfolds.

To this considerable extent, then, the monologue is a triumph for the Narrator. And it serves him in other ways as well. Fluid, free-formed, expansive, and completely unpremeditated, it arguably qualifies as the fluent improvisation that the Narrator had hoped to achieve on the stage, but did not. Moreover, it affords him a tangible brush with transcendence, as emerges when he last sets the scene for his tryst with the Girl. In doing so before, he had several times chosen to introduce a lark: "spiralling above us" (42), "singing" (43), "ascending" (49). And on each of these occasions—in fact, even when the lark was not explicitly mentioned (see 44 and 45)—the sound that was heard in the background was the cawing of crows, quite "insistent" (49). Thus did the Narrator's reverie mock him, even as he spoke. But in his last evocation of the idyll, sound accords with sense most congenially.

*The sound of water flowing. Birds singing. Summer country sounds.*
And so it came about that, just when I had thought it was all over, my hour came again, and again I stood once again I stood as in the old days I stood once again watching her dazzled by the brilliance of her stunned into joy at the sight of her, by the stream, by the tree, the wind lifting and shifting and lifting in her hair, sun lingering in its westward drift as though caught in the treetops, mountain sheering into the blue beyond while
*A lark, very distinct.*
a lark circled high above us, binding the hour in his silver chain of sound, and the river ran quick and clear at our feet, the rainbow and the brown trout jumping from it as though they had not freedom enough within it.

(54)

Through the music of nature, and especially the lark, which sings for the Narrator only this once, the scene fulfills its promise: it lives, however briefly. And in it the Narrator, too, comes alive: he actually experiences joy. In this limited sense, then, the monologue answers to the Narrator's need, affording him a momentary respite from despair. For one glorious instant, delicate but stirring, it brings his tuneless world into harmony.

"AND IT CAME into my head to sing." Whatever this comment may mean with respect to the Narrator—that he no longer trusts in words to do his bidding; that he has trespassed on an opera and is trying to fit in—it means something else again with respect to the monologue as literature. In particular, the comment implicates *Transfigured Night* in the long, elaborate history of jealous relations between music and words. At the risk of oversimplifying: whereas composers have envied, and attempted to emulate, the power of words to articulate concepts, poets have envied, and attempted to emulate, the power of music to give voice to emotions.[2]

As it happens, from the early Christian period through the mid-eighteenth century, western culture was inclined to give primacy to words. Music was widely regarded as words' handmaiden, especially by the church, a chief patron of the arts. Thus, song reigned supreme and composers, who were versed in rhetorical theory, turned frequently to rhetoric for insight into musical composition. By the time of Bach and Handel, music imitated speech through a host of devices, some of them arcane to modern audiences, others as familiar and easy to identify as the word-painting heard in the *Messiah* when the melodic line rises, for example, to represent the meaning of "exalted" or convolutes to give the sense of "crooked." So formidable was Bach, in particular, as a composer/rhetorician that he specifically drew praise on this account from a professor of rhetoric at Leipzig University. Yet even in his own day, Bach was thought to be old-fashioned; and the hegemony of words (which had long, if sporadically, been resisted by composers) was already in decline.[3]

Beginning roughly with Haydn and Mozart, in what has come to be known as the classical period, favor accrued to purely instrumental music, controlled not by verbal texts, but by musical themes and motifs, which were subject to harmonic development. As a consequence, words were eventually dethroned and music was installed in their place. Since that turn of events, music has been thought to set a challenge to writers. And if writers for their part have interpreted that challenge in ways from which composers have dissented, no matter. The misinterpretations have a measure of authority. For when writers determine to make language musical, it is their own sense of music that they imitate.

For a representative assessment of music from a writer in the modern tradition, we may look to Robert Browning: in particular, "Abt Vogler," which pays tribute to music as "the finger of God, a flash of the will that can," while calling painting and poetry, in contradistinction, "art in obedience to laws." Now music, in fact, is highly rule-bound, as Browning himself well knew.[4] Nonetheless, in the hearing, it may seem to be otherwise—not because of any fundamental lawlessness, but because of its ability to effect among listeners a powerful release of emotion. (In "Abt Vogler," for instance, the organist feels, through his own improvisation, the elation of boundless possibility, unfettered by the bonds of here-and-now.) This emotional immediacy is what writers have admired and sought, in different ways, to reproduce. In addition, they have adulated music for its apparent self-absorption, its ostensible indifference to non-musical ideas. Though musicologists dispute whether music is, in fact, inherently non-referential,[5] most listeners—as well as musicians—would contend that music is not *about* anything other than itself, even when it follows a program;[6] it is what it is and nothing further. To Walter Pater, in fact, this quality was a reason for contending that "all art . . . aspires towards the condition of music" (135). Music for Pater was the queen of the arts because, referring to itself alone, it could only be art for art's sake.

This is the context, then, into which Robert Ferguson steps with *Transfigured Night*. And even in the general terms outlined above, his play can be seen to have a musical dimension. For one thing, though it issues from a narrative of sorts, as the foregoing explication demonstrates, the monologue does not tell a story in any conventional sense. Witness the fact that, even when the Narrator's past comes into focus (insofar as it does), the monologue is still quite impossible to paraphrase. The point of the piece is not the story that it tells, but rather the manner of the telling. In this regard, the monologue aptly fulfills Pater's standard for judging the proximity of poetry to music: it exhibits a "perfect identification of matter and form" (Pater, 139)—a condition entailing "a certain suppression or vagueness of mere subject, so that the meaning reaches us through ways not distinctly traceable by the understanding" (Pater, 137). Given the monologue's suppression of "mere" history, so that listeners are likely to pity the Narrator without really understanding him, one can hardly imagine *Transfigured Night* better described.

As for monologue's manner of achieving coherence, its organizing principle rests not with the rudimentary plot recollected by the Narrator, but with the artful repetition of thematic material: the mountain, the tree, the lark, the balloon, the devastating question "Would you care for a slice of bread?" Here again the relation to music is clear. As Lawrence Kramer has observed, "Music and poetry . . . stand apart from narrative—even when they incorporate narrative elements—by embodying the other major way to organize time. Their structural rhythms embody a surplus of connective processes that in some cases . . . produces a vibrant fluidity that *baffles the will to distinguish and interpret*" (*Music and Poetry*, 10, my emphasis). Lulled by the rhythm with which images appear and recur in the Narrator's monologue, audiences lose the capacity, if not actually the will, to interpret what he says. And yet even in their bafflement, they cannot but recognize his ardor and distress. As in a heart-rending musical passage where the strings are heard to cry—"I suggested that certain parts be given the cello," says the Narrator, "as though the singer were too broken to continue" (45)—the monologue communicates emotion with the cogency of song.

Not just any song, however. It is the music of Schoenberg in particular to which Ferguson appeals, as his title makes plain. And indeed, Schoenberg's oeuvre—*Verklaerte Nacht*, to be sure, but later work as well—provides analogues for much that is distinctive in *Transfigured Night*. As a principal example, Ferguson's attempt to make words mimic music is a mirror reflection of Schoenberg's own efforts in *Verklaerte Nacht* itself, which he composed as a translation, a veritable restatement, of a Richard Dehmel poem. In fact, one of Schoenberg's commentators, Walter Frisch, has argued that Schoenberg's whole "musical development in 1899 can be seen as a reflection of his search to find a musical language appropriate to the poetry of [Dehmel's] *Weib und Welt*" (151), the volume in which the poem "Verklaerte Nacht" appeared. But beyond this correspondence to its namesake(s), *Transfigured Night* would seem to be further related to Schoenberg—primarily the Schoenberg of the atonal period—in several important respects. The morbid tone of the monologue and its improvisational quality, for instance, are both reminiscent of the composer. So, too, is the monologue's manner of varying, rather than merely repeating, thematic material. Most intriguing of all, the monologue is strongly suggestive of Schoenberg in its resistance to arriving at closure, not only in the matter of the Narrator's history, but even in the shape of individual sentences.

Consider first "Verklaerte Nacht," the poem, and *Verklaerte Nacht*, the music. In content, neither one bears much resemblance to *Transfigured Night*. The poem tells a tale of love perfected through an act of generosity: a grief-stricken woman confesses to her lover that she bears another's child, conceived in despair before she met him; the lover, for his part and without hesitation, accepts the child as if it were his own. Nothing could be further from the bitter isolation depicted in the monologue. As for Schoenberg's sextet, although it opens in a mood that is roughly appropriate to the Narrator—with an agitation and a yearning descriptive of the woman's state of mind—it ends by conveying the lovers' rapt accord through music that is positively luminous. The monologue, by contrast, ends in despair. Even the Narrator's moment of rapture, when the lark sings at last, seems frail by comparison. Being brief and illusory, it cannot compete with the sextet's expansive and tender conclusion. Nor is it meant to.

Whatever affinity obtains between the music and the monologue arises not out of mood, even less out of content, but rather out of striking similarities in the treatment of content. In particular, the music and the monologue both contrive to transcend what is sordid or grotesque in their subjects. Had Schoenberg's sextet, for example, captured Dehmel precisely, the music would have likely shared the poem's reputation. (If "Verklaerte Nacht" today seems somewhat maudlin, it was thought in its own day to be lurid, because sexually explicit. The poet, in fact, was summoned to court to defend the whole volume *Weib und Welt* from charges of immorality. See Frisch, 150.) Schoenberg, however, escapes Dehmel's shadow by expressing the spirit of the poem at the expense of its story. As Schoenberg himself put it many years later, when *Verklaerte Nacht* was recorded by the Hollywood String Quartet, he had sought "not [to] illustrate any action or drama," but only "to portray nature and to express human emotions": "It seems that, due to this attitude, my composition has gained qualities which satisfy even if one does not know what it illustrates; or in other words, it offers the possibility to be appreciated as "pure" music. . . . Thus, perhaps, it can make you forget the poem which many a person today might call repulsive."[7] Ferguson himself can make a similar claim. For *Transfigured Night*, too, "offers the possibility to be appreciated as 'pure' music"—a bravura performance in which the Narrator expresses emotions tied to an "action or drama" that might well be called repulsive, but that never quite comes clear enough to seem so. Moreover, in the matter of subduing irksome content, Ferguson succeeds against considerable odds, since words by their nature incline to "illustrate [an] action or drama" with fair specificity, as music does not.[8]

Where music can compete with words, and even enjoy an advantage, is in the evocation of emotion. And the particular emotional climate associated with Schoenberg—at least subsequent to *Verklaerte Nacht*, in the works that are regarded as atonal—has been aptly described as an "intense and morbid expressivity" (Charles Rosen, 13). Whether because of the painful chromaticism and "tortured harmonies" characteristic of atonality, or because of the specific texts that Schoenberg set to music (as in *Erwartung*, for example, where a soprano and orchestra cooperate to yield a nightmare vision), the composer has been credited with taking music for "a full-scale plunge into the subconscious."[9] In this respect, as well as in the improvisational quality of his atonal compositions, Schoenberg seems akin to Ferguson. For just as *Transfigured Night* appears spontaneous and formless—although the longer one studies it, the more premeditated it proves—so do Schoenberg's atonal compositions appear to unfold without plan. It has been said of *Erwartung* in particular that it creates the illusion of achieving "total freedom from the requirements of musical form,"[10] that it operates as "sustained free composition" (Payne, 35). Thus, in the liberties it takes with structure, as well as in its emotional coloration, *Erwartung* loosely resembles *Transfigured Night*. But only loosely, for this reason: that the music, being "'athematic' or 'nonmotivic' . . . , does not require [listeners to] recogniz[e] the motifs from one part of the work to another as all music from Bach to Stravinsky demands" (Charles Rosen, 41). Since such recognition, as we have seen, is a virtual precondition for interpreting *Transfigured Night*, there can be no detailed correspondence between the two compositions.

Yet if neither *Verklaerte Nacht*, nor *Erwartung*, nor any other single work of Schoenberg's seems "to form an intelligible pair"[11] with the monologue, still there are two distinctive features of the composer's technique that find a parallel in Ferguson. One is Schoenberg's preoccupation with the principle of variation in music; the other, his so-called "emancipation of dissonance," which resides at the heart of atonality. With respect to variation, Schoenberg's practice may appear inconsistent. For where he shunned motifs and themes in his atonal period (or used them so subtly that he was thought to have shunned them), in his twelve-tone or serial period he employed them extensively and quite recognizably, adopting "the variation concept in its most natural state— that of constant evolution" (Gould, 131). In both instances, however, this much remained the same: pure repetition was not to be allowed—or, as Charles Rosen elegantly puts it, "what returned was to be transformed" (64). Something similar, as we shall see, is true of Ferguson. Moreover, and perhaps more profoundly, Ferguson reproduces in language the general effect of the "emancipation of dissonance," a technical term signifying the freedom of chords to remain unresolved, so that in essence they lead nowhere. Whereas traditional narrative, like tonal music, gives audiences the impression of progressing toward some goal (the completion of the action, on the one hand; a return to the tonic chord, on the other), *Transfigured Night*, like atonal music, gives instead the impression of stasis.

But first to the issue of repetition and variation, both of which the atonal Schoenberg sought to avoid. In doing so, he forfeited the usual device for lending balance and length to a musical composition, as well as for achieving closure. (Only think of a classical sonata, in which the principal theme is stated in the tonic and the secondary theme in the dominant, after which both are elaborately developed—through numerous devices, but chiefly fragmentation—then repeated in the tonic to indicate the end.) At least partly as a result of curtailing repetition, Schoenberg, in his atonal period, had difficulty extending compositions beyond a brief, intense statement, like to Anton Webern's miniatures.[12] (Ferguson, in fact, explicitly alludes to Webern in *Transfigured Night*, more of which later.) What must interest us here is that, in seeking a solution to the problem of drawing compositions out to reasonable size, Schoenberg found his answer outside music: namely, in "the sense of logical continuity and varied pace to be gained from words," which he treated as "an all-important prop to musical construction in nearly all extended forms throughout [his] 'free' atonal period" (Payne, 17).[13] Marvelously, then, in the atonal Schoenberg, words took on the function of a musical device.

Not so in Schoenberg's later work, comprising his experiments with twelve-tone, or serial, music. Here the composer returned to the traditional principles of musical construction, at least insofar as variation is concerned. In fact, it is a tenet of serial composition that once twelve (or fewer) pitches have been stated in a particular order to form what is known as a tone row, variation inevitably follows. Witness the textbook explanation of serialism: "In spinning out the composition, the set or row can be repeated, broken into segments, transposed, turned upside down, stated backwards, and upside down and backwards simultaneously" (Christ, 378). Thus serial composers are said, "more than any other group, [to] have exploited different variation techniques in the twentieth century" (Christ, 446)—a fact for which Schoenberg, the creator of serialism, can take credit. As his most distinguished critic, Carl Dahlhaus, has observed, the "concept of developing variation [is] one of the central categories in Schoenberg's musical thinking" (128).

So, too, in Robert Ferguson's thinking about *Transfigured Night*, a work in large part built on variations that arise from the Narrator's obsessions. Variations, not repetitions. For as many times as the Narrator returns to familiar material, he never says the same thing twice. Not exactly; and sometimes not even approximately. Consider, for example, the following three versions (marked A, B, and C) of the Narrator's pastoral scene with the Girl.

A There we sat by the grey river, safe in the shadow of the mountain, and there we broke bread, and laughing and mindless scooped the waters of the river to our mouths, lifting the waters of the river to our mouths, and for just a moment the water seemed clear and bright, sparkling as it flashed from the shadow into the light, sparkling like . . . (*Pause*.) like . . .

(42)

B Unforgettable scene. The bright sun. The grey water. The white bread. (*Pause*.) The pale face, the grey water, the bright white sun, the flash of, the flash of the pale bread flashing in the sunlight before her grey face, grey against the grey of the water. *He tries again. The sound of crows.*

C The brilliant, the flashing brilliance of the sun on her pale face, the water trickling in veils from her fingers as she carried it in her hands from river to mouth. The scatter of her laughter as I sliced

the bread. The two of us. The sun and the bread and the mountain
and the water and the . . .

(45)

Although treating the same subject, the passages differ substantially. A,
for example, is fluid and coherent, until it stops short; B is terse and
disconnected, with nary a verb or a personal pronoun to bring it into
focus; while C, although rather more settled, is still composed of fragments rather than sentences, with the only true verbs being relegated to
the two dependent clauses ("as she carried," "as I sliced"). Moreover,
through all these transformations, though the scene remains unchanged,
there is remarkably little, if any, verbatim repetition. Thus from A to B,
the only word exactly carried over is "grey," with "waters" reappearing
as "water," and "flashed" as "flash" and "flashing." Even in C, only six
words recur from A and B both: "sun," "pale," "water," "river,"
"bread," and "mountain"—or seven, if one includes "laughing," which
reappears as "laughter." If such thorough restatements of basically identical material are not variations, what are they? They are as like to one
another, yet as distinct and individual, as any musical theme transformed
from a waltz, to a dirge, to a march, to a scherzo, to a fugue.

What is more, passage B, quite alone and in itself, is a miniature
example of verbal variation. For though every word in B is at least once
repeated, with "grey" receiving five reiterations, only two *combinations*
of words reappear, and then but once each: "grey water" and "the flash
of." Largely devoid of pure repetition, the passage takes its shape from
the changes that are rung upon its several basic units:

| | | |
|---|---|---|
| bright sun | bright white sun | sunlight |
| grey water | grey water | the grey of the water |
| white bread | pale bread | |
| pale face | grey face | |
| the flash of | the flash of | flashing |

The effect thus produced is very close to that of music, with sound taking
precedence over sense. Indeed, so sketchy is B that most of its meaning
arises from its context in the monologue: primarily, from the listener's
recollection of A; secondarily, from the clarification afforded by C. In a
manner of speaking, B distills the pure essence of A, intones that essence
briefly, then yields to passage C, which returns to conventional discourse,
no less poignant than B, but far less abstract.

Such a set of variations would seem perfectly designed to reflect growth
or change. The very word "variation" suggests, after all, some sort of
difference. And yet difference need not denote progress. As the French
proverb has it, *plus ça change, plus c'est la même chose*—a suitable

description of the Narrator's psychology and, by extension, of *Transfigured Night* itself. Given the Narrator's obsession with a single event to which he cannot be reconciled, he can hardly be expected to produce variations that represent conceptual advances. Thus, if it is literally true that the Narrator never (or rarely) repeats himself exactly, it is figuratively true that he never does anything else. "What return[s]" in his fervent disquisition may well be "transformed"—but in appearance only. Although the Narrator incessantly engages in motion, he does so without moving on. Hence he all but personifies stasis.

Now stasis, as it happens, is a defining characteristic of Schoenberg in his atonal period. For in giving up tonality, Schoenberg also gave up the forward-moving impulse produced, in tonal music, by the obligatory resolution of dissonances. Formidable as this technical concept may sound, no musical training is required to understand it—only an acquaintance with a simple melody like "Row, Row, Row Your Boat." To anyone raised in the western tradition of music, the tune associated with the last line of this song ("life is but a dream") leads relentlessly "home." In other words, even a listener unfamiliar with the song would know, for a certainty, how it ended, were the melody to be played but not finished: "life is but a . . . ." The tone associated with "a" is therefore said to be a dissonance, while the tone associated with "dream" is called a consonance—a tone providing stability or resolution. And in tonal music dissonances, whether in the melody or the harmony, are always resolved—if not by the musical score, then by the mind. Even when a resolution is withheld, listeners anticipate it (as in our song above), so strongly is a "home" tone implied. In purely atonal music, by contrast, dissonances are "emancipated": that is, individual notes and chords have no "home" tones to which to resolve. No particular note necessarily follows another; no tones are anticipated, because no tones are inevitable. An emancipated dissonance is thus "an event without consequences, an isolated sonority . . . ; it no longer leads anywhere" (Dahlhaus, 123). For this reason, "Schoenberg's free atonal writing" has been said to produce "an essentially static world. . . . For no matter how frenetic or otherwise the apparent activity, the vision remains rooted, unable to escape from obsessional self-regarding" (Payne, 25).[14]

Here, in an assessment of Schoenberg's achievement, is a telling description of *Transfigured Night* itself. Perhaps inevitably so. First, because the spirit of atonality finds an analogue in Ferguson's obsessionally self-regarding Narrator, whose frenetic talk leads nowhere. Second, because insofar as the monologue, like Schoenberg's music, creates an impression of stasis, it does so through musical devices: not only through the use of variations that root the Narrator to a single vision, despite all his apparent activity; but through something still more daring—namely, a linguistic version of Schoenberg's emancipated dissonance. In particular, just as atonal music declines to move toward resolutions of the sort required in conventionally tonal music, so *Transfigured Night* declines to move toward resolutions of the sort required in conventional narratives and even conventional sentences. Thus, little if anything in *Transfigured Night* ever reaches a conclusion. Instead, the listener is habitually left suspended in the tangles of a convoluted tale.

That the monologue's storyline is convoluted, we have already seen. What still remains to be considered is *Transfigured Night's* construction: especially, the way in which the monologue opens and closes. The beginning ("I dismounted, leaning my bicycle against a tree, and stood watching her") is actually the end, as eventually we learn; while the close ("And it came into my head to sing") is nothing if not a new beginning. Hence the Narrator's promise that "it only takes the end for all to become clear" turns out to be perfectly mischievous. There is simply no end, in a traditional sense, from which clarity can possibly issue. Indeed, the subversion of endings may be the monologue's principal motif. Note, for example, how the Narrator contrives, in recollection, to undo a curtain call taken by the Girl at what would seem to be the end of a performance:

> back she came, running back down the mountain track, and bowed low to the faces scattered pale across the darkness before us.
> *In the background the sound of applause from a large theatre with a full audience.*
> I made a quiet entrance.
>
> (41–42)

The play concludes in memory—then accommodates an unexpected entrance and moves on. Similar liberties are taken with subsequent (potential) conclusions: that is, the Narrator abruptly changes subjects and forges ahead. As a consequence, the monologue gives the impression of stretching out indefinitely, rather like the mountain that the Narrator describes in his W. C. Fields impersonation: "Why let me tell you sir we got mountains so tall it takes a man and two boys all day to look to the top of them, one lookin until he gets tired, an the other takin over where he left off from" (49). The logic of both monologue and mountain is the same: on and on they go.

So, too, with sentences. Sometimes they end prematurely—and thus never end at all: for example, I "set my teeth to the bark of the slender birch beside me, biting at it with the abstracted ferocity of . . . (*Pause.*) With all the tenderness of . . ." (41). Sometimes they exhibit so much reticence as to leave us hanging even at their close: "There was a mountain. (*Pause.*) I imagine it had some kind of symbolic significance. It's only a guess, but I imagine its significance was symbolic" (41). And in one extraordinary case, a sentence of gigantic proportions postpones its conclusion through more than three hundred words, while posing questions within questions, introducing interruptions within interruptions, and working variations on its thoroughly disheartening material.

> And what more natural, given the extent to which an actor can become involved in his part, what more natural—and why should she upon my entry be staring away after him?—what more natural than that—and why calling his name like that?—what more natural—if the man were no more than a name in her mind?—what more natural than that he should—if it were simply a name fed to her by the director?—what more natural than that an ex-lover—and if not, why was she staring away like that when I entered?—what more natural than that an ex-lover who makes his exit carrying with him still the memory unrequited, the unrequited memory, the unassuaged memory, the unassuaged memory, the unrequited, inassuagable memory of inexpressible things unlikely if not now then not ever to find expression, the inextinguishable memory of things left unsaid, and all that which must remain unsaid, words, words on words, mouldering, crumbling to the ground, subjected there to unspeakably, inexpressively massive geopsychological pressures over aeons of time until gradually an image crystallises, a mountain, perhaps, something having a purely symbolic existence, of the failures, perhaps, the disappointments, the sorrows, all the intolerable that cries out for the hiding shadow of symbol to fall upon it, subjected thus to the agony of leaving the stage with things unsaid, and the knowledge of memories in the making, and in his confusion, and because it's not always easy to describe but an actor may reach a point at which confusion blurs the distinction between, and in this confusion carrying his pain from the stage with him, what more natural than that an ex-lover should pursue a vendetta against me, not merely an image, in my policemanness, of high certainty of word, deed, and purpose, but his presumed successor in love, turning down the lights, as I struggled with my speeches?
>
> (44)

Although the sentence can be parsed, it contrives to confound interpretation by destabilizing the meaning of "ex-lover," which ostensibly refers to Don Sergei and yet clearly encompasses the Narrator himself. Ultimately, then, the statement takes its force not so much from its literal significance as from its emotional immediacy. In this respect, it both reads and performs like music, reifying feelings and extending them through time.

The Narrator, for his part, would annihilate time, as comes clear in his vaudeville routine when he gleefully smashes a watch. Such an action is consistent with his fear of conclusions, since if time could be stopped, the present would reign without end. Or would it? Perhaps timelessness is tantamount to suicide. If so, the only way to conquer time may be as music does: by marking time and shaping it, while living in and through it. Words, too, give shape to time, whenever they are spoken—and the spoken word can even sing, as *Transfigured Night* insists. Indeed, the monologue quite vies with song, thus yielding its last, and possibly most basic, similarity to Schoenberg: it becomes a form of *Sprechgesang* (song speech), a concept that Schoenberg introduced in his song cycle *Pierrot lunaire*. For Schoenberg, *Sprechgesang* (usually, if less precisely, called *Sprechstimme* or speech/voice) "stipulates precise pitches from which the voice slides downward, [creating] an artificial midpoint between ordinary speech and ordinary song" (Winn, 5). *Transfigured Night* seeks this midpoint, too, by aspiring to song through speech. And in doing so, it highlights an issue fundamental to many dramatists and poets, but especially to those who write for radio—the extent to which music and words are alike.


*Words and Music.* Here, in the title of his fifth and penultimate radio play,[15] Samuel Beckett discloses the general direction of his experiments with radio drama as a genre. From *All That Fall*, his first play for the medium, through *Cascando*, his last, Beckett increasingly used radio as a vehicle for exploring the musical potential of language. He even declined, after *All That Fall*, to use the term "play" for his radio work, choosing instead the term "pieces," which is distinctly, if loosely, musical in connotation.[16] Moreover, in his last two works for radio, Beckett introduced Music as an actual character, playing opposite Words in the first instance and Voice in the second. Little wonder, then, that Robert Ferguson should allude to Beckett in *Transfigured Night*, his own exploration into the musical dimensions of language on radio. Indeed, the devices reminiscent of music in Ferguson's monologue—principally, the suppression of narrative, but also the use of variation, as well as the absence of closure—all have analogues, perhaps even sources, in Beckett. Yet in Beckett, these devices have not been regarded as musical, either in intention or effect. *Transfigured Night*, then, stands not only as homage to Beckett insofar as it borrows his methods, but also as an invitation for listeners to reconsider his radio drama in light of its engagement with music.

First for the homage. Of Ferguson's two references to Beckett in *Transfigured Night*, we have already seen the lesser: namely, the Narrator's improbable characterization of *Waiting for Godot* and *Murder in the Cathedral* as "guaranteed crowd-pleasers," which his repertory company allegedly chose to perform as a way of counteracting a "general depression in the entertainments business" (49). At the very least, this nod to Eliot and Beckett creates a literary context for the Narrator's barren landscape and stalled sense of purpose. But there is more. By citing Beckett in particular, Ferguson inclines us to recognize a second, more important, allusion implicit in the Narrator's disastrous "improvisation," when he accosts the Girl-as-nanny from a park bench, only to be hauled away by Don Sergei dressed up as a policeman. Listeners familiar with *Krapp's Last Tape* will identify Krapp as the source of this scene—in particular, the recollection Krapp confided to tape on his thirty-ninth birthday:

> TAPE:  —bench by the weir from where I could see her [my dying mother's] window. There I sat, in the biting wind, wishing she were gone. [*Pause.*] Hardly a soul, just a few regulars, nurse-maids, infants, old men, dogs. I got to know them quite well—oh by appearance of course I mean! One dark beauty I recollect particularly, all white and starch, incomparable bosom, with a big black hooded perambulator, most funereal thing. Whenever I looked in her direction she had her eyes on me. And yet when I was bold enough to speak to her—not having been introduced—she threatened to call a policeman. As if I had designs on her virtue! [*Laugh. Pause.*] The face she had! The eyes! Like . . . [*hesitates*] . . . chrysolite! [*Pause.*] Ah well . . . .
>
> (59–60)[17]

The correspondences are unmistakable, with the narrators not only engaging in the same action, but even sharing the same respective circumstances in the present. Both are old, washed up, self-mocking. Both tell stories to themselves alone, essentially about themselves alone. By the time they tell these stories, which are circular and largely self-deceiving, both have said "Farewell to . . . love" (KLT, 57).[18] And both rehearse the past to the exclusion of living in the present. "Be again," says Krapp; "be again. [*Pause.*] All that old misery" (KLT, 63)—a reflection that equally suits Robert Ferguson's Narrator.

The essence of Krapp and the Narrator alike is utter self-absorption, mixed with a withering self-abnegation. This particular blend of contrary traits is a hallmark of Beckett on radio, extending from *Krapp's Last*

*Tape*, a stage play transparently influenced by the medium, through *Embers*, *Words and Music*, and *Cascando*. Ferguson thus captures, in his Narrator, the principal spirit of Beckett's radio protagonists, paralyzed by the desire to be and not to be, to speak and not to speak. In addition, in what well may qualify as the most curious moment in a monologue rife with curiosities, Ferguson pays Beckett a backhanded compliment by intimating just how difficult it is to render a static situation engrossing.

The moment in question arises in the selfsame scene with the nanny, in the very midst of Ferguson's extended allusion to Beckett by way of *Krapp's Last Tape*. The scene, for the most part, displays the Narrator forcing conversation on the Girl by milking his usual small range of subjects: his ever-present loaf of bread; and the issue of realism vs. symbolism, here engaged through the Narrator's recollection of his repertory company's production of *The Wild Duck*. Interrupting this flow of familiar banalities is the following unlooked-for exchange:

X:              I see you're reading a book there. What is it? Anything good?

NARRATOR:   She turned the book the right way up and read the title to me, a look of outraged uncertainty on her face. Improvising is hell.

GIRL:          Why yes, it's (*Pause*.) *The Death of Anton Webern: a drama in documents*.

X:              Oh. (*Pause*.) Who's the author?

GIRL:          Hans Moldenhauer.

X:              Is it interesting?

GIRL:          Fascinating.

(47)

Moldenhauer on the death of Anton Webern? On first consideration, the reference seems entirely whimsical. What has Moldenhauer, a music historian, to do with Ferguson or our agonized Narrator, not to mention Samuel Beckett? More, as it turns out, than meets the eye. For Moldenhauer quite rivals the Narrator—and Beckett's protagonists, too—in preoccupation with self. In particular, Webern is but the nominal subject of Moldenhauer's book, which actually narrates at length his own exhaustive, and numbingly uneventful, inquiry into the mysterious circumstances of Webern's death at the end of World War II. Every conversation of Moldenhauer's is retold in detail. Every letter he sent or received is reproduced in its entirety, from heading to salutation (thus the subtitle, "a drama in documents"). Every frisson he experienced as his search neared its end is recorded. And all for what? For the relatively minor discovery that an American soldier shot Webern by mistake—information that emerges from a single affidavit, which could better have been published as a note. Here is genuinely much ado about little enough, cast in a narrative incapable of "fascinating," so badly does it sag for want of action. Thus, the reference to Moldenhauer accomplishes this end: it suggests how much artistry a Beckett (or a Ferguson) must summon to engage a listener's interest in a self-centered narrator to whom little, if anything, happens.

Because unjustifiable, the length of Moldenhauer's book would invite criticism under any circumstances. But its subject matter makes it especially vulnerable, since Webern himself wrote tiny compositions, ranging in length from a maximum of ten minutes down to merely two. In fact, Webern's entire canon fills three hours only (Krenek, 3). Yet its significance is inversely proportional to its size, since musically it is intensely inventive and splendidly compact. In this respect, Webern may remind us of his teacher, Arnold Schoenberg—in particular, of the Schoenberg who found himself musically taciturn during his early experiments with atonality, a new language that both he and Webern came to speak with difficulty. Such a reminder does not come amiss in a discussion of *Transfigured Night*, with its alliances to Schoenberg on the one hand and to Beckett on the other. For it establishes a bridge of sorts between Schoenberg and Beckett, both of whom may be said to have made an unconventional kind of music: Schoenberg, through atonality and serialism; Beckett, as we shall see, through his radio plays. What is striking is that in both cases, the result was the same: a damming of the wellhead from which expression flowed. We have already briefly examined this phenomenon in Schoenberg (see page 71 above and note 12). As for Beckett, we will find that the more conspicuously his radio plays aspired to the condition of music, the shorter they grew. And why? Precisely because, in emulating music, they sought to relinquish the primary means by which length is conferred on a purely verbal text—the same means, as it happens, that Moldenhauer exploits in the absence of substantial discoveries about Webern's untimely death: the element of narration.

Now narration might seem to be all but inapplicable to Beckett, on or off the radio. After all, the bon mot about *Waiting for Godot* is that "nothing happens, *twice*" (Mercier, xii). But as Kristin Morrison has demonstrated, the stage plays of Beckett (and those of Pinter, too) operate by incorporating stories that the characters contrive to recount incompletely, with drama arising from the conflicts embodied in the way that these "vestigial stories" (27) are related.

> The telling of a story allows characters that quintessentially "modern," Freudian opportunity to reveal deep and difficult thoughts and feelings while at the same time concealing them as fiction or at least distancing them as narration. . . . The conflict between facing issues

and fleeing them is actually dramatized. In fact, in many plays by both Beckett and Pinter this conflict itself is the real action of the play. By choosing to tell a story, to *talk about* rather than to *perform*, to focus on a narrated past rather than on actual present, characters betray their deepest, most incompatible feelings. All that talk in Beckett's plays and in Pinter's plays is not for the sake of presenting thoughts and feelings directly, but rather for the sake of hiding them or at least disguising or distancing them.

(Morrison, 3–4)

If Morrison's comment pertains to Robert Ferguson no less than to Beckett and Pinter, the reason, of course, is that Ferguson's monologue has such striking affinities to Beckett. But from the nearer perspective of Beckett himself, Morrison's insight has this interesting catch: that it does not sit well with the radio plays, even with those that it seems to embrace with some ease.[19] For the plays that Beckett wrote to be performed on the radio struggle to be rid of a narrative element, even one as tentative as Morrison describes. And not coincidentally, the intensity of their struggle directly corresponds to the extent of their engagement with music, becoming strongest in those "pieces" that most urgently supplicate words to exhibit a musical dimension.

Evidently, in his effort to make language musical, Beckett developed a suspicion of narrative, like Pater and Schoenberg before him. In Pater, that suspicion inheres in the contention that when poetry aspires to the condition of music, it does so through "a certain suppression or vagueness of mere subject" (137). And what can better qualify as "mere subject" than a plot line, which, by laying stress on action, draws attention away from words in themselves? Schoenberg, too, implies that narrative is antithetical to music, when he comments that *Verklaerte Nacht* declined to carry over from Richard Dehmel's poem "any action or drama." As for Beckett, he appears to have arrived independently at much the same insight, principally through a process of experimentation that can be traced in his radio drama. But his mind may have well been prepared for this insight by Schopenhauer, whose notion of music (prefiguring Pater's) is cited in Beckett's study of Proust. According to Beckett, Schopenhauer "in his aesthetics separates [music] from the other arts, which can only produce the Idea with its concomitant phenomena, whereas music is the Idea itself, unaware of the world of phenomena, existing ideally outside the universe, apprehended not in Space but in Time only. . . ." (*Proust*, 70–71). When he came to write for radio, Beckett must have noticed that words on-the-air enjoy the singular opportunity to live as music does—"not in Space but in Time only."[20] As a consequence, his work for the medium increasingly engaged him in the effort to "produce [an] Idea" shorn of "its concomitant phenomena": namely, narrative and action.

How successful Beckett thought himself to be in this endeavor, which extends through six plays written over five years, we can only speculate. But considerable apprehension is implicit in his "Roughs" (two sketches for radio), as well as in *Words and Music* and *Cascando*, both of which cast Music as a character speaking solely through instruments. It is telling, moreover, that the affinities evident between Ferguson and Beckett with respect to words and music diminish after *Embers*—an indication, perhaps, that in his late plays for radio Beckett treads where others fear, in fact, to follow. We may anticipate, then, as will be argued below, that Beckett's radio drama leads to this conclusion: that words can surrender just so much of their impulse to narrate, and no more.

But let us start at the beginning, with *All That Fall*, Beckett's first work for radio and, as it happens, a play that discloses the fundamental tension between narration on the one hand and the potential musicality of language on the other. Most listeners asked to describe *All That Fall* would instantly resort to its plot, however modest: namely, Maddy Rooney's journey to and from the train that is carrying her husband home from work. Yet the play all but begs to be heard not as story, but as music. Indeed, from the strains of "Death and the Maiden" that we hear at the start of the work and again near its end, we may draw the conclusion that *All That Fall* seeks the status of Schubert's quartet.[21] Such an interpretation accords with Donald McWhinnie's efforts to impose a musical rhythm on the play when he directed it in its original BBC production.[22] It also gives a context to Beckett's insistence on the curious nature of Maddy Rooney's speech, which is idiosyncratic in more than its diction. To be sure, Maddy's "words" can be "bizarre" (13)—her own assessment—as when she calls Christy's donkey a "hinny" (12) with "great moist cleg-tormented eyes" (13). But when her husband later echoes her concern about her language, the specific words he ridicules are not, in fact, unusual:

> MRS ROONEY: No, no, I am agog, tell me all, then we shall press on and never pause, never pause, till we come safe to haven.
> [*Pause.*]
> MR ROONEY: Never pause . . . safe to haven. . . . Do you know, Maddy, sometimes one would think you were struggling with a dead language.

(34)

The joke here, no doubt, is that Mr. Rooney's criticism better applies to "agog" than to the words that he actually cites. But precisely for that reason, his comment may serve to redirect our attention from Maddy's vocabulary to associated matters, like her mannered turns of phrase (as in "safe to haven") and her repetitions (as in "never pause"), not to mention her refined sense of rhythm. Although speech of this sort is commonly said to be poetic, it may as easily be identified as musical. Certainly, it seems so in *Transfigured Night*, where Ferguson employs a similarly poetic speech in an explicitly musical context.

We may also discover a musical intention in Beckett's numerous references, as the play unfolds, to women in distress: Maddy Rooney herself, with her physical infirmities; the "poor woman" who plays Schubert all day long, "alone in [her] ruinous old house" (12); Christy's wife, who is "no better," and his daughter, who is "no worse" (12); Miss Fitt, who is "distray" (22), "just not really there at all" (23); Mrs. Tully, whose husband "beats her unmercifully" (33); and so on and so forth, straight down to the females who have died, including Maddy's own little Minnie, the hen squashed by Cissy Slocum's vehicle, and the child whom the "mind doctor" could not assist because "she had never really been born" (36). Every female in the play is in some sort of difficulty, real or anticipated—even the vehicles, all of which are designated (at least once, if not consistently) by feminine pronouns, and all of which keep threatening to fail. Thus, Christy's hinny "refuses to advance" (13); the back tire on Mr. Tyler's bicycle "has gone down again" (15); Mr. Slocum's limousine goes "dead" from "too much air" (18–19); and the train that Maddy goes to meet is late. Here, we may suspect, is Beckett's effort to express a pure Idea, in Schopenhauer's terms: the Idea, as the strain from Schubert has it, of Death and the Maiden. Yet if so, the Idea is anything but pure, so inextricably is it associated with its "concomitant phenomena"—namely, Maddy's journey to the station, and the suspense that is generated over the lateness of the train. As a consequence, the Idea is quite indistinguishable from a conventional literary theme.

Perhaps in planning *All That Fall*, Beckett failed to foresee how insistently the play's plot action, which is really rather slight, would urge itself upon the listener. In the abstract, a simple walk to and from a train station cannot have seemed likely to sabotage the musical design implicit in a recurring image of dead and dying women. But even a walk implies design of its own, however modest. And in this case, it suggests a three-part structure for the play: Maddy's progress toward the station; her wait on the platform where she meets Mr. Rooney; and their progress home together. Instantly comprehensible as an organizing principle, the walk overpowers the image, which is comparatively subtle in its structural force. Moreover, the importance of the musical motif in the play is further diminished by the small, persistent question of why the train is late. This

humble device for creating suspense—just a touch of expectancy to keep
the play going—runs away with the listener's attention. When Jerry
reveals at the end of *All That Fall* that "It was a little child fell out of
the carriage, Ma'am. [*Pause.*] On to the line, Ma'am [*Pause.*] Under the
wheels, Ma'am" (39), he admittedly offers a vivid addition to the play's
variations on Death and the Maiden, whatever the sex of the child. But
far likelier to give us pause are the narrative implications of his revelation.
For Mr. Rooney has earlier admitted to a "wish to kill a child" (31);[23]
and this confession, coupled with his evident reluctance to explain the
train's delay, firmly diverts our attention from musically motivated vari-
ations-on-a-theme to the suspicion—narrative in origin—that Mr.
Rooney himself may have caused the child's death.

Since that suspicion is at once unverifiable, yet impossible to silence,
the end of *All That Fall* must disorient us in the root sense of the word,
literally leaving us to wonder where we are. Have we arrived at the
solution to a mystery: namely, why the train was late? Or are we starting
out anew, attempting to determine if the death of the child was an
accident or murder? We know and do not know what demands to be
known. In this respect, *All That Fall* sets the stage for *Transfigured Night*,
where Robert Ferguson captures the same paradoxical spirit—certitude
shot through with doubt—by contriving for the Narrator to seem to tell
all, even while hiding the essence of his ill-conceived participation in the
opera *Maritana*. In *Transfigured Night*, however, Ferguson treats the
instability of the Narrator's confession as part of the monologue's musical
design, through association with Schoenberg's emancipation of dissonance. Beckett, by contrast, gives no evidence of seeing any musical
implications in his own play's lack of closure. And little wonder. For one
thing, his musical taste may not have embraced atonality,[24] where alone
in western music is the absence of closure an issue. For another, he
characteristically declined, in all of his writing, to arrive at definitive
endings, so that in courting ambiguity on radio, he was merely engaging
in his customary practice. We may therefore surmise that what Beckett
found instructive about *All That Fall* was not the musical potential of
his play's unsettled ending, but rather the tendency of the storyline to
interfere with the play's approximation to music. If so, such an insight
would account for the direction that he took in his subsequent experiments with radio. For Beckett's radio "pieces" are alike in forswearing
a narrative line. Of present action they have almost none. Of recollected
or recounted action, they offer less and less. Meanwhile, music becomes
their ever more urgent concern.

Witness *Embers*, the most important of these plays for comparison
with Ferguson. Written shortly after *Krapp's Last Tape*, *Embers* revisits

the stage play's conceit of an old man reduced to reiterating broken recollections. Its protagonist, Henry, is an aging, Krapp-like character obsessed with his past and with a story he had meant to tell, but did not finish, about Bolton, "an old man in great trouble" (94), who summoned a doctor to visit him on a "bitter cold" night (94) for some undisclosed purpose. Bolton's story—imparted in fragments, which are told and retold and revised in the telling—remains largely an enigma. So, too, does the tale of how Henry's father drowned. As for how, why, and when Henry's wife and daughter left him (if leave is what they did), we are not advised. Here, then, is a prototype for Ferguson's own fragmented and enigmatic narrative, which is further similar to *Embers* in entailing no action in the present, as well as in introducing independent voices into what nonetheless remains a monologue. Henry, after all, does relatively little except shuffle by the sea. And even in despite of his long scene with Ada—in fact, right in the midst of it—he remains "quite alone with [his] voice" (102), without which there is nothing: "Nothing all day. [*Pause.*] Nothing, all day nothing. [*Pause.*] All day all night nothing. [*Pause.*] Not a sound" (104). Thus, in its shape and its basic effect, as well as in such technical devices as the variations that it plays on words and phrases (as in "nothing" and "all day" in the excerpt above), *Embers* is closely akin to *Transfigured Night*. The monologues may not precisely mirror each other; but they are surely close enough that if Ferguson's is thought to release the musicality latent in language, then Beckett's must be thought to release it as well. Yet Beckett, unlike Ferguson, does not make such a claim. Rather, he emerges in *Embers* as preoccupied simply with acknowledging the rift between narrative and music.

So it is that Beckett characterizes Henry, who personifies narration in his impulse to tell stories, as hostile to music—almost comically so. Henry, for instance, regrets that Addie, his daughter, was made to learn piano and remembers her music master as a stereotypically irascible Italian who drove his young pupil to tears. Moreover, he associates rhythm—here described as "mark[ing] time" (93)—with violence, not only through the music master's beating out "waltz time with ruler on piano case" (98), but also through the stamping of a "ten-ton mammoth back from the dead," shoed "with steel" and prepared to "tramp the world down" (93). There may also be antipathy toward music in Henry's hatred of the sea, whose sound he seeks to drown with his incessant talk. For if he hears that sound as "sucking" (101)—"so strange, so unlike the sound of the sea, that if you didn't see what it was you wouldn't know what it was" (93)—the fault must be his own. Others, after all, from Homer onwards have heard the sea to sing like a siren. And on radio especially, the lapping of waves has musical implications: as Glenn

Gould observes in "Radio as Music," "sea sound" quite naturally establishes a "continuum" very like to the "base foundation" provided by the foot pedals on an organ (383). But since Henry would shut out that sound, if he could, he appears to embody Beckett's growing suspicion that a story—even one told in fragments—must shut the sound of music out of language.

*Transfigured Night*, of course, attempts to quell that suspicion. But it also concedes that the music extracted from words by a fragmented story must forever be distinct from the music of music. That is why the Narrator wishes to sing at the close of his monologue. And that is why Beckett, whatever his assessment of *Embers'* success in approximating music, tried to manage a nearer approach in subsequent plays. But how likely was his enterprise to prosper? This is the question that he ponders in his two "Roughs for Radio." And neither of the "Roughs" is optimistic.

Consider "Rough for Radio I," where a woman (She) visits a man (He, or Macgillycuddy) in order to bear witness to sounds that he hears "without cease" (107). The sounds, which are accessed by knobs as on a radio, turn out to be Music and Voice, both of which Macgillycuddy claims that he needs. What is more, he needs them to be separate. For when the sounds, to his surprise, occur "TOGETHER" (111), he grows frantic. "It's crazy!" he cries; "Like one!" (110). And believing the sounds to be "ENDING" (110), he calls for a doctor, who refuses to come, being otherwise engaged in delivering a child:

> HE:  [*With music and voice.*] Miss . . . what? . . . [*Music and voice silent.*] . . . a confinement? . . . [*Long pause.*] . . . two confinements? . . . [*Long pause.*] . . . one what? . . . what? . . . breech? . . . what? . . . [*Long pause.*] . . . tomorrow noon? . . . [*Long pause. Faint ping as receiver put gently down. Long pause. Click.*]
>
> (111)

If we postulate that Macgillycuddy is a writer (for who else depends upon music and words for survival?), and if we further interpret the togetherness of Music and Voice to signify copulation (for they are eminently marriageable, being "in the same . . . situation" and "subject to the same . . . conditions" [109]), we can understand this odd little parable to express Beckett's qualms about the outcome of his radio experiments. On the one hand, he fears for their failure, since the birth, being breech, is at risk of producing a stillborn. On the other hand, he equally fears for their success, since if Music and Voice are to yield something new, they must enter "confinements" (in other words, fall silent), thus depriving the writer of his needs. Either way, the writer suffers—a caveat for Ferguson, as for Beckett himself.

Nonetheless, Beckett blesses the union of Music and Voice by setting a delivery date for their progeny: significantly, "tomorrow noon," rather than today. The birth is delayed, we may suppose, because "Rough for Radio I" does not itself make words converge with music. Not if convergence presupposes the total (or near total) elimination of narrative. True, the first several pages of the "Rough" are nearly static. And true, too, these pages yield but a trace of a story from the past: "SHE: You asked me to come. . . . HE: I meet my debts" (107). But once She has departed, the sketch quite succumbs to narration. Not only does Macgillycuddy call the doctor, thus raising such story-bound questions as: what has gone wrong? will the doctor, though delayed, come in time? if not, will Macgillycuddy (whose fortunes seem allied to those of Voice and Music) survive in any case? But the conversation between Macgillycuddy and the doctor's receptionist also introduces a recollected story, however rudimentary: "who? . . . but she's left me . . . ah for God's sake . . . haven't they all left me? . . . did you not know that? . . . all left me . . . sure? . . . of course I'm sure . . ." (110). Although Beckett apparently tried in this "Rough" to sidestep narration altogether, his effort collapsed after only three pages.[25]

And what if he had, in fact, succeeded? Would anyone have listened—with approval? Not likely, to judge from "Rough for Radio II," where Beckett considers the fate of the writer who shuns the demands of narration: he is bound by his audience and tortured. Such is the predicament suffered by Fox at the hands of his own private audience, an Animator and a Stenographer cast in the role of sadistic interrogators. That Fox represents words-as-music is strongly suggested by the nature of his speech: alliterative, rhythmic, and so utterly lacking in narrative content that it easily illustrates Schopenhauer's notion of an "Idea" shorn of "concomitant phenomena." (Witness the longest of Fox's speeches—the one beginning, "That for sure, no further, and there gaze . . ." [119]. And consider, too, how short that long speech is. If eliciting music from words means refraining entirely from narrative discourse, then brevity is almost inevitable.) As for the Animator and the Stenographer, they can only be listeners in pursuit of a story: hence the sentence that the Stenographer reads from her notes about the soaping and death of a mole.

What must strike us, in reflecting on this sorry little tale, is that Fox, to whom it is attributed, cannot possibly have told it. Not, at any rate, in the form in which we hear it: namely, as a largely intelligible statement, in which events are related chronologically. For when Fox speaks himself, and not through the Stenographer, he can manage only snippets and hints of information that rarely converge on coherence. How, then, the tale of the mole? The Stenographer and Animator no doubt have made it up— probably by a process similar to the one they initiate when Fox surprises them by mentioning a woman and a brother:

> F: —fatigue, what fatigue, my brother inside me, my old twin, ah
> to be he and he—but no, no no. [*Pause.*] No no. [*Silence. Ruler.*]
> Me get up, me go on, what a hope, it was he, for hunger. Have
> yourself opened, Maud would say, opened up, it's nothing, I'll
> give him suck if he's still alive, ah but no, no no. [*Pause.*] No no.
> (119)

Evidently sensing here a narrative-in-embryo, the Animator and the Stenographer instinctively begin to enlarge on it: they marvel that the "notion brother is not unknown to [Fox]" (120), speculate that "what really matters is this woman" (120), observe that "someone has fecundated her" (123), and wonder "who got her in that condition" (123). Such interests all arise from a narrative impulse, as does the Animator's insistence on interpolating the phrase "*between two kisses*" (124) into the sentence about Maud. Although uncertain themselves "what exactly it is [they] are after [from Fox], what sign or set of words" (122), the Animator and Stenographer plainly suppose that whatever it is will take the form of a story. But given Fox's nature, it cannot.

The result is that misery abounds in this "Rough." Fox endures captivity and physical abuse—a metaphor, perhaps, for the deep internal suffering of writers, whose animators (that is, muses) lash them into creativity for the sake of stenographers (that is, audiences), who repeat what they hear without the slightest comprehension. The Animator and Stenographer, for their part, believe themselves imprisoned, too, as we discover from the last line of the play. "Don't cry, miss," the Animator exhorts his companion, who is verging on tears from the stress of a dispute over whether Fox had spoken of two kisses; "dry your pretty eyes and smile at me. Tomorrow, who knows, we may be free" (124). But if the interrogators' freedom depends upon their seizing what Fox has to offer, then their prospects for liberty are slight. They simply do not grasp that his conception of language is musical rather than narrative. Here, then, is an utterly nightmarish vision of the wages of avant-garde writing—so bleak an assessment that it seems to have disquieted Beckett himself. For alone among his radio "pieces," "Rough for Radio II" assumes a relatively conventional narrative form, hearkening after music only in Fox's few utterances. As a consequence, there is little here, if anything, that bears upon *Transfigured Night*—except for the warning that the risks of abandoning narration entirely may well be unendurable.

By contrast, *Words and Music*—the first radio piece that Beckett completed and permitted to be broadcast after *Embers*—points ahead again to Ferguson. For the piece relies firmly on the basic situation that Ferguson shares with Beckett: one in which an aging man (in this case, Croak) disconsolately muses on the face of a woman, long ago lost, "Who loved could not be won/Or won not loved/Or some other trouble" (131). What is more, Beckett here creates a radio protagonist explicitly determined to make his musings musical. (This, despite the "Roughs.") So it is that Croak has not one, but two servants who speak on his behalf: Words, whom he calls Joe; and Music, whom he calls Bob. These, Croak's "comforts" (127), alternate—and occasionally cooperate—in addressing the themes that Croak sets them: love and age, the twin obsessions that earlier enlivened Maddy Rooney (*All That Fall*), while disheartening Krapp (*Krapp's Last Tape*) and Henry (*Embers*). As Croak's very name insinuates, his own lot is disheartenment, for he has utterly been drained of life in living it. Thus, when Joe/Words speaks in sympathy with Croak, he mainly expresses regret and incurable longing—sentiments with which Music accords. But if in content and tone *Words and Music* resembles both Beckett's earlier radio drama and Ferguson's subsequent radio monologue, the piece is nonetheless unique in the way it is constructed. For neither Ferguson nor Beckett before *Words and Music*—not even in "Rough I"—introduces Music as an independent character actually engaged in a dialogue with Words.

The difference is portentous. Since conversation implies at least a modicum of mutual understanding, the mere fact that Joe and Bob can talk to one another raises the question whether words, in this semi-operatic composition, have finally attained the condition of music. And indeed, there is reason to argue that they have. For Joe/Words achieves musical effects whenever he speaks, while *Words and Music* as a whole goes far toward creating a musical (that is, a non-narrative) impression. Joe's opening disquisition on sloth, for example, functions less as a lecture than a song. Yielding little information about its nominal subject, it takes its *raison d'être* from the chance to produce variations on alliterative phrases like "powerful passion" and "pleasure or pain." Only witness how each of Joe's statements is followed by a restatement, in which word order changes for the sole sake of sound:

sloth is of all the passions the most powerful passion
no passion is more powerful than the passion of sloth

the mode in which the mind is most affected
in no mode is the mind more affected than in this

real or imagined pleasure or pain
pleasure or pain real or imagined

of all these movements and who can number them
of all these movements and they are legion

by no movement is the soul more urged than by this
  by this
  by this to and from
by no movement the soul more urged than by this to and—

                                                       (127)

(Here, we may note, is a prototype for Ferguson's own technique of variation in *Transfigured Night*: see pp. 72–73 above.) As for Joe's lazy response to Croak's call for a discourse on love—he repeats his old lines, with "love" substituted for "sloth"—this amusing maneuver not only attests to Joe's slothful disposition, but also produces the equivalent, in words, of a change of key in music, as when a theme is introduced in the major, then restated in the minor. Joe's musical pretensions no doubt reach their height when, taking "suggestions" (130) from Bob/Music, he creates a lyric poem—traditionally, the most musical of literary genres. But even Joe's subsequent foray into prose—namely, his description of Croak's intercourse with Lily—has the earmark of music about it, insofar as it largely dispenses with narrative detail. (This, although love affairs are custom-made for giving rise to stories.) In fact, *Words and Music* so stints on narration in general that it may strike us as finally expressing, in language, what Schopenhauer calls an "Idea itself": in this case, the persistence of desire in old age. The piece may be noticeably short, as if Beckett could not long persist in making language act like music. And it may, as well, yield half its length to the efforts of composers: John Beckett in the original BBC production; Humphrey Searle in Katharine Worth's subsequent British production; and Morton Feldman in Everett Frost's recent American production. But whatever its limitations, *Words and Music* stakes a potent claim to be considered words *as* music.

And yet: if *Words and Music* finds a way of freeing words from stories, how explain *Cascando*, which is mired in narration? In all other respects, this last of Beckett's pieces for the radio is essentially a twin to *Words and Music*. Thus, it features a Croak-like figure, called the Opener, who ostensibly governs two characters, Voice and Music, constrained to open and close (speak and fall silent) at the Opener's command. But whereas Words in *Words and Music* is indifferent to narration, Voice in *Cascando* is obsessed with it—or, more to the point, obsessed with producing narration in order to be rid of it. Thus, Voice's first statement is "— story . . . if you could finish it . . . you could rest . . . ," followed shortly thereafter by "no more stories . . . no more words" (137). The piece has hardly started, and questions abound. Why, for example, are stories and words here equated? Have we not just seen a radio piece in which words have, in fact, been agreeable to telling "no more stories"? If so, what can account, in this subsequent piece, for Beckett's curious return to representing a voice as a story-telling instrument chasing down the actions of someone named Woburn? Or have we simply misconceived *Words and Music*? Perhaps the piece is less successful than initially it seems in avoiding narration, so that Beckett in *Cascando* revisits the problem, though despairing of actually solving it.

A look back at *Words and Music* suggests that a new look indeed may be warranted. For if instead of attending to Joe in isolation, we follow how he interacts with Bob and with Croak, a narrative clearly emerges: a succinct little tale, in three parts, of how Joe/Words develops rapport with Bob/Music. In part one of this tale, Joe and Bob, although lodging together, do not fraternize. Rather Joe carps at Bob: "How much longer cooped up here in the dark?" he complains, "[*With loathing.*] With you!" (127). Even when Croak asks his comforts to "Be friends!" (127) and to discourse on love, Joe/Words stalls, cheekily recycling his comments on sloth. But when Bob produces music that is "worthy" of the theme (128), Joe is stung and retaliates by posing loaded questions:

WORDS:   [*Very rhetorical.*] Is love the word? [*Pause. Do.*] Is soul the word? [*Pause. Do.*] Do we mean love, when we say love? [*Pause. Pause. Do.*] Soul, when we say soul?
CROAK:   [*Anguished.*] Oh! [*Pause.*] Bob dear.
WORDS:   Do we? [*With sudden gravity.*] Or don't we?

(129)

Joe's point is apparently that Bob cannot specify or particularize concepts: although music can yield a sound "worthy" of love, words alone can assign love a name. So much for part one, which Joe dominates. Part two, by comparison, celebrates Bob. For when Croak introduces a second theme, age, Joe/Words promptly "falter[s]" (129). Only Bob/Music's "suggestion[s]" and "improvement[s]" (130) enable Joe/Words to eke out a poem for Croak: "Age is when to a man . . ." (131). Thus, part two chastens Joe by revealing his dependence on music, for all that he scorns it. In part three, as a consequence, Joe heals the breach with his rival—but not before seeking to prove his own prowess, now cast into doubt. So it is that Joe "violently" insists upon "Peace!" from Bob/Music (131), returns to the initial theme of love, and at last does it justice with a stirring evocation of intercourse in youth. When Bob shows approval for Joe's solo performance by producing an "irrepressible burst of spread-

ing and subsiding music" (132), Joe objects, but only "gently" (132).
For in truth he is ready to do as Croak wishes: that is, to cooperate with
Bob. To this end, Joe creates, with Bob's help, another poem: this one
(self-effacingly enough) about a place with "no words," where one
catches a "glimpse/Of that wellhead" (133) which is presumably the
source of all expression, antecedent to words and music both. The vision,
however, is unwelcome. In response to it, Croak drops his club and
shuffles off in despair. (Shades of "Rough I," where Macgillycuddy fears
a death when Voice and Music merge?) Meanwhile, Music produces a
"brief rude retort" to chastise Joe/Words for growing so familiar as to
dare to call him "Bob" (134). With a sigh Joe acknowledges that Bob
must forever—or, at any rate, for now—remain "Music" to him. And
thus the story ends, a neat little narrative charmingly dramatized.

Neat, because the moral is perfectly clear: words can come only so
close to approximating music and no closer.[26] Charmingly dramatized,
because the piece enacts the moral that it preaches: it is itself a kind of
poem that nearly succeeds in becoming words-as-music, only to fail when
a story unexpectedly materializes. No wonder that *Cascando*, written
shortly thereafter, takes the shape that it does. For in the person of its
Opener, *Cascando* produces an image of Beckett laboring over a radio
piece, attempting in vain to urge Music and Voice toward a place where
heretofore they have not ventured. Nominally, Beckett—as we may identify the Opener[27]—has a creator's control over Music and Voice, both of
which appear to arise "in his head" (139) and ought therefore to do as
he bids them. But in practice, these modes of expression are independent
characters, making "outings" (143) on their own, without the least regard
for Beckett, who merely turns them on and shuts them off. Thus, Music
speaks solely through the grace of its composer, with barely a suggestion
from Beckett himself.[28] (In this respect, the script is instantly distinguish-
able from *Words and Music*, where Bob is specifically directed to be
"soft" (128), "warm" (131), "discreet" [133], and the like.) Meanwhile
Voice is a veritable law unto itself—and ambivalent besides, being intent
upon telling the story of Woburn, even while wishing to be done with
telling stories altogether.

Inevitably, Voice achieves mixed results. On the one hand, it fulfils
the demands of narration by recording Woburn's actions: he rises from
a shed, makes his way across the dunes, lies down in a boat with his
"face in the bilge" (141), and drifts "out to sea . . . heading nowhere . .
for the island" (142)—a wisp of a story, yet enough of one, somehow
that Woburn has been rightly described as "more thoroughly visualized
than anything in the play . . . 'appear[ing]' as Opener and Voice never
will" (Worth, 212). On the other hand, Voice displays striking affinities
to music. Self-reflective and inward in most of its statements, it recits

its breathless comments at a pace that must discourage comprehension, redirecting the listener's attention to sound, and sound alone.[29] Thus has Marcel Mihalovici, the composer for the original production of *Cascando*, observed that "la voix . . . est en elle-même structure sonore ou musicale" (Zilliacus, 131). And thus, too, does Beckett-the-Opener reflect that "From one world to another, it's as though they drew together. We have not much further to go. Good" (141). Not much further, indeed, until Music and Voice converge upon each other, so alike have they grown in their aims and behavior. Yet they never arrive at the point of convergence. Rather they exit the piece in a state of perpetual seeking: "come on . . . come on—" (144), they say, then fall silent, deferring a conclusion forever. So near to the goal, and yet so far. This, then, is Beckett's own painful assessment of the outcome of his radio pieces: that however extensive the likeness they may draw between language and music, they never make the two speak as one.

True enough. But how could Beckett have predicted, let alone have overcome, the tenacious hold of narrative on language? Surely, it is wondrous that a story should emerge from the modest encounter that Bob and Joe enact in *Words and Music*. Wondrous, too, that Woburn should loom large in *Cascando*, though his role in the piece is so small. If Beckett intended, in his radio drama, to recreate words in the image of music by setting them free from narration, then his project was doomed from the start. And yet his doom is itself the very cradle of his glory. For Beckett's signal achievement on radio lies precisely in his vivid demonstration of how adamantly—indeed, compulsively—words contrive to tell stories, even when they least appear to do so. What Beckett establishes in his radio pieces is that words, in making sense, make narration, if only by a kind of innuendo. (Think, for instance, of the embryonic story that the Animator and Stenographer, in "Rough for Radio II," discover in Fox's remark about Maud. Think, too, of the poems that Words creates for Croak—"Age is when to a man" and "Then down a little way"— which both describe actions suggestive of narrative contexts.) For playwrights resolved to make language make music, Beckett's radio pieces thus present two alternatives. Either such writers must reduce words to nonsense—that is, to sound pure and simple—and thereby create *bona fide* words-as-music (a result that stands fair to be considered words-as-noise). Or they must settle, instead, for an approximation to music, in which words, while retaining their meaning and therefore their impulse to narrate, so attenuate narration as to subordinate the stories being told to the manner of their telling.

Robert Ferguson, as we have seen, selects the second alternative—with a nod to Beckett as his guide, and an appeal to Arnold Schoenberg as authority for his premise that a monologue composed à la *Embers* is

essentially musical. As for Beckett himself, he devised a cunning way to
unite the two alternatives in one. Only cast a glance at *Play*, a work
written for theater shortly after *Cascando*, in which three speakers—a
man and two women appearing merely as heads protruding from urns—
disconnectedly offer details about their jealous triangular relationship.
Beckett's stage directions call for the speakers to open and close as a
chorus, with their "voices faint, [and] largely unintelligible" (147) as they
chatter together.[30] Moreover, the text is to be delivered three times over,
always at a "rapid tempo" (147) and, if the director so desires, with
"variation[s]" (160) in the order of the speeches. The result is that *Play*
quite eludes comprehension, although in fact it tells a tale that can be
roughly pieced together from close study of the script. Thus, the music
of *Play*—a work that Beckett himself called "essentially a score for five
pitches" (Zilliacus, 103)—arises not from any absence of discursive
meaning, but from Beckett's willful suppression, in performance, of
meaning that is actually there.[31]

The same can be said for *Eh Joe; a piece for television*, as well as for
a number of Beckett's late stage plays, including *Not I*, *That Time*, *A
Piece of Monologue*, and *Rockaby*, all of which generate narratives,
however rudimentary, and all of which show such restraint in their use
of the stage that they patently bear closer ties to Beckett's radio drama
than to his work for the theater. *Not I* is of particular interest because
of Billie Whitelaw's comments about the rigors of performing it. (The
preeminent actress of Beckett's plays in English, Whitelaw worked on
her roles with Beckett himself in order to achieve precisely his intentions
with respect to tempos, rhythms, dynamics, and such special effects as
laughter and screams.) According to Whitelaw, *Not I* "goes at this
tremendous pace. I've been practising saying words at a tenth of a second,
I could see myself spelling them out like an Olympics clock. No one can
possibly follow the text at that speed but Beckett insists that I speak it
precisely" (quoted in Fletcher et al., 197). Here, then, on stage is the true
culmination of Beckett's experiments on radio: a play that, in telling a
story, impertinently contrives not to tell it at all, since "no one can . . .
follow the text at that speed." And the effect thus produced? As Whitelaw
remarks, in an image that could well have been Ferguson's, "It's like
music, a piece of Schoenberg in his head" (Fletcher et al., 197). Schoenberg, indeed. All roads lead to Schoenberg when the goal being sought
is the temple where words become music.

WHAT GLENN GOULD said of Schoenberg—that he "stood for most of
his life in the forefront of the avant-garde" (Gould, 108)—can equally

be said of Samuel Beckett. Still in all, Beckett's attitude toward language was conservative enough that he never consented to render words meaningless. It was narrative, not meaning pure and simple, that he took as a hindrance to his efforts to make language musical. Thus, Beckett's radio pieces, along with those of his stage plays that equally aspire to be heard as scores, not texts, are all of them articulate and, at least to that extent, conventionally literary. Radical though Beckett may have been in his pursuit of words-as-music, he never abandoned his regard for words-as-words.

The same cannot be said of John Cage—not, at any rate, the Cage who composed *Roaratorio*, a radio work bearing the curious subtitle "an Irish Circus on *Finnegans Wake*." (For Cage, the word "circus" refers to the "buddhist idea" that "there is not one center but that life itself is a plurality of centers.")[32] In essence, *Roaratorio* is simply a reading of excerpts from *Finnegans Wake*, replete with sound effects. But what excerpts! As Cage has designed them, they are abstract verbal units drawn from Joyce's novel according to perfectly arbitrary rules. The excerpts are intended to make no concession whatsoever either to the already nebulous story of *Finnegans Wake* or to the sophisticated wordplay implicit in the novel's language. Instead, they reflect Cage's "non-scholarly and naive attitude toward the book . . . , where experience becomes more to the point than understanding" (Cage, 79).

That Cage in *Roaratorio*, like Beckett in all of his pieces for radio, intended to make music out of language is suggested by his comment that "I wanted to make a music that was free of melody and free of harmony and free of counterpoint: free of musical theory. I wanted it not to be music in the sense of music, but I wanted it to be music in the sense of *Finnegans Wake*. But not a theory about music. I wanted the music to turn itself toward *Finnegans Wake*. And away from music itself" (Cage, 89). Moreover, that Cage, again like Beckett, found narrative to be incompatible with the music implicit in language—or, at any rate, irrelevant to it—can be inferred from what he says about Anthony Burgess's *Shorter Finnegans Wake*: "I've not seen it, but Norman Brown told me about it. It tries to give you the gist or story of it. But the story of it is exactly what it isn't. It's a larger thing than a single line" (Cage, 75). Even so, Cage's pursuit of words-as-music differs substantially from Beckett's in its fundamental purpose. For whereas Beckett, in attempting to render words musical, sought an unmediated engagement with Ideas in themselves (see pp. 81–82 above), Cage sought precisely the opposite: that is, immersion in language set free from "intention," free from "ideas" entirely.[33]

Cage's task in *Roaratorio* was thus to release *Finnegans Wake* not merely from its story, but actually from its conceptual content, while nonetheless preserving some semblance of the novel (presumably, its essence). But how? Cage's "first idea was to read the book through . . . [and] to make a list of the sounds I noticed mentioned in it. Recording these it seemed to me would bring the book to music" (Cage, 157). But to music without words—a prospect that Cage apparently found wanting. Perhaps the music made by sounds alone did not strike him as likely to "turn itself toward *Finnegans Wake*" sufficiently. Perhaps the omission of words by James Joyce, in particular, seemed unnecessary, given that Joyce himself had quested after "poetry as music" (Cage, 103).[34] Whatever the reason, the "circus" on which Cage eventually settled uses language throughout, although the words remain largely unintelligible because chanted indistinctly amidst a roar of random sounds that obscure them.

Since no form of notation has yet been devised that can reduce *Roaratorio* to print, the work cannot be read; it can only be heard. In this respect, it follows the example of contemporary experimental German-language radio drama, which tends to be acoustical, rather than literary.[35] Nevertheless, a fair impression of *Roaratorio*'s nature can be gathered from Cage's instructions for the creation of other circuses based on other literary texts.[36] A circus, Cage explains, begins with a "mesostic," which "means a row down the middle." In *Roaratorio*, the mesostics are built on the name of James Joyce, as follows:

> wroth withtwone nathandJoe
> A
> Malt
> jhEm
> Shen
>
> pftJschute
> sOlid man
> that the humptYhillhead of humself
> is at the knoCk out
> in thE  park
>
> (Cage, 29)

Writers (or is it composers?) seeking to create their own circuses are advised by Cage to take "the name of the author and/or the title of the book as their subject (the row) [and] write a series of mesostics beginning on the first page and continuing to the last." The procedure involves "finding the first word in the book that contains the first letter of the row that is not followed in the same word by the second letter of the row. The second letter belongs on the second line and is to be found in the next word that contains it that is not followed in the same word by the third letter of the row. Etc." Rows vary in length according to the wishes of the writer, who may also deviate from the formula in other ways prescribed by Cage. The resulting mesostics thus represent a complex combination of chance and design. Once composed, the mesostics are recorded on tape as "speech, song, chant, or sprechstimme, or a mixture or combination of these." (If Cage's reference to *Sprechstimme* calls Schoenberg to mind, it probably should. Cage, in fact, studied with Schoenberg, as he notes in his biographical sketch at the back of the volume *Roaratorio*.)

The next step is to "make a list of places mentioned in the book" and then "a list of sounds mentioned in the book." Recordings must then be made "in the places mentioned . . . and of sounds mentioned," after which the recordings must themselves be rerecorded "in stereo one at a time on a multi-track tape at proper points in time . . . following chance determinations a) of stereo position . . . b) of relative duration . . . c) of attack . . . d) of successions of loudness or loudness [sic], and e) of decay. . . ." When these rerecordings are mixed with tapes of the mesostics, along with "recordings of relevant musics (in performance by soloists)," the result is a circus like *Roaratorio* itself.

But what, we may ask, is *Roaratorio* itself? According to Cage, it is a translation of *Finnegans Wake* "into a performance without actors, a performance which is both literary and musical or one or the other" (Cage, 173). Both, one or the other—or possibly neither, depending on the listener's preconceptions about art. To anyone inclined to be skeptical of flamboyant departures from traditional aesthetics, *Roaratorio* must seem to bear a telling resemblance to Stoppard's description of Beauchamp's "master-tape" in *Artist Descending a Staircase*: "a bubbling cauldron of squeaks, gurgles, crackles, and other unharmonious noises" (21). For such listeners, there can only be high irony in the following acid exchange between Beauchamp and Donner:

BEAUCHAMP: If I had one good man placed high up in the BBC my tape would become art for millions, in time.
DONNER: It would not become art. It would become a mildly interesting noise instead of a totally meaningless noise.
(23)

Not that *Roaratorio* found an advocate at the BBC. Rather, it found its "one good man" at West Deutsche Rundfunk—the director, Klaus Schöning—with the result that it "was awarded the Karl-Sczuka-Prize for the best composition for 1979, [having been] felt to represent a convincing example of radio poetry that, at the same time, pushed forward the frontiers of the medium" (Cage, 153).

Even skeptics must concede some measure of justice in the jury's remarks. For whatever one's assessment of *Roaratorio* as art (or as art criticism, which seems closer to the mark), the work must be acknowledged as making a fearless, if reckless, approach to a particularly challenging frontier: the place where language and music promise to become indistinguishable. How, exactly, that promise can be realized is the question engaged by Ferguson, Beckett, and Cage alike, with increasingly abstract results. Which of their experiments comes closest to music? Listeners will differ in their judgments—justifiably so, since the matter is open to dispute. But what cannot be disputed is the centrality of radio to the endeavors of these, and other, playwright-composers.

Neither stage, nor film, nor television can effectively compete with the radio as a forum for words that make music. It is radio alone that yields appropriate conditions for releasing the music in language: namely, a performing space at once empty and dimensionless, from which words can emanate free of any material associations. To be sure, words-as-music can be staged or, for that matter, filmed. Witness Beckett's *Play* and *Not I*.[37] Even *Roaratorio* has been twice performed live by John Cage. But that is not the point. The point is rather that when Beckett and Cage (and Ferguson, too) determined to experiment with language and music, they conceived their experiments for radio. And no wonder. In order to accommodate words that make music, the stage and the screen must subvert their true nature, suppressing their appeal to the eye. For radio to do so, it need only be itself. Such is the particular virtue of the medium, its singular gift to the arts.

# Chapter Four

## THE MIND
### Arthur Kopit's *Wings* and
### Harold Pinter's *A Slight Ache*

•

Sighted people live in the world. The blind
person lives in consciousness.
(John M. Hull, *Touching The Rock:
An Experience of Blindness*, 202)

THERE ARE THOSE who would say that we *all* live in consciousness: that the world as we know it is a product of perception; and that save for our perceptions, nothing exists. Yet when sighted people give their assent to such proposals, they do so as a matter of faith or philosophy, rather than practical experience. Because vision is vivid, direct, and spontaneous, giving a coherent account of the world, the sighted seem to look through a window on reality, where things can be known as they actually are. By contrast, the blind must assemble their world, as an ever-emerging unproven hypothesis, from such small information as comes to them piecemeal. Trees are inferred from the rustle of leaves; a lawn, from the spring of the sod or the scent of mown grass; apples or pears, from their contours and textures, their tastes and perfumes. A world so discerned—that is, conceptualized, not witnessed—is patently constructed as an act of the mind. Nothing is there, for the blind or blindfolded, except what they sense (or contrive to be told about) and then visualize in approximate images: ideas of things, not things in themselves. When John Hull, himself blind, writes of living "in consciousness," his phrase thus embodies his daily experience: he meets his own mind where the world ought to be.

Such encounters, where mind is transparently what matters, are characteristic of radio drama, which posits situations that must then be imagined, exactly as if every audience were blind. To listen to radio is therefore, potentially, to plumb one's own consciousness—and frequently that of the characters, too, since a common device of the radio dramatist is to enter a character's thoughts. The feat may be achieved in a simple aside or by means of an extended interior monologue, often comprising the whole of a play, usually one in which memory is at stake (*Transfigured Night* and *Embers*). Alternatively scenes, or again a play in full, can filter present action through one character's perspective, with the curious result that objective reality turns subtly, inconclusively, subjective. So it is with *All That Fall* in regard to Maddy Rooney. The people Maddy meets on her way to Dan's train are there no less than she is; but since all that can be known of them is what she knows herself, we are better acquainted at the end of the play with Maddy's idiosyncratic shaping intelligence than with any of the people or things she perceives. What, then, does "there" mean in the context of the play? Where, exactly, is it? And who or what can claim to exist in such a place? The sole possible answer would seem to beg the questions—except on the radio, where the answer is a fact: nothing exists save perception itself (ours, and Maddy Rooney's as a function of our own).

Clearly, radio is fertile field for dramatists bent on exploring the mind in relation to objective reality. Especially for those who would objectify the mind in order to see how reality responds. On film or on stage, we know what we see, even when the spectacle is called into question. On radio, conversely, we know only what we know, because what constitutes spectacle is purely imaginary. As a consequence, radio inclines us to favor the action of the mind above the actuality of matter. This, without denying that the mind has its limits, insofar as the world may refuse to conform to the mind's impressions of it. Merely thinking does not make things so, even in radio's Berkeleyan realm. Nonetheless, by a paradox central to cognition, things can only be as thinking makes them—a fact that the radio is peculiarly suited to demonstrate.

Consider, for example, the case of a woman who has suffered a stroke and is thereby diminished (at any rate, changed) in her powers of perception and expression alike. In particular, suppose that she moves between free flights of fancy and efforts to recover the world that she has lost. If this woman's experience is dramatized on stage, her physical presence, her sheer corporeality, will constitute proof that the world she would recover is real, while the world of her fancies is . . . well, fanciful. Yet to the woman herself—Emily Stilson in Arthur Kopit's *Wings*—the problem of distinguishing reality from fancy turns out to be insuperable. Her mind, after all, has to serve as her arbiter: the very same mind that created the problem in the first place. At moments when this mind apprehends another world, how can she deny its validity? For that matter, how can we, if her experience is dramatized on radio? There is little, if any, true justification for discrediting Emily's fancies, or crediting her facts, when both of them come to us via a medium capable of validating consciousness alone, nothing less and so, too, nothing more.

To be sure, *Wings* creates the impression, immensely persuasive, that we can, indeed, verify features of Emily's experience, since she does so herself in her fashion. Emily, after all, knows her own mind to be injured and recognizes, too, that some of her perceptions are private and eccentric, while some of them are commonplace and shared by other people. Are not the shared perceptions facts? No doubt it is tempting for us, as for Emily, to think that they are. But such thinking is circular, certifying Emily's perceptions as valid because she and others so perceive them. True, *Wings* may not actively discourage this method of certification. But Harold Pinter's *A Slight Ache* does—at least on the radio, where the play emerges as a baffling mind game, which implicates the audience before the play's end.

In this game, a married couple, Flora and Edward, inflict upon each other their various impressions of the world that they inhabit. The winner of their game is the one whose impressions prevail when there is conflict—that is, a difference of opinion about the way things really are. But in matters of perception, no less than of ethics, might need not make right. A stronger personality can prevail against a weaker and nonetheless be wrong, as possibly happens when Flora charges Edward with mistaking the names of the plants in their garden. Moreover, circumstances may arise where personalities prove to be equally matched, as occurs when the couple meets a dubious matchseller. Edward perceives him as embodying a threat, presumably of death—and virtually dies of him. Flora perceives him as embodying life—and virtually consorts with him. Both characters cling to their disparate impressions, which cannot both be right, since they are mutually exclusive. And yet both of their impressions appear to be confirmed by the action of the play. Here, in short, is a conundrum, which a radio performance is sure to exacerbate. For given that the matchseller says not a word, how can we vouch for so much as his existence (never mind his identity) on radio, where utterance serves as our sole direct evidence that anyone actually *is*? We may be conscious of the matchseller and may even share that consciousness with millions of others in the radio audience. But nowise can we prove him to be real (or delusory). All that we can know of him is just that we perceive him. Anything further is open to challenge.

In effect, what *A Slight Ache* and *Wings* expertly exploit is radio's aptitude for creating indeterminacy, a condition conducive to contemplating consciousness. For not until we wonder whether what we know is true are we likely to consider how we come by our knowledge, and how inconclusive knowledge tends to be. Put *A Slight Ache* and *Wings* on a physical stage, and the plays forfeit much of their power to generate skepticism, which is central to their meaning. What a pity, then, that both the plays are known as theater pieces and that both have been published in their stage versions only, as if their origins in radio had somehow disserved them. Far from it. That the plays should emerge as enigmas on radio, when on stage they are relatively free of ambiguity, is hardly a disservice. The enigmas inhere in perception itself, as radio invites us to consider.

To BE CONSCIOUS, without being certain of what. This is Emily Stilson's predicament in *Wings*—and our predicament, too, insofar as we manage to share her perspective. That Kopit wishes us to share it is apparent from his comment in the Preface to the play: *Wings* is "so conceived and constructed that its audience can, for the most part, observe [the] realm that [Emily] is in only through her own consciousness" (xv).[1] But why is "for the most part" not "exclusively"? The play transpires, start to finish, within Emily's own ken. What is more, the play's whole action reflects Emily's experience so intimately that the dramatized events take their shape from her perceptions, coherent or chaotic, fragmented or complete, depending on her mental state. *Wings* should therefore strike its audience as fully, not just mostly, true to Emily's perspective; and the play should seem to offer not just distant observations of the realm that she inhabits, but habitation with her—in fact, through her. And so the play does operate, on radio. But not on the stage, where even Kopit's "for the most part" is unduly optimistic as a measure of our insight into Emily's mind.

By necessity, Emily Stilson on stage is strictly third person. Because we see her from afar, we know her as an Other, divorced from ourselves; and nothing that happens can close the separation. No matter that Emily's experience moves us; it does not directly involve us. From our seats in the theater, we watch what transpires, but we do not participate. Take the opening scene: what Kopit, in the printed text of *Wings*-the-stage-play, calls the Prelude. Entirely wordless, the scene displays Emily "reading a book" (7) while a clock close at hand ticks "louder than normal" (7), occasionally skipping a beat, and while the floor lamp to her one side and the table to her other "disappear into the darkness" (8). From the looks of "perplexity" (7), then "terror" (8), that pass across Emily's face, we can draw the conclusion that something outrageous is happening. But whatever it is—a mystery, at this point—it is happening to her, and not to us.

On radio, by contrast, the Prelude goes far to make Emily's experience our own in mood and meaning, if not actually in substance. The perplexity we only observe in the theater becomes an integral part of our response on the radio, since *Wings*—as recorded by Earplay, which commissioned it[2]—opens with sounds that resist interpretation, at least on first hearing. Even if we gather that the sounds tell a story, we remain in the dark (where the radio puts us) as the story unfolds—as a snatch of edgy music, electronically treated, gives way to the ticking of a clock, to a woman's labored breathing, and to several minor actions running roughly ninety seconds. The woman stirs, lifts a window admitting bright birdsong, goes outside, comes back in, runs the water at a spigot, drops and shatters a glass, staggers outside again, then lurches down a gravel path, where she voices a groan and falls silent. So much is so clear from the sound effects. But what does any of it mean? Is the woman young or old? At home or somewhere else? Alone or in company? Threatened or confused? Is she captured or murdered at the moment of crisis; or does she merely collapse from some shock or an illness?[3] There is simply no answering questions like these. We have raw information, but no means to comprehend it—a circumstance similar to Emily's own. For like a woman enduring the onset of a stroke (the Prelude's proper action, as eventually we learn), we are forcibly being estranged, through our blindness, from things we would otherwise recognize. Thus it is that, when *Wings* is performed on the radio, what happens to Emily touches us, too, if only in a manner of speaking.

This identification of the audience with Emily is firmly secured on the radio—while never so much as approached on the stage—in the course of the Catastrophe, the play's second scene, in which Emily is conscious but uncomprehending as people attend to her. The object of the scene is to create the effect of a stroke's "immediate aftermath," which Kopit conceives as "an experience in chaos": "Nothing at all makes sense. . . . The victim cannot process. Her familiar world has been rearranged. . . . she has been picked up and dropped into another realm . . . [where] time and place are without definition" (9–10). How this realm is portrayed in production must determine our entire reaction to *Wings*. But the portrayal itself is a function of venue. For while the stage, in attempting to summon the realm, can only represent it, the radio has a superior potential: it can actually succeed in reproducing it.

Consider in this context Kopit's prefatory "Notes on the production of this play" in the theater. He calls for the stage to appear "as a void," a feat he proposes to achieve through a "system of black scrim panels," some of them mirrored, that "confound one's sense of space" (3). Throughout the Catastrophe, Emily wanders in the corridors described by these panels, while "brief rhombs of color" (14) explode all around her, while "partial glimpses of doctors and nurses . . . appear and disappear like a pulse" (16) in the mirrors, and while the noises of engines and airplanes, of sirens and hospitals, of breathing and flapping and ripping and whispering alternate with snatches of Emily's voice as she tries to ascertain where she is and how she got there. Doubtless, a stage so designed is a suitable metaphor for chaos and for mental incoherence. But seen in itself and not figuratively, such a stage hardly indicates disorder. Rather it exhibits a formal simplicity, as well as a fundamental physical reality, which together affirm the very faith that the action seeks to undermine: faith that a world does exist independent from the mind, and that a mind in good order can connect with it.[4]

Not so on the radio. Here Emily's confusion must be felt as our own, since apart from her mind we can make sense of nothing—for the very good reason that there is nothing to sense. The notion of a "stage *as a void*" is redundant on radio, since a radio stage *is* a void by its nature. As a consequence, radio easily ratifies Emily's experience of the world gone awry, perhaps even gone away. When, for example, from the bewildering sounds that comprise the Catastrophe in the Earplay production, Emily is heard to say, "trees clouds houses mostly planes flashing past, *images without words*, utter disarray disbelief, never *seen* this kind of thing before!" (15, my emphasis), we have reason to empathize. Having listened through a Prelude consisting precisely of "images without words," from which we visualize little and understand less, we now find ourselves assaulted by words without images, which equally defy comprehension. Never *heard* this kind of thing before, is likely our response. As for Emily's questions—"What's my name? I don't know my name! Where's my arm? I don't have an arm! What's an arm?" (17)—they are our questions, too. Or they should be. For on radio Emily is not only nameless (as she is on the stage at this point in the play), she is also disembodied.[5] And being so, she puts her body—any body—into doubt. What *is* an arm, in fact, aside from our impressions of it? If we do not sense its presence, do we "have" it nonetheless? And if we do, where is it? In what form does it exist? Perhaps only in the form of an idea, which may (or may not) be chimerical. Such is the skepticism *Wings* provokes on radio, by depriving us of access to everything but thought.

The essential distinction between *Wings* as a stage play and *Wings* as a radio play can thus be summarized as follows. In *Wings*-on-stage, the world exists; what emerges as troublesome is how Emily perceives it. In *Wings*-on-the-radio, perceptions exist; what emerges as troublesome is how the world measures up. For all that the distinction may seem purely philosophical, in production it has dramatic moment. When produced on a stage, *Wings* is visibly earthbound, tethered to a set that, however indistinctly, makes visible Emily's external surroundings to the utter exclusion of her "interior landscape" (xiv). The images we glimpse in the Catastrophe,[6] for instance, are not of "trees clouds houses mostly planes flashing past" (15), although these are the ones of which Emily speaks. Rather we see "doctors and nurses" and "fragments of hospital equipment" (16)—images that correspond to Emily's plight. Similarly, during the Awakening, the set remains faithful to physical facts: we observe an attendant pushing a floor polisher, a bouquet of bright flowers brought to Emily's bedside, a pillow taken from a drawer and placed in her lap, doctors and nurses coming and going. By the last scene, Explorations, a rec room, a therapy room, and an office with a tape recorder manifest themselves with "a kind of normalcy" (52), leaving no doubt of *Wings'* general effect: it validates the world at the expense of perception. In the theater, *Wings* imitates material reality, to which it is consequently anchored. On radio, by contrast, it imitates thought, so that after its fashion it walks out on wings.

Wingwalking: a daredevil stunt from the early days of aviation, when barnstormers, frequently flying Curtiss Jennies purchased as war surplus, would show up at a fair, or fly low through a town attracting attention and drawing a crowd.[7] For a fee, they would either give rides to the public or embark upon exhibition flying, sometimes involving a wingwalker. This fearless individual would emerge from the passenger seat of the cockpit, stand upright and inch along the Jenny's lower wing, holding on to the stays, while the plane was aloft. In the best of the shows, acrobatics would ensue, with the wingwalker falling off the wing tip but not plummeting (thanks to a harness concealed by a jacket), or balancing erect on the Jenny's upper wing without visible support (the necessary wires not showing from below), or standing on the wing in defiance of gravity (aided instead by centrifugal force) while the plane looped the loop, perhaps several times over. Among the notable wingwalkers of the post–World War I era, a number were women, including Ruth Law and Vera May Dunlap, who were also superb aviatrixes. Thus, Kopit's depiction of Emily Stilson as herself having wingwalked and flown in her youth has a factual basis. So, too, does her stroke. For as revealed in the Preface, Kopit's model for Emily was an elderly, stroke-impaired former aviatrix, and wingwalker too, whom he met in the mid-1970s at the Burke Rehabilitation Center in White Plains, New York, where she was undergoing speech therapy of the sort that is dramatized at the start of Explorations. Thus verisimilitude, strange as it may seem, accounts for *Wings'* linking of "airplanes and brain damage—unquestionably a weird conjunction of subjects" (xii). Weird, but serendipitous. For in early aviation, Kopit finds a conceit that easily embraces the supramundane as it figures not only in Emily's thoughts, but also in radio's presentation of them.

The otherworldliness of flight (stirringly captured by Saint Exupéry in *Wind, Sand and Stars*)[8] serves in *Wings* as an analogue for Emily's aphasia after her stroke. In fact, flying is what Emily thinks she is doing when she wakes from her crisis and finds that her body is out of control: "Must have . . . fallen cannot . . . move at all sky . . . (Gliding!) dark cannot . . . talk (Feel as if I'm gliding!)" (15). As for her mind, from which everything familiar has vanished, it seems a polar landscape apprehended from the air:

> —all around faces of which nothing known no sense ever all wiped out blank white like ice I think saw it once flying over something some place all was white sky and sea clouds ice almost crashed couldn't tell where I was going right side up topsy-turvy under over I was flying actually if I can I do yes do recall upside down can you believe it almost scraped my head upon the water ice couldn't tell which way was up wasn't even dizzy strange things happen to me that they do!
>
> (17)

Here is a speech that, in several key respects, is quite out of this world. It is euphoric, to take the term colloquially; it is a free association completely disconnected from Emily's condition; it records an experience lived in mid-air; and it transports us to a place that is no place at all, having no definition, no scale or proportion, not even up and down. When delivered on stage, despite special effects—despite "whiteness. Dazzling blinding. . . . explosions of color . . . mirrors [creating] endless space, endless corridors" (14)—the speech contradicts what is perfectly evident: that the stage, as a platform, is fixed and secure, not at all like a plane that is diving and wheeling. But when heard on the radio, the speech has authority, drawn from the power of words in this medium to summon whole worlds into being—worlds that, however surreal, are compelling, as long as they exhibit internal coherence.

Now, for Emily Stilson, coherence is the rub. It is the quality of mind that she loses through her stroke and that all of her efforts are bent on regaining, with decidedly painful results. A coherent assessment of material reality requires, after all, that she recognize the fact of her own eccentricity: "No they're not mad, I am mad. Today I heard it. Everything I speak is wronged" (41). In addition, she must face the distinct possibility that she never again will be normal: "May not get much better even though I'm here. No, I know that. I know that" (55). Such knowledge, by virtue of "get[ting] the dark out" (64), is arguably good. But it also is bound to be an agonizing burden, even for one who "do[es]n't open up the door" to "the death thing, it comes in, I don't ask it, it just comes in, plays around in there, I can't get it out of till it's ready, goes out on its own" (65). At moments when her mind fully grasps her predicament, Emily evidently contemplates suicide, or at least capitulation to aphasia's ill effects: "Sometimes . . . how can . . . well it's just I think these death things, end it, stuff like sort of may be better not to listen anything no more at all or trying even talking cause what good's it, I'm so far away!" (64–65). The irony is striking. The more conversant with the natural world that Emily becomes, the more cause she has to think that she cannot converse. The closer she comes to being coherent, the more cause she has to fear that incoherence is her lot.

It is only when Emily wingwalks, so to speak, soaring where her mind alone can take her, that coherence becomes possible to contemplate. Take the passage referred to above—"all around faces of which nothing known" (17)—in which Emily exults in the "strange things" she finds herself doing. Though the syntax is strained, and though the exploit she describes is presented as a memory, not a current experience, still the speech has the general effect of imposing some order on what has heretofore been chaos. As the first sustained statement to be heard in the play, the speech gives the audience a sense of stability, for all that its putative subject is flight. So, too, there is something akin to coherence in Emily's later appeals to flight's perils as she formulates hypotheses about her predicament. At first, she remembers—or imagines—having crashed in the desert (à la Saint Exupéry) and concludes that she is waiting to be rescued: "just hold on they will find me" (24). Then she thinks she has been captured—"oh my God oh my God now I see now I understand they've got me oh my God" (26)—and has been taken to a "farm masquerading as a hospital. Why? For I would say offhand information" (34). No listening audience, in a radio performance any more than in a theater, is likely to suppose that these bizarre speculations are empirically true, since they are all of them belied by the syntactical and lexical distortions in which they are embedded: "upside down was I what a way to go felt embarrassed really glad no one saw me anyhow tubbish blaxed and vinkled I commenshed uh-oh where's it gone somewhere I flubbished please come back quackly quickly sickly quickly thank you anyhow there I was crawling like a rup like a what flop up what pop that's the way I felt the sand still can feel it actually hear the wind all alone somehow wasn't scared why a mystery"[9] (24). And yet no matter how odd or how oddly expressed, these same speculations display an inner logic insofar as they offer to account for information perplexing to Emily, and equally to us: for example, the fact that she is tied to her bed,[10] and that the people who surround her all fail to understand her. The logic may be false, but it is better than nothing. And better than the fact of her own limitations, as Emily eventually decides.

She flirts with the decision to abandon fact for fancy at the midpoint of the play, very soon after finally comprehending that, because of a stroke, she "can't make [her mind] do it like it used to" (44). "Sitting . . . on [her] bed" and lamenting her loss of "control" (46) over names (that is, over words), Emily yields to an impulse to "Close my eyes then, go to—":

> Here I go. No one talks here. Images coming I seem feel it feels better this way here is how it goes: this time I am still in the middle Stilson in the middle going out walking out wind feels good hold the wires hear the hum down below far there they are now we turn it now we spin! Looks more bad than really is, still needs good balance and those nerves and that thing that courage thing don't fall off! . . . And now I'm out . . . and back and . . . [WITH SUR-PRISE] there's the window.
>
> (46)

The passage is at once a pure hallucination and a lyrical description of what hallucination means: namely, hearing life only as a "hum down below" while turning and spinning through the mind's open space. Thus does wingwalking take on a metaphoric meaning, which extends to encompass the whole of the play. For in addition to describing how Emily thinks, the passage describes how *Wings* works on the radio, where (nothing being visible) the play is composed of "images coming" not directly to the audience, but only indirectly, through a single inter-mediary: that is, "Stilson in the middle." Any audience entrusting its experience to Emily surely requires "good balance and those nerves" to endure being lost with her, for fully half the play, in the "dark . . . space vast of . . . in I am or so it seems feels nothing much to go on really" (24). And yet the situation "looks more bad than really is." For precisely at her most confused and thus her most confusing, Emily is also most intriguing. The "wind," after all, does "feel good" when we wingwalk with Emily. The only question for the audience is how good, exactly? Good enough to recommend Emily's conclusion: all things considered, "feels better this way"?

Almost certainly so, if only as a matter of aesthetics. For *Wings* loses momentum once the mystery of Emily's condition is solved—once the play comes to earth, metaphorically speaking. In fact, the scenes that comprise most of *Wings*' second half (Emily's halting discussions with Amy, her therapy sessions, and her efforts to process scientific informa-tion) are pedestrian twice over by contrast to what has preceded them: in content, they are factual; in temperament, they plod.[11] To be sure, they can hardly do otherwise, given that their purpose is to represent the damage that Emily's stroke has done to her speech and her memory. Still, verisimilitude is small compensation for the loss of vivacity evident in *Wings* as it moves toward its close. Any audience at all, whether watching in a theater or listening on radio, must sympathize with Emily's struggle to limp—and, what is harder, to like it—while flight is still possible and utterly thrilling.

> MRS. STILSON [IN AWE AND ECSTASY]: As I see it now, the plane was flying BACKWARDS! Really, wind that strong, didn't know it could be! Yet the sky was clear, not a cloud, crystal blue, gorgeous, angels could've lived in sky like that . . . I think the cyclone must've blown in on the Andes from the sea . . .
> BLUE LIGHT FADES. WIND GONE, BELLS GONE, MUSICAL TONE IS GONE.
> [COMING OUT OF IT] Yes . . . [SHE LOOKS AROUND; GETS HER BEARINGS] Yes, no question, this . . . place better. [AND NOW SHE'S LANDED] All these people just . . . like me, I guess.
>
> (58)

Being like Emily, the passage reminds us, is pure exaltation as long as we fly. Only when we land, and make our minds conform to facts, do we find ourselves discouraged by the place that we are in. It is natural, as a consequence, to wish the facts away or, at the very least, to wish our minds their master.

As it happens, the radio can grant this wish. The stage cannot. For no sooner does the stage award substance to Emily's physical environs (principally, the hospital and rehabilitation center) than it proves her mental journeys insubstantial. Thus, when *Wings* is performed in a theater, flight emerges as escapist and completely self-indulgent, however we may empathize with Emily's impulse to pursue it. On radio, conversely, *Wings* authenticates flight, since the airwaves allow no distinction to be drawn between worlds that exist as a matter of fact and worlds that exist as a matter of thought. All worlds are alike on the radio: they are all of them mental inventions. That being the case, there is small rationale for us to favor those places that impress us as real over those that impress us as imagined. If Emily's flights take her soaring to worlds that are dubious but nonetheless alluring, radio permits us—without sentimentality—to approve her escape. And well that it does, since the last of these escapes, at the end of the play, would appear to be permanent and actively embraced.

So we can conclude from the last of *Wings'* monologues, in which Emily fashions herself "in a plane, a Curtiss Jenny, and it's night" (75). She is not "remembering," she says; "No . . . No, I'm simply there again!" (75). But where she is and what she is reliving—for "this is in another time" (75)—are not only her days as a wingwalker, but also the period recorded by the play, here interpreted figuratively. Thus, the monologue tells us that Emily is "lost," searching for "somewhere, Omaha, I think," but her radio "picks up only Bucharest" (75). (Recall that she was lost at the beginning of *Wings* and expecting, eventually, to "wisht or waltz away to some place like Rumania" [26].) As the monologue proceeds, "the clouds open up a crack, a peek," and Emily makes out beneath her "a field, a street" but "No place to land" (75). (Recall that a "knife slit opening of light"[12] marked Emily's initial, and exceedingly tenuous, reentry to common experience in the wake of her stroke. But unable to speak or even to gesture, she remained out of touch, hence deprived of a landing.) The situation is dire since, as Emily believes, she is "soon to be out of gas" (75) and therefore cannot fly for long. Nonetheless she "keep[s] circling" (76), as she is "scared to leave" what lies below (76), though it is only "this one small silly street in this one small town" (76)—a figure for the narrowness imposed by her aphasia. To leave, as she thinks, is to invite the possibility of "be[ing] inside something empty, black, and endless . . ." (76)—death or, its equivalent, oblivion. No wonder she is terrified to tear herself away. The result would be intolerable. Or would it?

Not if the monologue recapitulates the play. Remember, for example, that when Emily wingwalked (hallucinated) from her bed in the rehabilitation center, she found the experience gratifying: "Images coming I seem feel it feels better this way" (46). Similarly, only moments before this very monologue begins, she tells of a night when she "left [her] body" and floated "up there at the—[SHE SEARCHES FOR THE WORD; FINDS IT]—ceiling, and I looked down and I was still there in the bed! Wasn't even scared, which you'd think I would be . . . And I thought, wow! this is the life isn't it?" (74). Far from constituting threats of either emptiness or death, such flights were altogether life-affirming. Thus, it would appear that, in the monologue itself, all turns out for the best once Emily identifies circling as "a luxury [she] can't afford"—once she "pull[s] the nose up, kick[s] the rudder, bank[s], and head[s] out into darkness all in terror" (76). At least, she "Got to Omaha all right," or "Topeka, that was it!" (77). More to the point, her flight there exalted her: "God, but it was wonderful! [SLIGHT LAUGH] Awful scary sometimes, though!" (77). So far, so recognizable. So far, so benign.

But now something happens that we recognize and fear. We hear a "SUDDEN, SHARP, TERRIFYING FLAPPING SOUND" (77) of the sort associated in the Catastrophe with Emily's incoherence; then her speech becomes impossibly disordered:

MRS. STILSON [RAPIDLY]: Around! There here spins saw it rumple chumps and jumps outgoes inside up and . . . takes it, gives it, okay . . . Thank you.

PAUSE.
[EASIER] Touch her for me, would you?
PAUSE.
[EVEN EASIER] Oh my, yes, and here it goes then out . . . there on the wings?
PAUSE.
[SOFTLY, FAINT SMILE] Thank you.

(77)

Apparently, Emily has had another stroke—this one definitive, at least from our perspective, since nothing further follows: no landing in Topeka, or anywhere else. At the end of *Wings*, Emily is thus flying solo, unable for all that we know to return. By any ordinary standard, this conclusion should appall us, delineating Emily's final surrender to the very prospect "empty, black, and endless" (76) that had scared her. But *Wings*, of course, has striven to evolve another standard, as Emily reminds us with her poignant "takes it, gives it." The statement appeals to *Wings*' central contention, that whatever a stroke may take away from those it injures, it can give something, too: namely, mental autonomy, as embodied in the freedom to create one's own world through the generative power of one's mind. This is the gift for which Emily says "thank you," the last words she speaks—indeed, the last words of the play, as if *Wings* had a stake in her bittersweet triumph.

Assuredly it does. For what Emily has sought to achieve for herself—release from a suffocating physical context—is what *Wings*, for its own part, attempts to achieve in representing Emily to radio listeners. Thus, when Emily, moments before the play ends, says "Touch her for me, would you?"—apparently a third-person reference to herself, as her sense of her body begins to desert her—the radio listener has cause to demur, not only from necessity, but also from choice. Before Emily Stilson is fit to be touched, she must first be material, as she is in a theater. But no sooner do we see her as corporeal on stage than we know her to be flawed, absurdly indifferent to physical reality. Better for Emily to exist as just a voice, which takes precedence over its physical surroundings and thereby appears to control them. The control may be apparent only on the radio and may bespeak what we imagine rather than what is. But when what we imagine is all that we can know, as happens to us and to Emily in *Wings*, imagination easily passes for knowledge, filling dark and empty spaces with images and light.

"'EMILY . . . we're glad you changed your mind'" (73). These words—or something like them, to the extent that we can hear them in the Earplay production, where they fade in from a murmur—are spoken at the outset of *Wings* on the radio.[13] Delivered by a voice of indeterminate gender as well as intention (whether kindly, or mocking, or threatening, who knows?), they impress us at first as incomprehensible. But when Emily repeats them at the end of the play, we hear them in full and know just what they mean: that Emily's mind does not register reality so much as create it, now that her brain is egregiously injured. Such is the damage her stroke has inflicted. Yet when minds are sound and whole, they are hardly blank slates on which reality inscribes itself exactly as it is. From the myriad objects, events, and personalities that each of us encounters in the conduct of our lives, there are some we attend to and some we ignore—a matter of largely unconscious selection, which makes our realities individual, our own. What is more, we interpret whatever we see very much as we will, so that everyone's reality is idiosyncratic. Thus, for us as for Emily, our worlds are our creation. How we fashion these worlds in the act of perceiving them, how we test their authenticity, impose them on others, founder or thrive in them, depending on our luck: this, in effect, is the story of our lives—and the story as well of Harold Pinter's *A Slight Ache*, a radio play ingeniously crafted to weigh the subjectivity inherent in perception.

That perception is central to the meaning of the play is suggested at the outset by the first line of dialogue, Flora's question to her husband, "Have you noticed the honeysuckle this morning?" (9).[14] As it happens, he has not. Nor, though he says "I must look" (9), does he mean to. For Edward's way with the world, as *A Slight Ache* discloses, is to cloister himself from immediate experience, to stay in his house, in his scullery, his study, contemplating life at several removes from it, safe from what he takes to be the wholesale depredations of "usurpers, disreputables, lists, literally lists of people anxious to do [him] down" (35–36). So it is that his essays are "theological and philosophical" (23), addressing such abstractions as "the dimensionality and continuity of space . . . and time" (17). Even his research into Africa is remote: "Never been there myself. Studied the maps though" (23). One could almost say that Edward is not there, no matter where he is. So abstracted is his manner that he fails to hear the buzzing of a wasp in a jam pot (11), fails to hear the birds that are singing in his trees (28), keeps away from "noisy" places (25), savors scenes through a telescope rather than first-hand (35–36). By temperament, Edward is a reluctant perceiver. Since what impresses him worries him, he prefers not to see.

Flora is the opposite. At seven in the morning, she is out in the garden, relishing the plants and delighting in the weather. Later in the day, she again is outdoors, sitting "under the canopy" (28) among the trees and the birds. Whereas Edward in his heyday already was passive, taking wholly uneventful "excursions to the cliff," there to gaze upon "three-masted schooner[s]" from a distance (35), Flora appears to have been active in her youth, riding her pony, sometimes "unchaperoned" (31)—a risk that resulted in her rape by a poacher. "Life was perilous in those days" (31), she gamely reflects, in evident contrast to her circumspect husband, who longs for a time when his "life was accounted for" (35). Whereas Edward shuns surprises, Flora is all readiness. Whether literally "up to [her] ears in mud" (31) while struggling with the poacher, or only figuratively so while a Justice of the Peace, Flora is by nature a willing perceiver, drawn to the light and hence pleased that "today," as she twice thinks to mention, is "the longest day of the year" (10, 30).

Now two such contrary people cannot see the world alike, though they share the same space. What they see must conform to their separate personalities and justify their tendencies, inward or outgoing. Thus, Flora at the start of the play calls attention to flowers, which beckon, while Edward takes notice of a wasp, which is a threat. Their awareness of the world is thereby shown to be selective: what Flora sees corroborates her sense that life is good; what Edward sees corroborates his sense that harm lowers. Each is right, to be sure, if only partially and somewhat. But merely being right is not enough for either one of them. For their rightness to matter, they must each have the other's consent that it is so. That is why Flora insists upon Edward's accepting her names for the flowers in their garden: honeysuckle, clematis, convolvulus, japonica. Her aim is not to offer a short course in horticulture, but rather to wring out of Edward an admission that her judgment is sound. He concedes the point, but gracelessly: "I don't see why I should be expected to distinguish between these plants. It's not my job" (10). Then he sulks that the weather is "treacherous," though according to Flora the "sun [is] up" and the breeze is "light" (10). In Edward's opinion, the day becomes "good"—"Not a cloud," he exults (14)—only when a wasp's adventitious appearance lends his own judgment merit. Flora's fear of the insect, her concern that it will "bite" (11), proves that Edward's circumspection is, after all, warranted. What is more, he has the edge over Flora linguistically: wasps "don't bite," he informs her correctly; "They sting" (13). Most important of all, he has the courage and competence, as Flora does not, to disarm the "vicious creature" (13): he traps it in the jam pot, then scalds it by pouring hot water down the spoon hole. The maneuver turns out to be doubly successful. The wasp is disposed of; and the world, for the moment, becomes as safe and inviting as Flora would have it—sufficiently safe, that is, for Edward to contemplate acting on Flora's initial suggestion that he put up the canopy and "work in the garden" (14).

In effect, at *A Slight Ache*'s beginning, Flora and Edward negotiate a compromise, in which each of them yields to the other's perspective on the world that they inhabit. They do so, no doubt, because in fact they have no choice. For the fact is that flowers are benign and wasps menacing. In seeing them, the couple must acknowledge as much and accept the implications, however unwillingly. But what if something new appeared—something (or someone) completely unprecedented, quite *sui generis*, impossible to fathom from prior experience? How would they see/understand such a figure? This is the problem that is posed by the matchseller, whose baffling presence becomes the focus of the play. Very little about him is known or even knowable: just that he has stood at the couple's back gate for weeks or maybe months; that he holds a tray of matches, presumably for sale, although few prospective buyers ever pass along the road; that he looks to be old; that his outfit is slovenly; that he gives off a stench; that his boxes of matches are wet, perhaps with fungus. In short, he is a genuine enigma, impossible to classify in any common category or to comprehend in terms of any recognized function. Flowers bloom, wasps sting; but this matchseller . . . "What is he doing there?" (15). His absolute silence, which endures throughout the play, frustrates all efforts to answer this question. He can only be perceived, never truly understood. He lends himself, in other words, to pure speculation—a process in which the mind partly creates what it partly apprehends. Accordingly, the turns of mind that influenced Edward to notice the wasp, and Flora the flowers, express themselves again with respect to the matchseller. Edward sees him as a threat, a prohibition against "step[ping] outside the back gate" (15); Flora sees him as "harmless" (16), "a very nice old man, really" (15). And there matters would stand—more or less in equilibrium, with the couple at odds over what they observe—were not Edward afflicted by an ache in his eyes.

The first that we hear of this curious affliction is when the wasp is in the jam pot and Edward is proposing that "It'll drown where it is, in the marmalade" (12). No sooner does Flora devise a response, "What a horrible death," than Edward is said to be "clenching [his eyes], blinking them," as if something were in them, or as if he "hadn't slept" (12)—explanations he denies. It is just "a slight ache" (12), he tells Flora dismissively. But what is its source? Might the ache perhaps arise, as the context suggests, from the pain of perceiving the presence of death (or, more accurately, dying on the part of the wasp)? Or might it instead be the pain of perceiving that he is the one who must kill the wasp off, because Flora will not? Or is it rather the pain of perceiving pure and simple, when Edward by nature is closed to experience? Impossible to say from the evidence at hand. All that we can know at the start of the play is that the ache reasserts itself when Edward attempts to take refuge from the matchseller—in particular, when Edward has withdrawn to the scullery, where "only a corner of the garden" is visible, and a "very small corner" at that, albeit one in which Flora espies the old man and declares him to look like, of all things, "a bullock," hardly an image to calm Edward's nerves (17). The scullery has evidently failed as a retreat, and not just since its window gives a view of the matchseller, but also since Edward can hardly "intend to stay [there] all day" (18). "Aaah my eyes," he complains, as he grasps his predicament and as Flora confronts him with the necessary question: "You're frightened of a poor old man. Why?" (18). This is the question to which Edward's "slight ache," with all of its existential overtones, reduces. And this is the question that Edward must answer, if only to avoid looking foolish to Flora.

So it is that he resolves to have words with the man, and in his study no less—a thoroughly incongruous decision for Edward, given his reclusiveness. Flora herself doubts the wisdom of the plan: "Why don't you call the police?" (19), she proposes; "Edward, I could call the police. Or even the vicar" (20). But neither suggestion suffices—and no wonder, since the problem with the matchseller is not legal or spiritual. It is purely perceptual. As Edward remarks with apparent bemusement: "Every time I have seen you you have looked different to the time before" (37). How can this be? No less perplexing, he observes that "in appearance you differ [from Fanny, the squire's daughter] but not in essence. There's the same . . . [*Pause*.] The same . . ." (27). The same what? It behooves him to know. Even more than he needs to "get rid of" the matchseller (19), Edward needs to discover what the man represents—a mystery he proposes to solve by empirical means. But no facts are forthcoming. The matchseller *is* as he seems to whoever perceives him; for his silence and passivity give consent to all perceptions. He corrects no misjudgments, ratifies no truths. Hence those who would fathom him have to create him, revealing in the process their own casts of mind—exactly what happens to Edward and Flora.[15] In describing the matchseller, they describe their own traits: Edward, his sterility; Flora, her desire. And consequences follow for both husband and wife. Flora fairly blooms by the end of the play. But Edward's "slight ache" worsens into a "fever" (38)—a sign that what pains him is, of all things, his own mind in action.

To see how perception shades into creation, attend first to Flora, whose meeting with the matchseller, alone in the study, is more eventful than Edward's and also more direct. At the start of the encounter, the man's physical presence leads Flora to think of the poacher who raped her, while his perspiration moves her to mop off his brow. "It is a woman's job, isn't it?" (31), she comments. This conjunction of ideas—the rape, the woman's job—soon provokes her to contemplate consensual sex:

> Sex, I suppose, means nothing to you. Does it ever occur to you that sex is a very vital experience for other people? Really, I think you'd amuse me if you weren't so hideous. You're probably quite amusing in your own way. [*Seductively.*] Tell me all about love. Speak to me of love.
>
> [*Pause.*]
>
> God knows what you're saying at this very moment. It's quite disgusting.
>
> (32)

And so has the act of creation begun. In the course of several sentences, Flora has all but remade the old man in her own lustful image. He becomes as she wishes, an object of desire. Or *would* so become, were it not for two impressions that Edward has shared with her: first, that the matchseller gives off a stench (21); next, that the man is a "bullockfat of jelly" (29). If Edward is right in either one of these particulars, then Flora's attempt at romance is untenable. She is therefore obliged to evaluate these alien perceptions.

The first of them proves indisputable, though easily changed. Conceding that the matchseller's smell is "repellent," Flora determines to give him a bath (32), a simple and expedient solution to the problem. As for the status of his body, she neatly conspires to feel beneath his jersey, whereupon she discovers that "you're a solid old boy, I must say. Not at all like a jelly" (32). In short order, then, Flora has weighed Edward's notions and found them both wanting—a conclusion that frees her to proceed as she will. "I'm going to keep you, you dreadful chap, and call you Barnabas" (32), she says. And with the granting of the name, which means son of consolation, she effects a transformation in her vision of the matchseller. In fact, several transformations, each one of them consoling. She makes him her husband: "You came and stood, poor creature, at my gate, *till death us do part*" (33, my emphasis). She makes him her child: "I'll buy you pretty little things that will suit you. And little toys to play with" (33). And she makes him a replacement for the feverish Edward: "He's dying. . . . I tell you, he's very ill. . . . The man is desperately ill!" (33). No matter that these separate perceptions conflict. They are all of them equally cogent to Flora, hence all of them equally valid in her eyes.

Essentially, Flora has created the matchseller in three easy steps: she has assigned to him traits that comply with her own needs and character; she has assessed (and dismissed) competing perceptions of his attributes;

and she has given him a name as a way of affirming that, remade, he is hers. Could only Edward do the same. . . . But, alas, he cannot. Even to take the first step is beyond him, since his sense of himself is so vague and problematic as to keep him from knowing what he wants of other people. Being deeply uncertain what to make of himself, he is equally uncertain what to make of the matchseller, whom he describes as an "impostor" (19) when it is he himself who poses. Is Edward really, for example, a theologian and philosopher, as he says that he is—this man who has worked on an essay about space and time "for years" (17) without ever completing it, and who claims to be storing his notes in a scullery, where refuse from the kitchen is meant to end up? Was he ever "in commerce" (24, 25), as he purports to have been—this man who improbably characterizes commerce as "the weather, the rain, beaten from pillar to post, up hill and down dale . . . the rewards were few . . . winters in hovels . . . up till all hours *working at your thesis*" (24, my emphasis)? Is he an honorary squire in the eyes of the community, as he reports himself to be—this man who may "entertain the villagers annually" (22), but who sat out the "floods," according to Flora, while "whole families . . . drifted away on the current" (30); who, in much the same spirit, offers the matchseller a preposterous selection of alcoholic drinks, from "Curaçao Fockink Orange" to a "straightforward [!] Piesporter Goldtropfschen Feine Auslese (Reichsgraf von Kesselstaff)" (25), but who can think to do nothing more useful than to point out a chair when the old man starts "shivering" and "sagging" (27) in the study? After his fashion, Edward is finally no less of an enigma than the enigmatic matchseller, a fact that bodes ill for his chances of averting the chaos that the matchseller threatens.

It follows that Edward, if only he could, would do well to accept Flora's view of the matchseller as "an old man, weak in the head . . . that's all" (29). Nothing that he ever observes of the man contradicts this assessment. In fact, Edward's independent observations completely accord with Flora's early, if tentative, impression of the matchseller's infirmities—"I'm not sure if he can hear," she says, "or even see" (21)—a comment Edward echoes after meeting the man: "He can't see straight. I think as a matter of fact he wears a glass eye. He's almost stone deaf . . . almost . . . not quite" (29). Whether meaning to or not, Edward validates Flora's initial perceptions. He even grants her her simile, the matchseller as "bullock" (17), though he strips from the image its sexual import when he attributes to the man a bullock's "comprehension" (26) and the consistency of a "great bullockfat of jelly" (29). It would seem, then, that Edward, having yielded to Flora in the matter of the flowers, should yield to her again in the matter of the matchseller. In particular, having drawn for himself the conclusion that the matchseller is "very nearly dead on his feet" (29), he would seem to be obliged to agree with Flora's statement after Barnabas is christened, "He's dying" (33). But instead, Edward differs with Flora vociferously:

EDWARD: He's not dying! Nowhere near. He'll see you cremated.
FLORA: The man is desperately ill!
EDWARD: Ill? You lying slut. Get back to your trough!
FLORA: Edward . . .
EDWARD: [*violently*]: To your trough!

(33)

Aside from being cruel, the outburst is foolish, committing Edward to negate what in fact he has perceived, solely in an effort to prevail over Flora.

That he persists in this folly, perverse as it may seem, is consistent with his character. For Edward is occupied through most of the play in various forms of negation.[16] At the outset, of course, there is the killing of the wasp. Then there is Edward's opinion that the matchseller is somehow an impostor, a term that essentially robs the old man of any semblance of identity: he is *not* what he seems, while what he is remains unknown. In addition, there is Edward's unreliable memory, which at least in the case of the squire's third daughter, slips with Freudian import.

Three daughters. The pride of the county. *Flaming red hair* . . . The youngest one was the best of the bunch. Sally. No, no, wait a minute, no, it wasn't Sally, it was . . . Fanny. Fanny. *A flower.*

(22–23, my emphasis)

Oh, I understand you met my *wife*? . . . Fine figure of a woman she was, too, in her youth. Wonderful carriage, *flaming red hair.*

(24, second emphasis mine)

If the daughter, as seems likely, is none other than Flora, then Edward's apparent indifference to her name can be seen as a rejection of her person. (Note that he is heard to say "Flora" but once in the course of the play [27]—and then under pressure, having lost his composure.) As for Edward's own name, he would like it forgotten: "Do not call me that!" (18), he barks when Flora calls him Beddie-Weddie, which indeed may be offensive; but later he demands that she "stop calling [him] Edward" (29), as if even his adult name were best set aside. More so even than the monks who are his neighbors up the lane, Edward is bent on renouncing the world, including on occasion his very sense impressions. By Edward's own testimony, there have been times in the past when he felt overwhelmed and, in consequence, actually ceased to perceive:

I would take shelter, shelter to compose myself. Yes, I would seek
a tree, a cranny of bushes, erect my canopy and so make shelter.
And rest. [*Low murmur*.] And then I no longer heard the wind or
saw the sun. Nothing entered, nothing left my nook. I lay on my
side in my polo shorts, my fingers lightly in contact with the blades
of grass, the earthflowers, the petals of the earthflowers flaking,
lying on my palm, the underside of all the great foliage dark, above
me, but it is only afterwards I say the foliage was dark, the petals
flaking, then I said nothing, I remarked nothing, things happened
upon me, then in my times of shelter, the shades, the petals, carried
themselves, carried their bodies upon me, and nothing entered my
nook, nothing left it.

(38)

Awake but insensate, Edward enters here a death-in-life, interment in a
living grave if only he knew it.

That we know it for our own part should help us appreciate how much
hangs on Edward's taking the matchseller's measure, rather than retreat-
ing in fear of him. Nothing less than Edward's being—his existence as a
sentient, intelligent creature—depends on his ability to form a persuasive
account of the man, even if one that persuades only Edward. Flora
thrives, after all, upon seeing the matchseller as husband, son, and invalid,
though no one else is likely to see him as she does. But Edward cannot
move beyond his negative impression (the matchseller as impostor),
cannot put in its place an affirmative image—a failure he acknowledges
at the end of the play and attempts to explain as best he can. Seeing the
matchseller clearly, he proposes, has proven impossible because external
conditions have never been right. According to Edward, whatever his
perspective (the "roof," the "drive," the "scullery"), and whatever his
accoutrements ("dark glasses," "light glasses," or "bare eyed"), he has
been hampered by the elements: by "driving snow," "thick fog," or
"blinding sun" (37). Perhaps he is right. But since Flora twice demurs
when Edward talks about the weather—once early on when he says it is
"treacherous" (10), and later when he speaks of having seen a "summer
storm" in which the matchseller curiously "stood without moving"
(21)—we may wonder if Edward's barometer is accurate. Even Edward
seems to wonder; for without any warning, he abandons this theory and
devises another, which supersedes the first: "Not that I had any difficulty
in seeing you, no, no, it was not so much my sight, my sight is excellent—in winter I run about with nothing on but a pair of polo shorts—no,
it was not so much any deficiency in my sight as the airs between me
and my object—don't weep—the change of air, the currents obtaining in
the space between me and my object, the shades they make, the shapes

they take, the quivering, the eternal quivering—please stop crying—nothing to do with heat haze" (38). This, then, is Edward's last word on his predicament, his final attempt to comprehend why his comprehension falters. And considering that such a task is self-contradictory, the marvel is precisely that this second theory rings so true.

Rings true, that is, as metaphor, if those quivering shapes that cause Edward concern—that obtain *between* himself and his object of scrutiny—are taken to issue from *mutual* perception. They can then be understood as the visions and re-visions that are bound to occur when one person looks at another, sees himself being seen in return, and adjusts his initial impression of the viewer (and possibly himself) on the basis of (what he imagines to be) the viewer's impression of him. Such quivering occurs between Edward and Flora when they speak of the flowers, the wasp, and the matchseller, all three of which are pretexts for the couple to watch themselves watching each other, as they jockey for position in their race for authority. A similar quivering also occurs when each talks with the matchseller, even though the man never breaches his silence. For silence, too, can lead to perturbations in relationships. Thus Flora, after judging the man to be a mendicant, discovers in his muteness permission to regard him as begging for love—and as begging it from her, now restored to her youth, not to mention her innocence, "picking daisies, in my apron, my pretty daisy apron" (32–33). Flora, in short, takes a look at the matchseller, sees her first impression quiver and, hearing no dissent, exploits the occasion to resolve the blurred image (of herself as well as him) into one she approves. With Edward it is much the same, yet altogether different. For Edward looks first at himself and only after at the matchseller, finds that what quivers is his own self-regard and, hearing no consent to any self-account he offers, loses his faith in his power to resolve any image whatsoever.

The perceptual link between Edward and the matchseller is cited explicitly by Edward himself in the interlude between the men's sessions together. Repeating to Flora his charge that the matchseller is merely an impostor, Edward hastens to add: "And he knows I know it. . . . And I know he knows I know it. . . . And he knows I know" (29). The comment confirms that "the currents obtaining in the space between [Edward] and [his] object" of scrutiny (38) arise from incessant exchanges of impressions. But impressions of what, in this particular case? Not of the matchseller, as Edward proposes, but of Edward himself, to judge from the results of their initial encounter. Despite the self-assurance that Edward evinces on waving the matchseller into his study—"Here I am. Where are you?" (22)—his confidence (mock or real) soon ebbs away. When the man does not sit, though Edward offers him a chair, any one that he wishes—when the man does not acknowledge the roles Edward plays, whether squire or scholar or peddler or bully, except insofar as he retreats into shadow upon Edward's demand that he "Get back!" (26)—when the man proves indifferent, even oblivious, to Edward's very presence, Edward registers the strain in his own personality. He forgets Flora's name, as we have already seen. He loses track of his intention to banish the man and all but recommends that he remain in the area: "I can tell you, in my opinion you won't find many prettier parts than here" (23). And he cedes to the matchseller virtual control of their whole interaction: "I can't possibly talk to you unless you're settled. Then and only then can I speak to you. Do you follow me? You're not being terribly helpful" (26). By the end of the scene, the same Edward who said "Here I am" at the outset is lost to himself. The matchseller meanwhile is found, at least by Edward, to "possess most extraordinary repose" (24), or some similar quality that Edward cannot name ("Well, perhaps that's not quite the right word . . . repose"), let alone himself display. Whereas Edward had expected to rout the old man, the tables have turned. Edward, instead, now flees his own study, flustered and frightened, in an evident panic.

Thus, this irony arises: that by the time Edward comments to Flora that "I could not possibly find myself in [the matchseller's] place" (28), he is already there. At the end of the play, then, when Flora hands Edward the matchseller's tray, she is not herself forcing on Edward an alien identity; she is merely acknowledging a *fait accompli*. As for how this particular fact has been accomplished, the answer is that Edward has utterly failed at the give and take of mutual perception. Bad enough for poor Edward that he cannot, like Flora, give the matchseller traits fit to complement his own. Still worse, he can find nothing wholesome to take from the matchseller's ostensible impressions of him. What Edward takes, to his detriment, is a sense of himself as either laughable or piteous, he cannot tell which.

You find that funny? Are you grinning?

(35)

Laugh your bloody head off! Go on. Don't mind me. No need to be polite.

(36)

You're crying . . .
[*Pause.*]
[*Moved.*] You haven't been laughing. You're crying.
[*Pause.*]

You're weeping. You're shaking with grief. For me. I can't believe
it. For my plight. I've been wrong.

(37)

Although Edward would rather be pitied than scorned, neither reaction
is good for him. The pity induces him to think of hibernation, of times
when he hid in a "nook" (38) like a grave. And the scorn that follows
fast on this sign of his mortality effectively serves to annihilate him:
"[*Slowly, in horror.*] You *are* laughing. You're laughing. Your face. Your
body. [*Overwhelming nausea and horror.*] Rocking . . . gasping . . .
rocking . . . shaking . . . rocking . . . heaving . . . rocking . . . You're
laughing at me! Aaaaahhhh!" (39). Edward's "Aaaaahhhh!" may be a
protest against his extinction. But still he succumbs: that is, he ceases to
frame independent perceptions and thus ceases, in essence, to be.

Edward's loss of independence comes instantly clear in the wake of
his crisis, when without any warning he sees the old matchseller not, as
before, through eyes of his own, but through Flora's instead. "You look
younger. You look extraordinarily . . . youthful" (39), he says to the
man, in what constitutes complete capitulation to his wife's way of seeing.
The moment is shattering—the more so since Edward must construct
Flora's image of the matchseller *de novo*. She never, after all, entrusts
Edward with her sense of the matchseller's youth or his sexual appeal.
(Recall that she develops these impressions in private and that, rather
than share them with Edward, she staunchly maintains that the man is
"ill" and "dying" [33].) To be sure, Flora does betray her tendency to
prurience: this, through the sexual overtones present not only in the
names of the flowers she identifies (clematis, convolvulus, and honeysuckle), but also, and more pointedly, in her characterization of the
matchseller as a "bullock let loose" (17) in the garden. As for Edward,
he appears to be aware of these overtones, to judge from the insult that
he chooses for Flora when she tells him what transpired in her meeting
with the matchseller: "You lying slut" (33), he calls her. Even so, it is a
distance from detecting Flora's lust to perceiving the matchseller as Flora's
lust would have him. And when Edward traverses it, he does so incau-
tiously: he leaves his own bevy of impressions behind. That his new
perspective jolts him is readily apparent from the question that he asks
before lapsing into silence: "Who are you?" (39), he wonders with respect
to the matchseller. But the answer would be obvious even were Flora not
heard in the distance, calling out "Barnabas?" as if in reply. The
matchseller, at least in this last incarnation, is fully and exclusively Flora's
invention, now fully and autonomously apprehended by Edward.

What began as a straightforward difference of opinion between Edward and Flora about the matchseller's identity thus ends as a mind-game

in which Flora prevails. Edward not only sees, but sees for himself, that the matchseller is everything Flora has discerned. Yet since Flora has discerned a young rival for Edward, and a rival who effectively does Edward down, Edward's fear of the man now emerges as prescient. Just as Edward had predicted, the matchseller proves to have been an impostor, if only insofar as he is not what he seemed. What is more, this impostor's effect upon Edward is anything but salutary, as Edward foresaw. Hence—cruel trick of fate—Edward vindicates his own beleaguered view of the matchseller precisely by rejecting it in favor of Flora's. The action of the play, then, has contrary lessons to teach to these thoroughly contrary characters. For Flora, the lesson is: perceiving makes things so. For Edward, it is rather: *not* perceiving makes things so. Accordingly, the play's closing image shows Edward insensible, Flora alert, and the matchseller just as the two of them have made him: youthful and hale, impressively virile, no matter the truth of his physical condition.

No matter? If so, then this same closing image—unstable; open-ended; above all, immaterial—cannot be conveyed in a theater. Put *A Slight Ache* on stage and the matchseller's physical condition is no mystery: it is easily deduced from his physical presence. To look at the man is to see him as he is, irrespective of Flora's and Edward's opinion. And his appearance being known, the couple in turn can be known (that is, judged) by their opinion's validity. Is the matchseller cast as decrepit and obtuse? Then the couple emerge as completely deluded. Does the matchseller change in appearance and demeanor at the couple's least suggestion as the play runs its course? Then the couple are sane, though their world is surreal. Is the matchseller simply a void on the stage, an absence where a man is reputed to be? Then the couple demonstrably hallucinate. Only one of these options can apply per production; the choice is the director's and, once it is made, the performance is constrained by it. Yet nothing in the playscript recommends any choice whatsoever. On the contrary, the script keeps its silence with respect to the matchseller's appearance, no less than his identity.[17] Hence performances, too, should be silent on this point. And for very good reason: when silence is observed—as it is on the radio—*A Slight Ache* invites us not merely to witness the mind-game enacted by Flora and Edward, but actually to enter a mind-game ourselves.

Now the object of the game that we ourselves are meant to play is actually no different from Flora's and Edward's: we must simply attempt to make sense of the matchseller. But we play by different rules from those governing the couple. For when we hear *A Slight Ache* on the radio—hear it, that is, without seeing it—the matchseller's silence guarantees that there is nothing we can know of him first-hand. Whereas the couple can see the man directly, we cannot. We observe him through comments made to him and about him. We see him, in short, not in and of himself, but by and through others exclusively. What is more—what is worse—nothing said about the man goes without contradiction, so that nothing we come to believe of him is necessary. Here is a game that the better part of wisdom would advise us not to play. But before we can decline, we are committed. No sooner do we hear Edward mutter "He's there" (14) than we start to construct a mental image of the man—an image that we shape and refine at the couple's direction, until the portrait of the matchseller that eventually emerges begins to impress us as flawed, incoherent. But by then it is too late to disown the whole enterprise, to pretend that the portrait, whatever its defects, has not been produced. An idea once thought cannot be unthought; the matchseller, once imagined, cannot be unimagined. He has to be accommodated. But how?

The answer is familiar: we can cast him in our mind's eye as protean, changing over time as the couple contend; or we can cast him as fixed in his initial decrepitude, irrespective of the couple's later view of him; or we can cast him (in retrospect) as merely a figment, a chimera by which we were fooled at the first. The three choices are the same as those mentioned above with respect to the stage; and each of the choices defines, as above, the couple's state of mind, representing their mental condition as sane or deluded or hallucinating. But here, in the context of radio, our own condition too is defined by our choice—and not only defined, but assessed. In apprehending the matchseller, do we perceive him as protean? Then we identify with Edward when he says to the man, "Every time I have seen you you have looked quite different to the time before" (37). But that way lies fever, in Edward's case at least—a strong indication that the play takes this view to be misguided. Do we instead perceive the matchseller as an old and harmless mendicant, never more and never less? If so, we are very like Flora: in the absence of clear confirmation that our vision is sound, we subscribe to an arbitrary view of the man because it suits us—behavior that plainly encourages error. As a third and last alternative, do we leaven our perceptions with distrustfulness sufficient to persuade us that the matchseller is purely a chimera? Then we wilfully ignore a fact that argues to the contrary: namely, that though Edward dearly wishes the matchseller gone, he is nonetheless unable to wish him away. The fact is one that Edward appears to acknowledge when he says to the man, "In appearance you differ [from Fanny/Flora] but not in essence" (27). And the acknowledgment in turn entails a warning to the listener. See the matchseller simply as airy illusion, fit to be regarded as null, non-existent, and Edward and Flora also risk invalidation, since characters on radio are all the same in essence: they exist because we think they do; they have no other being. Kill one, kill all, is thus potentially the consequence of dematerializing the matchseller through an annihilating skepticism.

So it is that *A Slight Ache*, when broadcast on radio, involves us in a mind-game without a solution. All three of our alternatives for seeing the matchseller turn out to be defective; yet we have to choose one of them nevertheless. This being the case, the second alternative, which commits us to an arbitrary view of the man as consistently decrepit from the first to the last, has several advantages. It produces, for one thing, an image that is stable, hence true to our customary notions of the world. This, as opposed to an image that youthens in defiance of time (the surreal alternative), or that vanishes abruptly (the skeptical alternative), destabilizing Flora and Edward in the process. What is more, the only defect of the second alternative—that it *may* produce error—is tentative, not sure: perhaps we are actually right about the matchseller in thinking him infirm, for all that he remains an impenetrable mystery. And even if we err, there would seem to be no penalty. Not judging, at any rate, from Flora's example. For Flora, too, devises an arbitrary image—and one that is patently wrong if ours is right. Yet she flourishes anyway, secure in her conviction that her perceptions of the matchseller are valid because she perceives them and others concur. If *A Slight Ache* when heard as a radio play thus posits a world where perceptions can never be known to be true, Flora seems to offer a modus vivendi, suggesting that, whether we see what we will or will what we see, we only need *treat* our perceptions as true and, in the event, they will not disappoint us.

Would that Flora could be trusted in this matter. She cannot. For a moment's reflection reveals that she is lucky, not wise, in her dealings with the matchseller. Just consider: were the matchseller's merchandise dry instead of sodden, were he manipulative not mute, vicious not docile, Flora's modus vivendi would certainly have failed her. Compare her, for example, and Edward as well, to Max Frisch's Biedermann (a contemporary Everyman in *Biedermann and the Firebugs*), whose encounter with a very different species of matchseller—that is, with an articulate and unmanageable arsonist—results in conflagration. The comparison is warranted by the uncanny similarities between Pinter's play and Frisch's.[18] Both plays, in particular, employ the same formula—"He's there" (14); "He's still there"(B5)[19]—to introduce us to a stranger who purports to be a "hawker" (B5) enormous and threatening: in *A Slight Ache* the matchseller resembles a bullock; in *Biedermann* the hawker, Schmitz, declares himself a "wrestler" and a "heavy-weight" at that (B6). Biedermann, like Edward, has a simple intention: to "throw [Schmitz] out with my own hands if he doesn't beat it immediately" (B5). Yet when Schmitz seeks out shelter in Biedermann's house "because it's raining so hard outside" (B7)—and here we may remember the matchseller standing in a storm without moving—Biedermann decides against calling the police (as Edward calls neither the police nor the vicar to deal with the matchseller) and rather permits the rude menace to stay. Hence Schmitz takes up residence in Biedermann's attic, sipping Biedermann's Beaujolais (think of Edward's many liquors) and dining on goose (which Flora, too, serves for lunch). Meanwhile, the Chorus (in a verse that could well have been written of Edward) reflects upon Biedermann's refusal to admit what he cannot but know, that Schmitz is an arsonist:

> Blinder than blind is the faint-hearted,
> Trembling with hope that the thing is not evil
> He gives it a friendly reception,
> Disarmed, tired out with terror,
> Hoping for the best . . .
> Until it's too late.
>
> (B24)

Blindness to truth, whatever the cause—whether bravado as with Biedermann, or confusion as with Edward, or miscalculation (perhaps) as with Flora—provides no protection against the apocalypse, according to Frisch. Schmitz (a.k.a. Beelzebub) torches the house and all its inhabitants without any regard for how Biedermann perceives him or tries to befriend him—a fact that puts Flora's success with the matchseller in dismal perspective. Flora succeeds, insofar as we can tell, because she meets no resistance; that is, she succeeds, unlike Biedermann, because she does not fail. This is as much as we can gather from her triumph. As for what is wise and what is not (like what is true and what is not) we cannot deduce it from Flora's experience.

The eponymous slight ache in Pinter's subtle play is thus ours no less than Edward's when we hear the play on radio. For *A Slight Ache* on radio cleverly traps us in a perceptual maze that we cannot negotiate—a maze that for Pinter betokens the human condition. Indeed, precisely in addressing this condition in relation to the theater, Pinter offers observations that apply to *A Slight Ache* with startling exactitude, though the play is not a subject of discussion.

The desire for verification on the part of all of us, with regard to our own experience and the experience of others, is understandable but cannot always be satisfied. I suggest there can be no hard distinctions between what is real and what is unreal, nor between what is true and what is false. A thing is not necessarily either true or false; it can be both true and false. A character on the stage who can present no convincing argument or information as to his past experience, his present behaviour or his aspirations, nor give a comprehensive analysis of his motives is as legitimate and as worthy of attention as one who, alarmingly, can do all these things. The more acute the experience the less articulate its expression.[20]

No character in Pinter fits so nearly as the matchseller this description of one who "can present no convincing argument or information" about his past, his present, or his motives. The passage, in fact, needs but one simple change to capture *A Slight Ache* precisely: it is not as a character "on stage" but on radio that the matchseller serves to express Pinter's point, that a "thing is not necessarily true or false; it can be both true and false." Only radio releases the matchseller to articulate this mind-confounding meaning, which is all the more acute, all the more powerful, for being spoken in absolute silence.

> Minds that have nothing to confer
> Find little to perceive.
>                                    ("Yes! thou art fair")

In context, this elegant statement of Wordsworth's acknowledges the transformative power of love. Because lovers are blind, as the adage insists, they perceive in a loved one a beauty that, in fact, they confer, not discern. But, then, lovers are hardly unique in this regard, as modern philosophy and psychology, too, have endeavored to teach us. In all of our various acts of perception, we are obliged to be creative, though to what extent we cannot know. Nor, in the ordinary course of events, does the question arise with much frequency. On radio, however, the question is ubiquitous—hence never more intriguing than when radio drama contrives to address it directly.

The paradox of radio—that we cannot see, yet see distinctly—is the medium's gift to the playwright who seeks to exhibit the mind as a maker, not just an imbiber, of reality. As for the mind on exhibit in a radio performance, it is finally none other than the listener's, caught in the curious process of fabricating exactly those things it appears to observe. To hear Kopit's *Wings* on the radio, then, or Pinter's *A Slight Ache*, is to recognize ourselves—our own perceptual predicament—in characters blinded by disease or eccentricity. What these characters say on the radio, and in no other medium, is *mon semblable, mon frère*. And loath as we may be to acknowledge that kinship, we must yet admire radio for making us perceive it.

# Chapter Five

## THE WORLD
## David Rudkin's *Cries from Casement As His Bones Are Brought to Dublin*

•

Oᴄᴛᴏʙᴇʀ 1964. It is very nearly fifty years since the British con-
victed Roger Casement of treason, hanged him, and consigned his
remains to the Pentonville limepit. And in all those fifty years, while
Casement mouldered in the lime with all manner of miscreants—among
them, the notorious wife-murderer Hawley Harvey Crippen, the last
man before Casement to swing from the Pentonville gallows—the Irish
were endeavoring to recover Casement's corpse. Sir Roger Casement:
British traitor, Irish martyr, international cause célèbre with his so-called
Black Diaries (authentic or forged?) describing innumerable homosexual
encounters on each of three continents. For almost fifty years, Roger
Casement was history. But in 1964, he was once again news. Whether
"as a curry to the Irish immigrant working class" or from a sense that
his bones had been harbored "so long, they're not even symbolic . . .
any more," the British were finally exhuming Casement's "sulphura'ed
and potassified remains" (8)[1] and transporting them to Ireland for hon-
orable burial. Wherever Casement was remembered, the media would
rally to report the event. And radio would play its part.

What part, exactly? In fact, several over time. As a purveyor of news
when the corpse was exhumed, radio would broadcast the facts (and no
doubt some opinions) about Casement's significance and the disposition
of his body. Nine years later, as the forum for David Rudkin's *Cries from
Casement As His Bones Are Brought to Dublin*—a docudrama so original
that it all but reinvents the genre—radio would promulgate a radical
reinterpretation of both Casement and his relevance for modern Ireland.
And on the night after *Cries from Casement* was aired, radio would host
a discussion about Casement and the play, thus promoting consideration

of how historical drama differs from conventional biography. Three different, if related, responses to a matter of social and political import; three means by which radio lays claim to the world.

Such a claim customarily derives its authority from the accurate and objective presentation of facts about a world event or figure—precisely what radio news is intended to provide. Biography, too. And since Rudkin's *Cries from Casement* takes its motive from the news (the return of Casement's bones) and embraces biography (through flashbacks to his life), it gives the facts about Casement due prominence: his humanitarian activities while he served the British crown in Africa and South America; his knighthood; his subsequent conversion to Irish nationalism; his treasonous negotiations with Germany at the start of World War I, when he sought to promote the cause of Irish independence; his trial, his conviction, and the sentence of death; the worldwide pleas for mercy, quieted by Britain's discovery and private circulation of his homosexual Black Diaries; his execution in summer 1916. But for Rudkin, the facts are the least of the matter, since he finds them devoid of "Casement's personal presence."[2] As Rudkin contends, the "concrete evidence" alone cannot conjure "a living sense of Casement *the man*" (Kilt, 72). For that, the bare facts must be leavened by "something . . . speculative and intuitive" (Kilt, 72)—a demand inconsistent with news and biography, but perfectly suited to drama. Insofar, then, as Rudkin succeeds in making Casement live—that is, in answering to Casement's request in the body of the play: "Say of me something I inly, by my own definition, am" (30)—he gives radio access to more than mere facts in its engagement with the world.

Admittedly, where Rudkin ventures in depicting Casement's inner self is highly controversial. In particular, Rudkin interprets Casement's homosexuality as the catalyst for his political development. (Having studied Casement's diaries in the Public Records Office, Rudkin doubts that they were forged.)[3] As Rudkin via Freud would have it, Casement's "emancipated anality"—that is, his ability to revel in "forbidden anal pleasure"—freed him to repudiate those tenets of Western imperialism by means of which anality is sublimated: namely, "punishment, industry, capitalism itself" (Kilt, 74, 75). So it was that Casement, as Rudkin understands him, rejected the excesses of colonial rule in Africa and Peru, finding the widespread exploitation of the native populations to constitute a "psychic sexual delirium" (Kilt, 76). And so it was too—again, according to Rudkin—that Casement, born in Dublin of a Northern Irish family, came to see the plight of Irishmen as largely identical to that of African blacks and South American Indians. Hence Casement's gradual conversion from an early jingoistic British loyalty to an ardent Irish nationalism.

Strikingly audacious, Rudkin's theory about Casement has raised hackles. Indeed, of Casement's two principal modern biographers—Brian Inglis (*Roger Casement*, 1973) and B. L. Reid (*The Lives of Roger Casement*, 1976)—one has actually characterized the theory as "crazy." Or so, at least, Rudkin reports in his reconstruction of remarks Inglis made during the aforementioned panel discussion on BBC radio.[4] Even Reid, who respects Rudkin's argument, remains unconvinced. The theory, he finds, is "ingenious" but flawed, "lead[ing] finally to too much simplicity" (xv). It would seem, then, to be Rudkin whom Reid has in mind when he writes, near the end of his book, that the "English laid the trap of Casement's 'degeneracy,' the Irish fell into it with enthusiastic truculence, and the rest of us have had to argue about it in all helplessness. But it is time to have done with that issue. Casement's homosexuality is interesting, but it is not the heart of the matter" (451). This, in the face of Rudkin's contention that "where Yeats said Love had built his mansion"—namely, in the place of excrement—"I think Casement's saintliness built his" (Kilt, 76). Nonetheless, Reid approved of the play to the extent of paying it a tacit compliment: he took the trouble, in the text of his biography, to mention and identify virtually every minor figure who appears in *Cries from Casement*—even the murderer Crippen, who historically had nothing to do with Roger Casement, but who emerges in *Cries* as Casement's pestering gravemate. Moreover, as the plural use of "lives" in Reid's title suggests, Reid concurs with Rudkin's view of Casement as "many-personed, many-voiced"(24)—a man of "deep dividedness" (Reid, xvi).

From an historical perspective, Reid's approval carries weight as a kindly rejoinder to Inglis's censure. But from the perspective of radio drama, neither censure nor approval is the crux of the matter. What matters is rather that scholarly biographers have actually attended to Rudkin. It is relatively rare, after all, for historical drama to be treated as history, or to be admitted into public debate over matters of historical record—in this case, the debate over the authenticity of Casement's Black Diaries, which for decades were believed to have been forged by the British (and which may still be so considered in Ireland). That an exception has been made for *Cries from Casement* is telling. For if the play has been held to a standard of historical accuracy generally reserved for documentaries, the explanation lies not just in Rudkin's temperament, which indeed is rather scholarly, but also in the ease with which radio is understood to speak to world affairs. If for no other reason than that radio is everywhere an organ of the news, the medium readily appears authoritative—a quality that Orson Welles brilliantly exploited in *The War of the Worlds*, where a simulated news report alleging the landing of aliens on earth was widely taken to be real. In a sense, something similar has happened to Rudkin: his simulated biography of Casement has been judged as "real" history. But Rudkin, unlike Welles, does not seek this result. In fact, in defending himself from Inglis's objections to the authorial license he has taken in the play, Rudkin contends that there is an "essential, qualitative difference between a Casement dramatised against a background of 1970s Ireland, and a Casement sedulously biographised within a strictly documented context of his contemporaneous own" (Kilt, 71). And though that difference may unsettle historians, it in no wise negates what Rudkin has called "the morality of my more schematic, polemical approach, as compared with this particular historian's more orthodox scrupulousness" (Kilt, 71).

The morality to which Rudkin appeals is implicit in his vision of Casement as an "example [for] modern schismatic Ireland" (Kilt, 70). From Casement's "thorny and bitter story," Rudkin draws an "urgent Irish moral" (Kilt, 71): namely, "that North and South have no real future, until they discover their own shared common Irishness" (Kilt, 73). Until, that is, they heal their partisan divisions and become one neutral whole. For them to do so would be tantamount to their emulating Casement, at least as Rudkin has conceived him. For the Casement of *Cries* is a fragmented figure whose agonizing struggle for inner coherence ultimately leads him to repudiate patriotism. Claimed as English by the English and as Irish by the Irish, Rudkin's Casement discovers that neither claim is valid, since each would diminish him: the English, by denying his Irish heritage; the Irish, by denying his Northern roots; and the two of them together, by scorning his homosexuality, the wellspring of his being. Such a Casement has no choice but to forge a private self, in defiance of England and Ireland both. And to this neutral private self, heretofore unknown and mute, Rudkin gives a public voice through the agency of radio.

Why radio? In part, no doubt, because it accommodates quotations from Casement's private diaries (and Rudkin quotes extensively) without violating their essential interiority. Although radio communicates with millions of listeners, it can nonetheless be intimate, since voices on the air, in being out of sight, can contrive to seem not heard but overheard. In addition, radio so effortlessly tolerates changes of scene, tone, and mood that it leaves Rudkin free to construct *Cries from Casement* in Casement's own image: that is, "schizoid" and "kaleidoscopic" in its "multiplicity" (24). Thus, in substance, the play is not only a biography of Casement, but also a review of Irish history from its origins, a defense of homosexuality, an indictment of the capitalist greed at the heart of Western imperialism, and an impassioned plea for a peaceful settlement to Irish civil unrest. As for its form, *Cries from Casement* is equally various, proceeding by turns as a docudrama, a dramatized narrative, a standard academic lecture, a conventional interview, a series of news flashes, even a pageant play. That such relentless variety is far better suited to radio than theater follows from the fact that radio is never discommoded by the physical implications of changes in action, no matter how frequent or abrupt they may be. For these reasons among others, Rudkin has characterized the text of *Cries from Casement* as "radically radiophonic" and has published the play in the form it took on radio, not in the much altered version produced on the stage by the Royal Shakespeare Company.[5]

It is radio, then, that gives Rudkin a means of apprehending Roger Casement and delivering him, live, to the world. That this particular apprehension is purely metaphoric, Rudkin knows. He indicates as much not only by conceding that his approach to biography is "schematic" and "polemical," but also by incorporating Crippen into *Cries*. For Crippen, among fugitives from justice, was the first to be captured with the aid of a wireless—a literal apprehension, indeed. Thus does Crippen yield one kind of triumph for radio, and Casement another. Yet this much the two have in common: that they equally exemplify radio's propensity to seize upon events that might otherwise elude us.

ALTHOUGH EPIC in scale and conception (running almost to three hours in performance and involving many dozen speaking parts), *Cries from Casement* nonetheless begins *de minimis*: with background information for the audience.

AN ACTOR WITH
A NEUTRAL VOICE:    Who's Who. Sir Roger Casement: QM,CMG, Knight. Born county Dublin eighteen-sixty-four, father a soldier, Ulster Protestant, mother a secret Catholic. School, Ballymena. University, none.

AN ACTOR WITH
AN ENGLISH VOICE:   Distinguished career in Foreign and Intelligence services of Victorian and Edwardian Empire. E.g. eighteen-ninety-two, Assistant Surveyor to Niger Protectorate; eighteen-ninety-four, acting vice-consul, steps taken to stemp out local human secrifice. Eighteen-ninety-nine, personal schemes to frustrate Imperial Germany's anti-British manoeuvrings in Boer War. Nineteen hundred, Queen's Medal for service in Saith Efrica.

| | |
|---|---|
| NEUTRAL: | Nineteen-hundred-and-three, investigates and documents slave-labour atrocities in Belgian Congo rubber colonies. |
| ENGLISH: | Nineteen-eoh-five, Companion of the Order of Sint Michael and Sint George. |
| NEUTRAL: | Nineteen-hundred-and-ten, investigates atrocities in rubber colonies of Portuguese Amazon. |
| ENGLISH: | Knighted. |
| NEUTRAL: | Nineteen-fourteen, the Great War: Casement moves freely in Germany as Kaiser's guest, recruiting an anti-British Brigade among Irish POWs there; negotiating German military assistance for a rebellion in Ireland. |
| AN ACTRESS WITH AN IRISH VOICE: | April the twenty-first nineteen-sixteen: lands on Ireland's south-west coast with fruit of his mission. Arrested within hours; brought to London; interrogated; imprisoned in Tower; tried; hanged. |
| ENGLISH: | Judicial process perfectly proper. |
| IRISH: | On paper. |

(7)

What could be more unassuming than this simple recitation of the facts? Or more devious? For though the information given here is utterly straightforward, the manner of its telling is not. We may note, in particular, Rudkin's decision to fragment the Who's Who by dividing it among three different voices; his designation of the specific accent and gender of these voices; and his extension of the biography beyond Casement's death to encompass the enmity caused by his hanging. Each of these choices embodies some feature of Rudkin's special insight into Casement, so that the prologue in essence interprets the facts while ostensibly merely reciting them. We only need know how to listen.

Admittedly, the primary function of the prologue is to introduce Casement to an audience unlikely to have heard of him. As Rudkin would have it, the name of Roger Casement provoked from the British a flat, derisive "Who?" (8) when, in October 1964, Harold Wilson's newly elected Labour government succumbed to entreaties from Dublin and announced its decision to surrender Casement's bones to the Irish. Even a listener steeped in Irish history might know little more of Casement than the nature of his treason: that is, his efforts during World War I to negotiate with Germany, on the theory that "England's difficulty is Ireland's opportunity" (46). Largely missing from the world's collective

memory is the tale of Casement's struggle to secure the human rights of
native Africans pressed into slaving for rubber in Leopold's infamous
Congo, then of his similar work on behalf of the Putumayo Indians
ravaged by the Portuguese, again in search of rubber, in Peru. If the
prologue is intended to cure this amnesia, it does so with concision and
simplicity.

But why the three voices? Voices, as it happens, that Rudkin insists
on identifying, not only in print, but even in performance, by contriving
for the microphone to eavesdrop before showtime on the assembling of
the cast by the producer, John Tydeman.

> TYDEMAN:          Right. Could we have quiet from the studio, please?
>                   I want three voices. Neutral voice: Sean, that's you;
>                   and I think if you stand central, that'll be right. I
>                   know you're Irish, but, I mean, the voice is very
>                   neutral.
>
> SEAN BARRETT:     (*Archly*) Thank *you*.
>
> TYDEMAN:          Bill, English voice; I think that's decidedly you . . .
>                   here. Irish voice: Peggy, over here on your left.
>                                    (transcript from the tape of the play)

Neutral, English, Irish: the trio looks remarkably similar—although not
quite identical—to Casement's poignant self-assessment, midway through
the play: "Three times an exile," he muses of himself: "Irishman in
England. Ulsterman in Ireland. Queer in the world" (30). Perhaps no
one could have made such inconsistencies cohere, particularly after pe-
riods of self-imposed exile in the jungles of the Congo and Peru. But for
Casement, the comment bears witness to a fundamental psychic dis-in-
tegration—a virtual condition of his existence.[6] As Rudkin explains in
the role of the Author, a part he spoke himself in the BBC production
of the play, Casement's diaries present a "contrast of messages" (11),
revealing a personality that over time "begins to fragmentate" (22),
becoming "many-personed, many-voiced" (24). It seems fair, then, to
regard the tripartite Who's Who as a figure for the various selves that
Casement struggled, all his life, to accommodate.

Understood in the light of the facts they recite, particularly as those
facts are elaborated by the rest of the play, the three voices suit Casement
both perfectly and poorly, as would seem to be inevitable for a man who
was forever in the process of becoming something other than the thing
he was. Consider, first, the "Neutral Voice." In speaking of Casement's
birth and schooling, along with his efforts to expose *de facto* slavery in
Europe's distant colonies, this voice represents the Casement who was
free of partisan attachments, being fundamentally a citizen of the world.

Was there ever such a Casement? Rudkin seems to say there was, if only by default. For the Casement he depicts throughout a third of his play is, properly speaking, neither Irish nor English. How could he be Irish when, for most of forty years, he remained apolitical with respect to Irish issues? It was not, after all, until "nineteen-five" that he produced "a Sinn Féin pamphlet calling on Irishmen to refuse conscription"—a pamphlet that, moreover, he only "*co*-authored" and then published not openly, but "anonymously" (20, my emphasis). And how could he be English when he knew, to his pain, that the "English have a God, an ancestral demon, tribal, to whom my racially inferior sense can never be attuned" (20) and when his work for the Crown was received with mixed emotions? It might be grudging, but it would not be wrong, to assert that Casement's investigations into slave labor in Africa and South America were conducted as much in despite, as on behalf, of the British Foreign Office. That Office did, after all, have the cheek to respond to his "atrocity report on the Congo" by "request[ing] him to tone it down: 'International good manners'" (19)—a response that they repeated when he reported on Peru. Thus the Casement who agitated for colonial reform must, in some sense, be regarded as neutral—despite his Irish background, and despite his long employment by the British Crown.

Even so, that employment cannot be entirely ignored. The figure that Casement cut in the world was necessarily affected by the fact that he was England's representative abroad and that the Crown did eventually decorate him for exemplary service. It is therefore appropriate that the names of his specific decorations—the Queen's Medal, appointment to the Order of St. Michael and St. George, and finally knighthood—should be recited by an "Actor with an English Voice." For this actor, too, is one of Casement's several selves. Inevitably, Casement, at the end of all, was partly English, however ambivalent he may have been about his honors (which he contrived neither to accept nor to reject), and however acutely he may have regretted that he "very nearly did become [an Englishman] once! . . . I had accepted Imperialism. . . . I was on the high road to being a regular Imperialist Jingo" (quoted in MacColl, 57). This is the Casement whom Rudkin conjures up, near the start of the play, to fulminate against the Irish patriot, John MacBride, for engaging in treason in South Africa.

CASEMENT: (*jingo*) A certain renegade Irish Major, MacBride by name, is in the pay of the Boers, and moving freely among their Irish prisoners of war, in an endeavor to recruit from them, for service against Her Majesty, a so-called Irish Brigade. This shows the despicable lengths to which Her Majesty's enemies will go, to induce men loyal to their Queen to be false to their allegiance and dishonour their oaths.

(11)

Yet only sixteen years later, in 1916, Casement would himself be recruiting an Irish Brigade from the prisoners of war held in Limburg. By then, his "jingo" intonations, specifically called for above, would be gone. The Casement who had spoken with "the voice of Empire at [his] beginning" (16) would have undergone a "turnabout" (11) and been replaced by the Casement who spoke with "the voice of Ireland at [his] end" (16).

That the Who's Who should represent this voice of Ireland as female ("An Actress with an Irish Voice") is significant. It is not just that Ireland has traditionally been perceived as a woman, or even that Casement had literally adopted his country's persona when, still in the employ of the British, he wrote nationalist articles for *The Irish Review* under the pseudonym of Shan Van Vocht, the poor old woman (MacColl, 101). More to the point is the fact that Casement took his sole "delight," as the Author puts it, "in being at the receiving end of other men's virility" (17)—that he adopted, in other words, the female role in his sexual relationships. Moreover, at the time of his trial he saw himself, if only in a single, small respect, as being womanly: "How white my hand has suddenly become, blue veins on it standing out like string. A woman's hand" (61).[7] And yet, for all that the feminine gender applies to him, Casement was decidedly not female—a fact that introduces the troubling question of how "the [female] voice of Ireland at [his] end" (16) could have any better suited him than the jingoistic voice that he had earlier rejected.

As the prologue seeks to intimate, it did not, in fact, suit him. If it had, it would have surely been the natural voice for telling of Casement's activities in Germany. But instead, the voice that conveys this information is neutral.

NEUTRAL: Nineteen-fourteen, the Great War: Casement moves freely in Germany as Kaiser's guest, recruiting an anti-British Brigade among Irish POW's there; negotiating German military assistance for a rebellion in Ireland.

(7)

Are we intended to see Casement's pro-Irish efforts as no more partisan, finally, than his work on behalf of the victimized peoples of the Congo and the Portuguese Amazon? The Irish would be scandalized to think so. And yet the prologue does not assign an Irish voice to Casement till he steps on Irish soil. Moreover, even then, it fails to stick. For though the voice of Ireland attempts to have the final word on Casement by bringing his life, and thus the prologue, to a close, it does so on a note so decidedly querulous (deriding the English contention that Casement was afforded due process in court) that the voices regroup and begin again.

ENGLISH: Judicial process perfectly proper.
IRISH:   On paper.
         *(Pause)*
NEUTRAL: Diaries. 'Black Diaries' so-called. A sodomite journal, purporting to be Casement's: leaked to press before and during trial; circulated internationally after, countering world agitation for a reprieve.
ENGLISH: For forty-three years thereafter, the Heome Office find it would be against the public interest to yield to presshah and confirm whether or not the Diaries in fact exist.
NEUTRAL: Nineteen-fifty-nine, a pirate transcript is published in Paris.
ENGLISH: Nineteen-fifty-nine, the Heome Secretary of the Day agrees to make the Diaries available, for limited inspection, by persons approved.
IRISH:   Casement's body. Committed to the Pentonville limepit—previous incumbent, Crippen. Requests for return of his remains to Ireland, over a period of forty-nine years repeatedly refused.
NEUTRAL: And then, one day—

                                                                    (7–8)

The result of this "coda," as it were, to the prologue, is that the play is at last introduced by a voice that, instead of being Irish, is neutral.

Why should the Neutral voice prevail? The coda itself offers little explanation. It merely confirms that the other two voices bear a tenuous relationship to Casement. The English voice is now a total stranger to the man, speaking solely for the Home Office and for England's attempt to obliterate Casement by refusing any access to his diaries—by shutting him up, so to speak. (Inevitably, by the perverse irony of all such attempts, the refusal kept Casement and the issue of his diaries alive among the Irish for over half a century.) As for the Irish voice, it speaks but once, and then of Casement's body, which by 1964 had been reduced to "a chest of sulphura'ed and potassified remains" (8), little enough for the voice to represent. The Casement who endures, the Casement of the diaries, belongs to the voice that is Neutral—a curious status for an Irish martyr, and one that the unfolding play must justify.

And so it does, almost from the start. For there are early signs that Rudkin will not settle for a view of Roger Casement as exclusively the property of Ireland. Literally lecturing not far into the script, in the role of the Author, Rudkin cautions his listeners against "mythologiz[ing] Casement, rejecting those aspects that seem not to fit a hero. I think we must take the whole man. Perhaps the whole man is more a hero even, than his Irish part" (17). Although primarily attempting, in this passage, to prevail upon the Irish to accept Casement's homosexuality, Rudkin is also promoting a supra-national view of Casement's significance: "What is [Casement's] triumph? This. Through horror, sickness, danger, sodomy, farce, he hacks out a new definition of himself. For that, is he a hero: and not for Ireland only" (24). For whom, then? Presumably, for all the world, for men of every race and nationality, for "man" as a neutral being, free to forge a self that yields to no external forces—or that yields, like Roger Casement, to many forces, mutually exclusive, yet all of them acknowledged and embraced: "I had voices in me no King nor Cardinal would like to hear. But they were mine, Casement's voices, mine, all mine: the voice of Empire at my beginning, the voice of Ireland at my end; the voice that championed negro and Indian; the social charmer, the moral agitator; the voice of the Foreign Office; the voice of Sodom. All are Casement, all one man; like many bloodstreams, fuelling one discordant heart" (16). By necessity, that heart, in assimilating discord, must end by being neutral; for if it ended up as Irish, it could not be British ("the voice of the Foreign Office"), too.

Just how partial, how transient, is Casement's Irish identity emerges poignantly in Rudkin's portrayal of Casement, late in the play, in his role as Irish martyr. When arrested for treason, only hours after he had swum to shore from the German vessel that transported him to Ireland on Good Friday before the Easter Rising, Casement temporized but briefly: "I pretend, for the last time in my life, to be an Englishman" (58). By Easter Sunday, when he had been removed to Scotland Yard in London, he could face interrogation squarely: "Who am I? I tell them" (59)—a simple, but moving, assertion from a man who, years earlier in the jungle, had doubted he knew who he was: "The Queen's Medal I've never worn. As much in my own right am I here. What right is that? As Casement myself. What self is that? What brief is that?" (14). But if the "brief" that Casement had on Easter Sunday, 1916, was definitively, undeniably, Irish, it had the peculiar effect of diminishing his "self," to judge from his sense of what, in fact, he had become at his preliminary trial: "I fidget, scratch my neck, bite my nail, pinch my cheeks, squeeze my eyes; look up the ceiling, down at the floor; reach into my breast pocket, pull out nothing; raise my eyebrows, relax them, deepen the furrows on my head. *A shadow, the man of me gone*" (61, my emphasis). Here, at the moment when Casement can finally say who he is, he feels himself, nonetheless, missing.

What he mourns in referring to "the man of me gone" is most certainly a loss of self, and not a loss of masculinity. True, the trial corresponds to the public disclosure of Casement's homosexuality. And true, it is during the trial that he looks upon his hand and sees it as a "woman's" (61). But homosexuality is never, in any play of Rudkin's, equated with effeminacy. Rather, acknowledgment of sexual preference, whatever it may be, is for Rudkin fundamental not to gender-identity, but to self-identity. Thus it is that Casement can claim to have "saved my*self*" (my emphasis) by going "down, down [where] my lusting took me, intill a secret undergrowth deep deep beyond the pierce of social light" (44). When the "man" in Casement leaves him, what he loses is the self he saved—a self confirmed, not threatened, by his homosexuality. The threat to Casement's self arises not from his lust, but from the forces that imprison him, strangling the man he has become. What forces, in particular? The English, literally, with their imprisonment of his body. And the Irish, figuratively, with their efforts to imprison his soul.

That the Irish are at war with Casement's soul is intimated shortly before his death, when Casement—wishing to convert to Catholicism so that he might "identify with the Irish nation through their predominant faith"—is asked "to repudiate [his] scandalous public and private acts" (67). The request, though it comes from the Westminster Cardinal, accords with the Irish distaste for unsanctioned sexuality. But as Casement refuses to recant—"I could not. All I had done, was of my self" (67)—he succeeds, at least for the moment, in sacrificing nothing of his hard-won identity either to the Church or to the country of his birth and his martyrdom. Yet once he is dead, the Irish perforce have their way with him. They mythologize him, as Rudkin has indicated, by insisting that his diaries, with their record of his secret homosexual encounters, have been forged. And when his bones are delivered to their care, they bury him in Dublin, not "in Antrim, to [his] specific dying wish" (76). Object though Casement may, he is helpless in his coffin, as another Cardinal, this time Irish, mockingly reminds his ghost:

CARDINAL: Balls to your specific dying wish, we've got you now.
CASEMENT: Am I a property, then? Eminence? A relic of sacred
     bones? Oh, don't let your young men in their worship
     come too near till *me*! And my writings, will *they* be a
     national treasure, too? Or will they go down on your
     index, Tubberguts DD?
CARDINAL: I'm disgusted at you. Lie down. Be a good hero, shut
     your mouth. Be a good patriot, lie down.
CASEMENT: (*quite Paisley-like*) I'll not lie here! Sand me till Panton-
     ville again! Next time, do the job right! Straight! Oh

Ireland, weeper of tears for a man yous do not know
nor want to know, I'll not lie here, give me the
huppucruts of England, at least I am an honest anamy
there! (*climax*) I'd liefer be a traitor by their lights than
a patriot by these!

(76)

So possessive and thus soul-destroying are the Irish, at whose mercy the
"sulphura'ed and potassified" Casement now finds himself, that he prefers the English hypocrites, who at least acknowledged what he was,
even though they killed him for it.

No wonder Rudkin cautions, at the outset, that the play "will be no
dialogue for admirers" (9).[8] If admirers are those Irish who, like Robert
Monteith, regard Casement as "the man who eliminated self,"[9] then they
have nothing in common with Rudkin, for whom Casement is the quintessence of self-seeking. As Rudkin would have it, Casement "went down
to Dublin . . . , committing [him]self with open eyes to the ecstasy and
danger of [his] newborn forbidden selves" (45). And it is precisely in
embracing these selves that Casement becomes, for Rudkin, "preposterous and magnificent by turns" (45), his only mistake being his failure to
anticipate how his patriotism would license his country to appropriate
and then destroy his individuality.

This lesson about patriotism, which is only implied (though strongly
so) in *Cries from Casement*, is made explicit in another play of Rudkin's:
*Penda's Fen*, broadcast by BBC TV as a "Play for Today" on 21 March
1974, less than fourteen months after *Casement* was aired. Stephen, the
hero of *Penda's Fen*, suffers a crisis of identity similar to Casement's; for,
as Stephen discovers in the course of the play, he is both homosexual
and adopted. In other words, he is a stranger to his society both by
nature and by blood. How Stephen learns to cherish his strangeness,
which seems to him at first both unnatural and immoral, is a story that
complements Casement's, particularly in the vision Stephen has of the
price he will pay if he chooses to reject his inner demons and conform.
Dreaming of an archetypal couple whom he thinks of as the mother and
father of England, Stephen perceives that yielding to these ostensible
parents would mean consenting to a gruesome rite of passage in which
his hands are chopped off at a block. Self-mutilation is the price of
yielding wholly to one's country in all of its personal, social, and religious
demands. So Stephen intuits; and so Casement discovers, when he yields
to the Irish and finds them conspiring to amputate his Ulster roots along
with his sexual identity.

Ironically, these amputations cannot serve the Irish any better than
they serve the outraged corpse. For when the Irish deny Casement's

Northern-ness, they deny as well his relevance in the "dance of death" (74) that is their history. As Casement proposes while he lies in state awaiting burial, "My relevance is, that I am coming Home" (75); or, as he puts it when he finds he has been exiled to a Dublin grave, "Relevance on relevance, me in my life a symbol of Ireland's seceding, a token of her fracture in my death" (77). But to betoken fracture no less than homecoming, Casement must be recognized as Northern, a concession that the Irish will not make. Moreover, his relevance is compromised still further by Ireland's rejection of his homosexuality. For as Casement (and Rudkin) would have it, "the white lily of [Casement's] patriotism grew out of his backside" (45). This is the contention that Casement's biographers, Inglis and Reid, find so ludicrous. But is it? When Rudkin insists that Casement could rebel against England only because his "lusting" introduced him to "a sacred misrule [that] show[ed] up the rotten fiction of all law" (44), he is merely contending that sexual nonconformity primed Casement for nonconformity in general—a reasonable enough proposition.

To be sure, Rudkin himself, in "The Chameleon and the Kilt," developed a sophisticated Freudian argument as a means of explaining how Casement's homosexuality was related to his willingness to defy English law and to engage in all manner of "misrule." But the relationship makes sense without reference to Freud. And even if clarification is needed, the place to look is, once more, *Penda's Fen*, where homosexuality lends Stephen, like Casement, the strength to reject common standards of morality. When the Mother of England attempts to lure Stephen to her fold by asserting, with deep religious overtones, "You are our Child of Light. You have to be born in us. Then you become Pure Light" (81), Stephen looks to his sexual (as well as his racial) identity for the courage to defy her: "No! No! I am nothing pure! . . . Nothing pure . . . My race is mixed, my sex is mixed, I am woman and man, and light with darkness, mixed, *mixed*! I am nothing special, nothing pure. I am mud and flame!" (81). Just as Casement's "lusting" introduced him to a "sacred misrule," so Stephen's homosexuality reveals to him his own potential to become a "sacred demon of ungovernableness" (83). And in finding that potential, as Rudkin explains, Stephen "has 'discovered himself'. No more now, can the myth of being pure anything afflict him or cause him to afflict mankind" (81). This is the state of grace (unorthodox, admittedly) to which Casement, too, aspires.[10] But being dead, he is deprived of Stephen's power to escape from his oppressors. He is subject to the will of a nation determined to afflict him, and all of mankind, with the myth that they have made of him.

Casement's sole escape, while the Irish persist in their willfulness, is through the vehicle of Rudkin's play. Only a playwright, as distinct from a biographer, can take the liberty of adopting a "schematic, polemical approach" (Kilt, 71) to Casement's life. Only a playwright can posit that, though Casement died an Irishman, he later shed his Irish self as surely as he "slough[ed his] English shell" (45), becoming at the end of all a Neutral voice with a decidedly unpatriotic message for his countrymen:

> Courage you must show. Courage without. Courage within. Delve delve delve deep in your heart, to find it to say: 'I am of this land.' One colour fears another, fears its extremeness. But colours mix. First they must meet. Ireland, Ireland, transcend this trauma. Sons of Ireland, cease looking for your sunrise in the west. Tear this old bitch Erin off your backs. She'll squeal and claw off skin and flesh from your bones, but rip her off, be free of her: trample her down where she belongs, beneath your feet, to be the land you live from, not your incubus and curse.
>
>                                                                    (78)

To hear this plea and yield to it is to accept a profoundly subversive proposition. For what Casement says, however strained the syntax, is that the Irish, having been their own "incubus and curse," must now contrive to be, themselves, "the land [they] live from," destroying the historical abstraction that passes for Ireland and forging the country anew. How? As Casement forged his Neutral voice: by delving deep within—"Down, down my lusting took me" (44)—and finding it to say, of the various extremes that constitute the depths, "All are [Ireland], all one [land]; like many bloodstreams, fuelling one discordant heart" (16). Where Casement once became a type of Ireland, now Ireland must become a type of Casement, attaining a voice that is Neutral in order to be healed.

DEFENDING Brecht's *Galileo* against the charge of historical inaccuracy, Eric Bentley has observed that "[l]ike *Saint Joan* and all other good history plays, *Galileo* is about the playwright's own time" (Bentley, 14). Clearly, the same can be said of *Cries from Casement*. However voluminous Rudkin's research into Casement's past, however abiding his respect for the facts he uncovered—and neither is in question—Rudkin had a personal motive in writing the play: he sought to find, in Casement's life, a moral for contemporary Ireland.

Rudkin's notion that a life of courageous self-seeking could serve as a model for Ireland's renewal emerges again in *Ashes*, his stage play of 1974. Although principally an exploration of a couple's futile efforts to conceive a child or, barring that, adopt one, *Ashes* includes a haunting monologue on Northern Ireland, the husband's native land. Having travelled to Belfast for the funeral of a relative killed in a terrorist bombing, the husband arrives at the following insight: "We have been a great people. Twice in history our Protestant existence here has turned a tide of tyranny back: now we are on the anvil a third time. Can we rise to the occasion this third time, then? turn a third tyranny back? the tyranny of our own—(*Now it hits* COLIN, *and the clarity of it is freeing him:*) *inheritance?* Our inheritance is glorious, we are a— But all that has to be behind us now. Shed. I just—I just think we just have to—try to see, what new selves we can rise up out of this, and become" (59–60). The message is, of course, the same as Casement's. And the messenger bears, roughly speaking, the same relationship to Ireland that Casement does: he is an estranged, but affectionate native son, whose private struggles obliquely reflect the nation's public dilemma over how best it can honor its heritage, and "where best—no, not where best; where at all we go now" (*Ashes*, 58).

But if *Cries from Casement* is as much about contemporary Ireland as it is about Casement himself, it is also about history and biography in general. Casement's comment about his indictment for treason—"The facts might be in [it]; the truth was not" (62)—implicitly raises the question of where the truth in historical matters resides. Rudkin himself asks the question, as well, by opening the play with the succession of facts that comprise the Who's Who. If these facts were sufficient to tell Casement's story, the rest of the play would be superfluous. And yet the rest of the play, in expanding on the facts, tells us nothing that is not already latent in the prologue, if only we could rightly interpret its voices. The truth would thus seem to reside nowhere else but in the facts, which nonetheless do not suffice to make the truth perceptible.

The paradox is one that interests Rudkin. He touches on it lightly when, speaking as the Author at the start of his research, he depicts himself seated in the Public Records Office, London, with all of Casement's diaries (the facts *par excellence*) before him, but emptiness the only thing he senses there: "Casement? Casement? I touch. I open. You are nowhere near. I feel nothing" (12). Though soon enough the man approaches, speaking words that could well have appeared in his diaries (and some of which did), the implication remains that even Casement's own utterances may lack life, and hence truth. Casement himself says as much when he asks, "Where is my speech? Was it ever my speech? I—am—unvoiced . . ." (30). Taken strictly in context, the words refer only to Casement's rejection of English in favor of Gaelic, the language that he thought to be properly his own, though he never succeeded in learning it. But broaden the context just slightly, and the words become ironic. What, after all, could Casement be, on the radio, if not a voice? And whose speech but his own could he be voicing, particularly when Rudkin through much of the play has liberally quoted from the historical Casement?

Just how much direct quotation Rudkin uses would be impossible to say without reviewing all of Casement's correspondence and whatever else of his is still sequestered in the Public Records Office. But to judge from the Grove Press edition of *The Black Diaries* (full of errors though it is) and from the passages of Casement that appear in the biographies written by MacColl, Inglis, and Reid, Rudkin borrowed freely from his sources, making changes primarily for the sake of the dialogue (or, as frequently happens, the monologues).[11] The play thus stands fair to be considered a docudrama. But if it is, it is also a critique of one. *Cries from Casement*, with its expostulating corpse, is, for example, a good deal less like Hochhuth's starkly realistic *The Deputy* than it is like Shaw's *Saint Joan*, a thoroughly imaginative interpretation of reality replete with Joan's posthumous appearance. Moreover, nothing in *Casement* reflects the confidence, which Peter Weiss expressed in *The Investigation*, that facts can be trusted to speak for themselves. Weiss may propose in the "Note" to his play that "Only a condensation of the evidence can remain on the stage. This condensation should contain nothing but facts." But the standard set by *The Investigation*—which is surely the ultimate docudrama, being purely an edited transcript—is cast into doubt by *Cries from Casement*; for the truth, in Rudkin's play, is most difficult to fathom in precisely that scene which is most factual: the Who's Who.

Rudkin's manner of constructing *Cries from Casement* suggests that, docudrama notwithstanding, facts are woefully short of dramatic intensity, even at their most authoritative. Facts do not, that is, live. What creates the impression that they do, when they do, is the playwright's ability to animate them. The facts of the Who's Who, no less than the facts of Casement's diaries and letters, can aspire to life only through the playwright's art, which for Rudkin involves bold experiments in form. Thus, insofar as *Cries from Casement* yields a "living sense of Casement *the man*" (Kilt, 72), it does so by actually being, in itself, all the contradictory things that Casement was: fragmented, hesitant at first about its own identity, waylaid by the lure of Irish history, recalled to a sense of itself that grows increasingly assured, but haunted to the last by a sense of incompletion, of inadequate closure.

That the play reflects Casement's fragmented nature is obvious. Its two major actions—the one involving Casement's bones; the other, the historical Casement—interrupt and intersect each other in a dizzying pattern, which itself is interrupted by the intrusions of the Author and by the wholly unexpected review of Irish history that occupies the center of the play. Moreover, as if to emphasize how sharply it is splintered, the action pauses twice to describe itself as "Fragments from the Author's *projected* play" (25 and 26, my emphasis)—a description that has the mind-boggling effect of suggesting that whatever we are listening to is not the Author's play on Casement, since that play still remains to be written. Clearly, what Rudkin is after is not a dependable sense of coherence. At least at the outset, he fashions a play that is ardently seeking its identity, and fearful that its "self" may be as yet so rudimentary as not really to exist at all. What more faithful imitation of Casement, as Rudkin understood him, could there be?

Still, despite the appearance of chaos, the play proceeds in measured steps to produce a living Casement by degrees. When Casement first appears, he is nothing but a heap of bones (or maybe, being "sulphura'ed and potassified" [8], just the molecules that bones resolve to). Moreover, he is mixed, perhaps indissolubly, with the poisoner Crippen: "'tis anybody's guess," says one of the gravediggers sent to retrieve Casement's skeleton, "what's goin in this box" (10)—a comment that might equally apply, at this point in the play, to the fragments of Casement being broadcast through the box that is the listener's radio. For even when Casement starts to speak in his historical person, his voice is mediated, as it were, by the voice of the Author. In one instance (Sequence III), he seems less to be himself than an emanation of the Author's research. In another (Sequence V), he appears to be an echo of the Author, lending authority, in his own voice, to the Author's opinions as expressed in a lecture to a literary society in Belfast. Even in Sequence VI, where Casement speaks on his own, without the Author's prompting, he must still be summoned forth, introduced as a less-than-autonomous character in the Author's future play. Thereafter, as a sign of his increasing self-assurance, his presence will grow in extent and significance, until by Sequence X, Casement will dominate the script. What is more, his bones will have taken on the task of relating the story of his capture, trial, and hanging, so that the historical and the dead man will essentially have merged. Thus it is that Casement gradually evolves into a single mesmerizing voice that indeed appears to live.

But before this virtual galvanizing of Casement can occur, Rudkin treats us to a curious interlude: a thirty-minute "panorama of 'istoree" entitled "The English civilize Eyeland" (31). A more eccentric interpolation of history into drama can hardly be imagined. And yet, eccentric or not, it is entirely, if against all probability, justified. Simply on biographical grounds, it has a certain validity. It is the treatise that Casement would presumably have written, had he acted on the wishes he expressed in a letter of April 1907 to his friend Alice Green: "What a delightful book *The English in Ireland* would be if written by someone who knew the subject. I wish we had a Max O'Rell who knew his ground properly and could write. I get too angry to write about these things and this abominable people in their dealings with Ireland. . . ." (quoted in MacColl, 56–57). But far more important is the fact that, on dramatic grounds, the history is perfectly attuned to its moment in the play. "Say of me something I inly, by my own definition, am . . ." (30), says Casement immediately before the history is initiated with a "colossal gongstroke."[12] Given this introduction, the whole panorama must serve as an answer to Casement's request—at least the answer that will, of necessity, serve if he "inly, by [his] own definition," insists on being Irish. For to be Irish, as Rudkin establishes, is to be lost in the sweep of Irish history, as Casement here is lost throughout twelve entire pages of dialogue. Though he tries, at the start, to remind us of his presence with an innocent remark about the Scots being "Irish who learnt how to swim," he is firmly instructed to restrain himself: "Shut up Casement, back in your box" (32). The only part of Casement we are able to see in this section of the script is the part that Irish history can accommodate, which is significantly less than the Who's Who contained. Despite himself, Casement is subsumed by his country; and hence so is the play that represents him, as long as the history lesson lasts.

What Rudkin has managed here is wondrous. Not only does the Irish panorama reify the particular threat that Ireland poses to Casement's identity (the threat of displacing him entirely); it also establishes exactly why his Irish background so allured him. As Rudkin describes Irish history, it consists of many issues that equally apply to Roger Casement. Virtually from the dawn of time, for instance, Ireland was embattled and divided, north and south—a predicament that reflects, in political terms, the fragmentation of Casement's personality. In addition, for all that it was passionately Catholic from 432 A.D., the country nonetheless "persist[ed] for seven centuries in certain heterodoxies at variance with Rome" (32), much as Casement persisted in his own heterodoxy when he himself embraced the Catholic faith. Invaded and conquered, the country found itself pacified over and over by the successful English policy of "inseminat[ing] the North" (33)—a policy repeated, metaphorically, in Casement's own person, since he was both Northern and, in effect, inseminated by English ideals for the better part of forty years. Still, even when thoroughly colonized, Ireland harbored in her "grievances a potential revolutionary seedbed on England's doorstep" (36), just as Casement must have nurtured "inside [his] consular Victorian im-

perialistic shell, [a] hidden rebel seed" (11). Given correspondences like
these (and other items in the panorama similarly resonate to facts in
Casement's life), it seems almost inevitable that Casement would eventually be attracted to his native land. What seems altogether less inevitable is that a playwright could have actually succeeded, as Rudkin has
here, in making an extended history lesson serve as both a reflection of
a character's soul and a caution that his soul might soon be forfeit.

Perhaps historically the forfeiture occurred. But in Rudkin's reconstruction of the life, Casement emerges from the panorama stronger than
before. At least temporarily, his Irish past has quickened, not sapped
him, by awakening him "to the Congo- and Putamayo-like predicament
of his own land."[13] Rather than needing to be conjured by the An-
nounceress, as if depending on her summons for his very life, Casement
now displays the energy to spar with her, asserting in Sequence VIII the
justice of his anti-English attitudes. In Sequence IX, too, he governs the
action, which has unprecedented narrative coherence. Although actually
composed of many fragments, with rapid cuts from one bit to the next,
the sequence manages to give the impression of perfect continuity. It
thereby suggests that Casement, throughout his year in Germany, succeeded in imposing some measure of order on his heretofore divided
personality, however disappointing his reception by the Germans. The
irony, of course, is that the more self-assured Rudkin's Casement becomes, the closer he comes to being hanged by the English and appro-
priated by the Irish, so that body and soul he is obliterated. It is thus
when he most cogently is most himself—that is, when his voice is heard
at length and when attention to his story is unwavering—that he speaks
of himself as a "shadow, the man of me gone" (61). Casement's search
for self is doomed to incompletion because, except in Rudkin's play, he
is not long permitted to remain what he has striven to become.

Even this theme of incompletion finds expression in the play as a
structural motif. For time and again, scenes aspire toward a closure they
do not, in fact, achieve. We have already seen that the Who's Who is
prevented from closing on the comment "Judicial process perfectly
proper" by a querulous response ("On paper") that forces it on. A similar
frustration of closure occurs when, only moments later, an English Crier
expresses the hope that, with the delivery of Casement's bones to Dublin,
"we shall at last have washed our 'ands of the problem of Ireland for
ever" (9). "If you want to do that, mate," replies the Man in the Street,
"put all the Irish in a box, shove it aht to sea and sink it!" (9)—a
recommendation that suggests the Irish problem will remain with the
English indefinitely. And so it goes. Sequence II concludes with "*Guitar-
dissonance, left unresolved*" (11, my emphasis). Sequence III concludes

with Casement, at the age of thirty-nine, discovering "a man, a me," only to revert to his habit of pretense, which guarantees continued instability: "Hush hush, rob's colony, cock's felony. English again" (15). Sequence IV ends with Crippen's loaded (and unanswered) question, "Which vein of your heart, though, akooshla makree, will Mother Ireland want?" (17). Sequence V cuts to silence at precisely the moment when violence is meant to break out against the Author: "Where is the Orange bastard is slanderin our heroes? (*quiet, dangerous*) Blow out his eyes" (25). Sequence VI ends with Casement's request for something yet to follow: "Say of me something I inly, by my own definition, am . . ." (30). And the history, which fulfills that request, closes with a passage from Elgar that itself never reaches proper closure: "*Its penultimate tutti chord is combined with a sharp unison deathshot sound. Its final chord is not heard at all: a second deathshot replaces it precisely*" (42, my emphasis). Even Casement's hanging is accomplished without resolution: "I heard the lever pull," says Casement; but for our part, we hear only "*Silence*" (68).

Ultimately, the unheard lever and the unfinished Elgar are eloquent as metaphors of all that lies ahead for Casement and for Ireland. The lever that declines to drop reminds us that, though Casement dies, his life is hardly over. In death, he must live on as Ireland's hero, not to mention as the spokesman and embodiment of Rudkin's own ideas about heroism. As for Elgar, the works of this composer have a special and personal meaning for Rudkin, to judge from *Penda's Fen*. The music of Elgar—in particular, "The Dream of Gerontius," when Stephen plays it on the organ—causes an illusory "jagged veinlike crack" (74) to appear in the church where Stephen's father is a pastor. The meaning of this vision would seem to be related to what *Penda's Fen* identifies as the "one hope for Man only": "That when the great concrete megaCity, chokes the globe from pole to pole, it shall already have, bedded in some hidden crack, the sacred seed of its own disintegration and collapse. Disobedience, chaos, out of those alone can some new experiment in human living be born" (*Penda's Fen*, 49). Thus, when Elgar is played in *Cries from Casement* as a frame for "Statistics of Dublin Rising" (42), it seems fair to imagine that Rudkin thinks of this Rising as having contained the potential for some new experiment in human living. That potential, however, died a-borning (as the unfinished chord seems to indicate) when the leaders of the Rising were summarily executed by the English. Hence still in the future for Ireland is Elgar's last chord, along with the "Last Disobedience and new . . . Resurrection" (*Penda's Fen*, 70) that his music appears to represent.[14]

The play therefore ends on a prophecy—or rather a plea, since prophecy implies an assurance of success (and completion) that Casement does not have. He can direct his successor James Anderson, an Ulsterman, to go "down into Ireland's blood," there to find his "own belonging" (78). And he can "plead with [the Southern Irish], to find it in their hearts to say to [Northerners]: Come in, and look out. Come in" (78). But, imprisoned in the grave, he cannot act to make his vision materialize. Nor can he, or Rudkin, know what coming generations will perceive when they look out, beyond the current boundaries of Ireland, toward a concept of nationhood yet to be imagined.

Once, in life, Casement "doodl[ed in his diaries] to see how they look, various forms of a name for a nation that did not yet exist" (23). Now, on his behalf, Rudkin fashions a play, infinitely various in form, that seeks to give Casement a name, an identity, that the Irish can use in remaking themselves into still another nation that does not yet exist. No doubt the play, in pursuit of this end, takes some liberties with Casement, just as it takes a host of liberties—and audacious ones at that—with the conventional structure of drama. But in doing so, it justifies Rudkin's proposition that disobedience produces resurrection. For the play brings both Casement and drama to life by disobeying all but its own inner truth as it "struggl[es] obscenely"—or beautifully—"to be born" (24).


OF ALL THE MAJOR FACTS about Casement that appear in his biographies, the only one that Rudkin fails to mention is that Casement was singularly handsome. Such a point of information could not have been animated on radio, which may well be why Rudkin omitted it. For in virtually every particular, *Cries from Casement* proves Rudkin precisely attuned to his medium's range and limitations. What radio can capture is sound, not appearance. Therefore Rudkin discounts Casement's face altogether, never mentioning its beauty, while acknowledging only in passing that Casement towered over others (68), being exceptionally tall. Rather, Rudkin gives Casement an iridescent voice—an endowment that, in fact, can be justified historically from comments by Ernest Hambloch, Casement's Vice Consul in Rio: "He was an easy talker and a fluent writer. He could expound a case, but not argue it. His greatest charm was his voice, which was very musical. He must have been aware he had great powers of persuasion, yet I think he was quite unconscious of the charm of his voice" (Inglis, 163). It would seem that Rudkin fixes on a truth about Casement when he allows the voice to represent the man.

Nonetheless, something other than historical happenstance appears to have motivated Rudkin to write his play for radio instead of the theater, as may be gathered from his "Thoughts on Staging the Play," a brief essay that was published as an afterword to the text of *Cries from*

*Casement*. Radio, it seems, appealed to Rudkin in part because of the polemical nature of his material, and in part because of the vast span of time and emotions to be covered. Rudkin argues, for instance, that radio handles polemic more tactfully than theater: "Once actors are physically carrying [a] polemic, and having to project it out and up at the house, there is a danger that the tone of the evening will become strident and aggressive; the audience will then have good reason to withdraw whatever goodwill they came with" (81). As for the scope of the material, Rudkin wanted the play to be performed without an interval, so that the audience could achieve "a sense of the various 'bloodstreams' of the play gradually and indeflectibly achieving confluence" (82). In the theater, an intermission would have had to be included; even on radio, as Rudkin concedes, its absence is a risk, given that the play runs to nearly three hours. But a radio audience can stand and move about while they listen; and radio, being prerecorded, can compensate an actor for the fact that playing Casement is physically punishing: "The monologue of X is possible for a radio actor because he can record it section by section, and establish for himself a fresh threshold at the beginning of each take; a stage Casement has to manage the whole course of it in one clear run, and may find it calling for changes of focus and gear he simply cannot make" (82). Rudkin knows whereof he speaks when he observes that "there could hardly be a more radically radiophonic text than this one" (81); and the comment pertains not only to the script's broader outlines, but also to its smallest details.

In particular, the text of *Cries from Casement* depends, in large part, on the kind of "subtle resonances" that radio alone can communicate. As Rudkin explains:

> Because [the play] was to be heard in a box, I set most of the action *in* a box—this was the best way for me to fix those boundaries within which my inner ear could most effectively work. You can see from the page, there is hardly ever a voice raised; you can see how fractional, but telling, are the differences between one broken accent and another in sequence IX; Casement's range of emotional colours might be colossal—but the vocal palette is largely *internal*. A radio actor (a thoroughly professional and very skilful class of man) need only shift his voice by a thousandth of an inch as it were, to achieve a resounding change of effect.
>
> (81)

So it is, near the start of the play, that Casement is directed to move from a *"faint hint of Ulster tinge"* (14), to a *"stage Ulster voice"* (16), to a speech that is *"black, quite Ulsterish"* (20), to a *"dark, slow, 'lust' voice*" (21), and finally to a voice that is *"sotto, a little Irish"* (25). Such distinctions are minute, requiring scrupulous vocal control on the part of the actor (in the BBC production, Norman Rodway) and, on the part of the medium that broadcasts the play, a receptivity to delicate differences in timbre, tone, and accent. In this respect, radio excels. For proceeding sans costumes, sans gestures, sans every conceivable physical distraction, radio isolates and highlights a voice, making even its slightest inflections conspicuous.

What emerges, then, on radio at Rudkin's behest is a very private Casement. Private in his secret sexuality, as well as in the confidential mood that his vocal modulations establish. And yet surely this Casement is nothing if not public, with his audience of millions and his summons to the Irish to redefine their purpose and their nationhood. Such contrariety is basic to Rudkin's conception of Casement—and basic, as well, to the medium at hand. For radio is Janus-faced: one face looks inward, discovering a world that Rudkin rightly describes as Cartesian (you're inside the character, seeing what he sees, thinking what he thinks);[15] the other looks outward, engaging a world of empirical fact—the world of news, sports, and weather, along with feature presentations and even most drama. Rudkin's feat in *Cries from Casement* is to have shown us both faces of radio at once, the private and the public together.

In the preface to *Ashes*, Rudkin posits that the playwright's proper mission with respect to matters private and public is to mix them indissolubly: "I believe the dramatist's function in a society to be to transmute the idiosyncrasies of personal life experience into metaphors of public, political value to mankind."[16] What medium can better comport with this function than radio, with its propensity for introspection on the one hand and for the dissemination of ideas on the other? Indeed, radio is surely the medium of choice when a dramatist like Rudkin depicts a protagonist like Casement, whose personal idiosyncrasies are egregious and whose political message is volatile.[17] For not only does radio facilitate the transmutation of private affairs into public metaphor; but it literally domesticates the enterprise by transmitting it into our living rooms. There is truth, then, in Casement's observation near the end of the play: "My relevance is, that I am coming Home" (75). Whereas in life, as Rudkin tells us, Casement longed for a home but never found one ("Not even a flat of his own here in Ireland. At his trial, he was formally described as 'of no fixed abode'" [19])—whereas even in death, he was essentially displaced, being buried far from Antrim, where he wished his bones to rest—he does come home at last on the radio, having found, in this vibrant yet intimate medium, a means to be known and hence possessed.

# Chapter Six

## THE STAGE
## John Arden's *Pearl*, and
## *The Bagman*, Too

•

**P**earl: John Arden's radio play "about a play within the play."[1] A play, then, about "Esther," a "chronicle-history in five acts" written for the stage in the early 1640s by the fictional dramatist "T. Backhouse, gent." (47), with assistance from his mistress, Pearl. A play, too, about the several plays that "Esther," for its own part, is about: Shakespeare's *Julius Caesar*, which it emulates; Ben Jonson's court masques, which it spurns; Racine's own *Esther* and his later *Athaliah*, which it resembles; Schiller's *Wallenstein*, which it recalls. And one further play as well, for which it serves as a metaphor: *The Island of the Mighty*, a chronicle history in three parts written for the stage in the early 1970s by John Arden himself, with assistance from his wife, Margaretta d'Arcy. Thus does *Pearl* earn its name as a pearl of a play, lustrously layered with theatrical history.

But at the heart of *Pearl*, what grain of sand, what irritant, provokes the pearl's development? What else but yet another play, again by John Arden and again for the radio: *The Bagman; or The Impromptu of Muswell Hill*, a grim little fable with the cheek to suggest that the theater is devoid of all redeeming social value. Here is a suggestion that must rub a playwright raw, till he transmutes it into something less abrasive. Hence Arden's transmutation of *The Bagman* into *Pearl*, a work that may not altogether vindicate the theater, but that does discover merit in its past. Of the plays, then, that *Pearl* may be said to involve, *The Bagman* is the one that *Pearl* most nearly is "about," so that *Pearl* at last emerges as a double curiosity: a radio-play-about-theater about a radio-play-about-theater.

Only think of the audacity. That a radio play should reckon with the stage, and should do so twice over, not only in itself, but also by means of a play to which it answers . . . is it not disproportionate, rather like a pygmy in contention with a giant? And a pygmy, in this case, that would swallow up the giant whole. Or so we may conclude from *Pearl's* extraordinary moxy in incorporating, into its radio action, full-blown productions of Shakespeare and "Esther" on stage. (Shades here of *The Bagman*, which stages several puppet shows on radio.) It appears that, in composing *Pearl*, Arden overrated radio considerably. Either that, or the radio, as a medium for drama, is by no means so humble in relation to the stage as circumstance seems to suggest.

What cannot be denied about radio drama is that, praise it however we will or we may, the laurels go to stage plays nonetheless. Whether because plays produced on stage inherit the glory of the theater's many triumphs, or because the theater exacts the equivalent of homage by imposing special disciplines on spectators (we must purchase a ticket, dress for the occasion, travel to the show, and sit quietly throughout), or merely because stage plays have extended runs that keep them in the public eye for months or even years, drama in the theater persuasively asserts its own importance. As a consequence, stage plays are widely reviewed; they are nearly always published; and the best of them are readily received into the canon of world literature. Radio plays, by contrast, go unheralded, except for those few that, from some combination of luck and distinction, gain the dubious prize of being transferred to the stage. There they acquire prestige and attention, but only in their theater dress. *Under Milk Wood*, for example, is well-beloved by many who imagine it a stage play, though it was first produced on radio and belongs nowhere else.

Now, were theater fundamentally superior to radio (as a diamond, for example, is superior to glass), this state of affairs would be perfectly reasonable. As things stand, it is perfectly irrational. Bare boards, after all, are without intrinsic worth; and even an elaborate set inspires admiration chiefly as a physical correlative for ideas conceived in the mind of a playwright. The value that we choose to impute to the stage issues not from its essence, but rather from its function as a vehicle for drama. To depreciate radio is thus passing strange, since it patently serves the same function as the stage, with only this difference: that in presenting a play, the radio proceeds without material props or a theatrical space—a limitation that may tax a playwright's talents, but that in no way inhibits the expression of ideas through dialogue. Indeed, in a play such as *Pearl*, where the idea under scrutiny is theater itself, radio can pose a formidable challenge to its arrogant rival, the stage.

The particular challenge that *Pearl* represents is partly aesthetic (insofar as the play ends with visual effects that the stage would be hard put to realize), but in greater part moral, reflecting Arden's fear that the theater is merely a frivolous pastime, when it ought to be a tool for social justice. Such is the burden of *Pearl*'s central action, carried over from *The Bagman*, where the theater proves completely irresponsible. In *The Bagman*, conceived as a new *Pilgrim's Progress* with Arden himself in the role of a pilgrim mired in Vanity Fair, the stage does no more than to mirror the world as a pessimistic Arden thinks to find it: a place so corrupt that even martyrdom offers no access to paradise. Endeavor though he may, Arden cannot make the theater work for good in such conditions, perhaps because what good might be is largely indeterminable. And yet given that *The Bagman* is half fairy tale, half nightmare, the question arises if its nihilistic outlook truly squares with reality. Arden ventures, then, to offer an answer in *Pearl* by rewriting *The Bagman* as historical drama. Set at a time when change is imminent—when insurrection is brewing in Ireland, civil war in England, and religious fervor everywhere—*Pearl* features a playwright, Tom Backhouse, who labors to influence politics through theater. His efforts, however, are fruitless. Events proceed apace, outstripping Backhouse utterly, while consigning his world—not to mention his play about Esther—to ruin.

So far-reaching is the debacle in *Pearl*'s final scenes that the indictment of theater implied there may appear to extend to all drama. Nonetheless, it does not. Arden's references to Shakespeare and Jonson, to Racine and to Schiller, are sufficient to remind us that eminent dramatists have turned their attention to fundamental questions of political morality. And who is to say that the truths they have spoken about abuses of power have not had salutary consequences for policies of state—or at least for the behavior of individual spectators? Were Arden completely disillusioned with the theater, he would hardly have appealed to such playwrights as these in his effort to say so. What is more, he would hardly have said so in a play—even if "only" a play for the radio. In fact, precisely by resorting to an underrated medium, Arden argues in support of the theater's potential. For if radio, despite its supposed inferiority, can actually catch our conscience in *Pearl*, then the contemporary stage can do so as well. It need "only" follow radio's example.

AMONG the various distortions of history that Arden permits himself in *Pearl*, the foremost no doubt is his depiction of Backhouse as a dramatist motivated by republican sentiments. "I have no knowledge," Arden admits, "of any writer who made a serious endeavour to present republican ideals upon the professional stage at this period [the 1640s]. If it had been possible, say, for John Bunyan to have written plays and had them produced, our theatre would have found for itself a very different history. By Bunyan's time it was not only too late: it was ideologically inconceivable. Yet Bunyan's genius was of a very similar nature to that of the authors of the late-mediaeval morality plays: a true theatrical instinct runs through every line of *The Pilgrim's Progress*." Standing as it does in Arden's preface to the play, this intriguing speculation may appear at first a key to *Pearl*—a forthright invitation to observe how theater fares with a secular Bunyan, Tom Backhouse, in charge of the show. And yet Backhouse, when we meet him, displays none of the mettle we associate with Bunyan: neither the severity, nor the dogmatism, nor the willingness to act on his beliefs at any cost. Although Backhouse has convictions that are genuine enough, he is singularly cautious in his efforts to promote them, recoiling from deeds that risk sowing the whirl-wind. Thus, the figure that he cuts is essentially pallid, the more so in light of Pearl's ardor and daring. No wonder the play bears the title it does: it is Pearl that *Pearl* vaunts, not Tom Backhouse.

Still, the reference to Bunyan is not idle. It directs us to *The Bagman*, a play broadcast eight years beforehand, in which Arden not only antic-ipates *Pearl* by taking for his subject the political and social utility of drama, but in which he also substantiates the "theatrical instinct" that he would have us appreciate in Bunyan. More fearsome than charming when rightly understood,[2] *The Bagman* unfolds as a Bunyanesque fable based loosely, but tellingly, upon *The Pilgrim's Progress*. Thus, just as Bunyan in the *Progress* falls asleep within a den, where he dreams about Christian, so Arden in *The Bagman* falls asleep in Highgate Wood, where he dreams about himself—or, more precisely, about his adventures on account of a bag that he buys (a proverbial "pig-in-a-poke") from a "portentous oracular condemnatory old hag" hawking heather (B39).[3]

If the bag remains unopened for rather longer than we might expect, the reason is apparently that Arden (as author) needs time to secure the connection between his own work and Bunyan's. So it is that Arden (as character and Narrator) slings the bag across his back—in the manner of Christian, burdened down by his sins—and crosses a moor that arises before him where the Muswell Hill Road used to be. His progress takes him south toward what was once Highgate Hill, but now "might have been Mount Zion for as much as *I* could recognize" (B43)—the same mountain that was Christian's destination, to be won on a perilous journey. Arden, too, faces peril: namely, an attack by starving women, who covet his bag for the food they suppose it contains. But before they can dispatch him, he is rescued by Riders and brought to a latter-day Vanity Fair. (We can recognize the place from the townspeople's custom of referring to the folk in the outlying wilderness as "outlandish men" [B63, B69], the same term by which the people of the original Fair denominated Christian and Faithful.) Here Arden, like Christian, is ogled, interrogated, even beaten—whacked twice, in any case, by a minister with a cane, who insists that he open his bag.

Finally, then, the cord is cut, the bag is upended, and its contents are revealed: a troupe of wooden puppets, stock characters all, who so delight the crowd with the show they perform—a morality play about politics— that Arden is spared any further mistreatment. Instead, he is offered asylum in the town, along with "peace and quiet . . . agreeable surroundings . . . appreciative audiences . . . plenty of opportunity for experiment . . . unlimited funds" (B65)—everything, in fact, that a playwright requires. Or does he? We shall see for ourselves as *The Bagman* proceeds, disclosing, as it does, the significance of its allusiveness to Bunyan. For the play now evolves into a proper "Playwright's Progress," in which Arden must contend with the principal temptations that can spirit a writer from the path of righteous action within a body politic. (Tom Backhouse, take warning: for the lessons of *The Bagman* will have bearing on *Pearl*.)

As in Bunyan, the temptations that *The Bagman* explores are primarily spiritual. True, Arden-as-Narrator succumbs to the lure of such worldly delights as his Vanity Fair lays before him: lust, in the form of a Young Woman sent to entertain him in his bedchamber; luxury, in the environs of "the King's private garden" (B80). But the woman, when importuned, denies him her favors, on the grounds that "it's not that kind of dream at all" (B70); and the garden, though "very indolent and agreeable" (B80), dissolves at a touch, being just a dream *within* a dream, an illusory illusion. There is nothing here, in short, to corrupt the playwright's politics: nothing to dissuade him either from "diagnos[ing] society's] weaknesses and discover[ing its] public perils" (B61), or from offering "subversive encouragement to insurrection and revolution" (B63). Nor does anyone in power attempt to dissuade him: not the ministers of state, who explicitly decline to control him, resolving instead only to "suggest directions: that is all" (B65); nor the King's Ambassador, who may fulminate that Arden "deserves to be suppressed," but who tolerates him nonetheless, defying him "to do [his] worst" (B74); nor the King of the sumptuous garden, who professes to welcome Arden's view of the court as "a crowd of posturing exquisites" (B78), although this "truth about ourselves" (B79) makes him squirm. It would seem, then, that full artistic licence is Arden's for the taking. And yet, set his little puppets to perform as he will, he achieves no good end with his spectacle. As Arden concedes in the frame of *The Bagman*, even before he embarks on his dream:

> I could not boast, like Cicero,
> That I had saved the state,
> Nor yet, like Catiline, that I had tried

My fiercest best to have it all destroyed.
If, on this soggy Thursday, I should fall down dead.
What of my life and death would then be said?
'He covered sheets of paper with his babble,
He covered yards of stage-cloth with invented people,
He worked alone for years yet was not able
To chase one little rat from underneath the table.'

(B37–38)

An unsparing confession of impotence. But what can account for the Narrator's plight? Neither material comforts, nor the lack of them, if *The Bagman* speaks true, but rather his spiritual failings: initially, his pride in his art; thereafter, his despair in the world.

To be sure, in his role as the Narrator, Arden is so diffident as to seem quite incapable of pride. "From my childhood ever," he declares, "I had felt great fear/Of a crowd of strange men who would stare at me and jeer" (B56). By instinct, then, Arden effaces himself under challenge: laughing companionably, for instance, when the King's "enormous Ambassador" (B74) pelts him with eggs; half-kneeling to the King despite his Republican principles. "Never willingly give offence, not me—a disposition always, so I thought, to be both meek and courteous" (B75). But on stage this disposition grows presumptuous. To his own pure amazement—and without any evident conscious intent—Arden emerges as both arrogant and menacing when he undertakes to lead his little men. In their company, he behaves like "a very old and cantankerous dragon . . . growling and orating" (B58), like "Adolf Hitler at his worst" (B59), like "Hitler in the Berlin bunker" (B78), like Savonarola, Cromwell (B85). Here, indeed, is pride altogether overweening, cocksure of its authority, and utterly oblivious to political threats. So it is that Arden overhears, yet overlooks, the ministers' debate about whether to muzzle him. Discounting present danger, he spends his time exulting in "the power and the splendour of my little men, so newly revealed to me, so manifold in possibility, so outrageously out of proportion to the amount of actual work I had done—they had been absolutely given to me, from where I knew not, and by whom I knew not. But it appeared that they were mine: and I alone was capable of inspiring them into their motions" (B65). If Arden escapes from the ministers' lair, he has only his captors to thank for his liberty: it is they who release him, while he, for his own part, does nothing whatsoever to save himself from danger. How, then, can he hope to commandeer his little men to save the world? His pride, by interfering with his judgment, disarms him.

Not that the puppets seem likely to reform the state in any case. Only see how their audiences respond to them: for the most part, by failing to heed them. Thus, though the townspeople cheer when the little men dramatize a violent civil war entailing regicide and the founding of a Republic, these very same spectators, the show being done, turn directly to business as usual: the trying and executing of brigands "in the name of His Majesty" (B64). Similarly, the King of the sumptuous garden and his numerous courtiers persist in their indolence, though the little men burlesque them every day. It would seem, then, that Arden's didactic presentations are taken no more seriously than the "indecent excitement" (B50)—a dance-cum-striptease, a "most depraved performance" (B66)— that was featured on stage when Arden entered the town. Let the puppets appeal to the crowd as they may, life within Vanity Fair goes on just as before. The little men achieve nothing, with one exception only: they inspire "a mood of rebellion" (B70) in the fierce Young Woman, slave to the state, who is sent to sleep with Arden but refuses to do so. (Note her well. For just as Arden-the-Narrator will appear in *Pearl* as Back-house, the Young Woman will appear as Pearl herself.)

Are the puppets, then, "weapon[s]" (B85), tools of revolt, if only for a minority of spectators? Hardly, as Arden discovers to his pain. For though his "heart burn[s] with zeal" (B85) for the Young Woman's cause, and though he "dedicate[s] . . . [his] little men" (B85) to her group of co-conspirators, "who rise in anger/Against the tyrant and oppressor" (B84), the puppets piteously decline to perform as men of war: "If you bring us into battle/You bring us only unto grief and woe/Fracture and breakage that we cannot repair" (B86). As for the Woman herself, she insists that Arden set aside his puppets for a cudgel—a demand that he rejects. Thus, when the rebellion is discovered and ruthlessly crushed, she attributes the debacle to Arden himself: "We are betrayed by this fool with his bag—he has wasted our time and distracted our attention" (B86). Theater, the woman appears to suggest, is not only irrelevant to politics, but actually destructive of it—destructive even of such political movements as the theater itself may engender.

What an antidote to pride is here. Believing himself "a forsworn traitor" (B87) to a cause he had admired, Arden wakes from his dream in despair. His puppets have vanished—and, with them, his erstwhile satisfaction in their antics. Where once he had reveled in his little men's power to make audiences "see themselves in a truthful mirror" (B86), now Arden suspects that there is greater social value in "a bag full of solid food" (B88) than in one containing puppets who may well be "attractive . . . But what are they for?" (B57). They are not, it seems, for waging war, though they emerge from an Army-issue kitbag. Nor are they for toppling or reforming the government, though they perform, at least initially, on a government stage from which ministers conduct affairs of state. They are apparently for nothing beyond "watch[ing] . . . rows and rows/Of people watching them" (B58) as they ape the crowd's condition and behavior. But of what use is mimicry in a world where some starve while others steal, where some slave while others rule, and where the universal passion is for power, not for good? This is the question implicit at *The Bagman*'s close; and nothing in the play suggests an answer. Indeed, Arden's final comment—"All I can do is to look at what I see" (B88)—is a candid admission of helplessness in the face of the world's pressing needs. He can neither change what he sees nor cause others to bring about change for the better. He can only look on, while the powers-that-be commit murder and pillage, and while those who are despoiled plan spoliation in return. As the Young Woman says of her rebellion, "There is nobody any good to anyone, nobody and nothing—except to burn the whole town down" (B82).

Now drama, of course, can burn nothing in earnest, even at its most incendiary. So if a purifying fire can alone save the world, then Arden and his puppets provide no salvation, not even for themselves, and *The Bagman* emerges as a tract against theater such as Bunyan himself might have written. Might, that is, if Arden-as-author were a worthy successor to Bunyan-as-Christian. As it happens, however, he is not. For insofar as *The Bagman* is a new *Pilgrim's Progress*, it describes a journey twice removed from Christian's in its outcome: physically removed, because Arden is trapped within Vanity Fair for the length of his dream, whereas Christian travels on to the heavenly Jerusalem; emotionally removed, because Arden is cruelly imprisoned in spirit, having evidently slipped into the Slough of Despond. As Christian informs us, this slough "is such a place as cannot be mended; it is the descent whither the scum and filth that attends conviction for sin doth continually run . . . ; for still as the sinner is awakened about his lost condition, there ariseth in his soul many fears, and doubts, and discouraging apprehensions, which all of them get together, and settle in this place; and this is the reason for the badness of this ground" (Bunyan, 58). Christian, for his part, clambers out of the slough, thanks largely to Help, who lends him a hand. But Arden, quite alone, remains mired in despair, which envelops both his puppets and himself. So it is that the puppets' performances—which are "informed," after all, "by [Arden's] own personality" (B63)—yield in one case the "ominous" conclusion of carnage all around (B60), in the other such "diverse and perverse setting-to-partners" as can hardly be considered a conclusion at all (B78). And so it is, too, that Arden's dream recapitulates a number of biblical stories, in each case subverting their traditional meaning—a sure indication that Arden is spiritually lost.

Note, in this regard, how Arden's nightmare (for that is what it is) commences: with an action akin to Adam's temptation and expulsion from Eden. But if Arden is Adam, allured by the promise of "some fresh brief sexuality" (B40) of the sort that ensued from Adam's bite of the apple, where are his Eve and his Eden? The one is a hag; the other, Highgate Wood in a forlorn condition, a "cold park . . . [where] dead leaves blew between my feet . . . [and a] dream rose up at me . . . in a turbulence of sand and torn scraps of cigarette papers" (B38). This place, from which Arden is driven with his "dunnage" (B42), is clearly no paradise, but rather a world lost to grace before Arden ever enters it. Accordingly, the figure who drives Arden from the Wood is neither a god nor an angel, for all that he imitates the cherubs east of Eden by brandishing his spike "like a sword of living flame" (B42). He is rather a narrow-minded, punishing Park-Keeper—a "guardian of the public amenity" (B42), as distinct from public virtue.

If this mockery of Eden turns the Bible topsy-turvy, so do several of *The Bagman*'s other scenes. Witness, for example, the song about Pharaoh, with his dream of seven fat cows, seven lean. Whereas the story in the Bible tells of famine averted, here it is refashioned so that everything ends badly:

> 'Joseph Joseph—
> What does it mean?'
> Joseph said to Pharaoh:
> 'You are dead and gone.'
>
> (B51)

Consider, in addition, *The Bagman*'s depiction of Calvary: a "living man" nailed to the trunk of a tree, screaming in vain "for the freedom of the people," while begging for "a spoonful of water" (B47). According to the Rider who interprets the spectacle, this crucified Jesus is "nothing, he don't signify" (B47). But a Christ who is nothing signifies much, betokening a world in which redemption is impossible. In such a godforsaken place, Christ may still be a king—the "true King," in fact, of Vanity Fair (B81, identifiable as Christ from his pleas for both liberty and water). But such a Christ, such a King, is less divine than despairing. Indeed, the King's physical condition—for twenty years he has been "chained to the wall" of a "derelict shed" (B81)—closely allies him to Bunyan's Despair, a man "shut up . . . in [an] iron cage" and "shut . . . out of all the promises" (Bunyan, 78). As Despair describes his plight, "There now remains to me nothing but threatenings, dreadful threatenings, fearful threatenings of certain judgement and fiery indignation, which shall devour me as an adversary" (Bunyan, 78–79). The same judgment would appear to await Arden's King, as well as the people who live in his realm. For without a risen Christ to intercede for their sins, they can only be headed for damnation. No doubt this is the reason that they stink from the mouth, "such bad breath they all had in this place" (B71). Physically as spiritually, they are rotting from within.

Here, then, is a genuine vision of hell. But is the hell itself genuine? Or is it, as Bunyan would likely contend, just the fevered expression of a transitory sickness in the playwright's own soul? How Arden eventually answers these questions is a matter of some moment for the practice of his art. For if the world is, in fact, irredeemable, then politically and socially challenging drama can never be more than a mirror of our sins, and Arden himself must be morally suspect. As the Ambassador of the Great King across the water puts it:

> You set afoot unauthorized imitations of people you should despise and you blow them out like bullfrogs with the imagination of their strength. *At* the same time, however, you reserve to yourself a sharp pin with which you can at your own convenience prick their distended bellies and explode them into nothing. The first part of your programme, from my point of view, is abhorrent. From the point of view of the underdog people to whom you address yourself, the second part is likewise. Therefore you are very bold, and a man to be objectively admired: or else you are a hedger and a fencesitter, and a contemptible poltroon.
>
> (B74)

These being the alternatives, no wonder Arden shrinks from them. No wonder he writes *Pearl*.

As if in answer to *The Bagman*, *Pearl* tests the proposition that the world can be redeemed—or, at any rate, improved—by concerted moral action in which drama plays a part. Given all that is at stake, the test is necessarily severe. So severe that, strictly speaking, it cannot be passed. The mere setting of *Pearl*, early 1640s England, predetermines that the play must end badly: with a bitter civil war in which a king will be executed, his subjects slaughtered wholesale, and all society subjected to a political and religious fundamentalism that will stultify the land for very nearly twenty years. Accordingly, insofar as *Pearl* rings changes on *The Bagman*'s motifs, it mainly reconfirms *The Bagman*'s pessimistic outlook, imposing an historical context on Arden's grim fairy tale about a playwright's good intentions on the ruthless road to hell. Yet there is more to *Pearl* than this alone. For presiding at the spectacle are four substantial playwrights—Shakespeare, Jonson, Racine, and Schiller—whose example suggests that there is honor in drama, and possibly even political wisdom. If Arden can emulate playwrights like these, might not drama yet reclaim its former worth? Such is *Pearl*'s wish, which in essence is fulfilled, although late and imperfectly, as befits a fallen world.

HAD THE ENGLISH CIVIL WAR been a glorious revolution instead of the debacle that it was, the power of the crown would have transferred without bloodshed to the Parliament, Cromwell's terror would have been averted, and Ireland would have won her independence in negotiation with the Parliamentary Party. So *Pearl* instructs us by means of a plot that valiantly endeavors to yield these results, though the past by definition is immutable. At issue, then, in *Pearl* is not the question of ends—not What might have been, had things been otherwise?—but the question of means—Had things been otherwise, what might have made them so?[4] To judge from *The Bagman*, the answer can hardly be theater. Yet the theater is precisely the answer *Pearl* chooses to explore. Taking up, as it were, where *The Bagman* left off, *Pearl* rushes where *The Bagman* feared to tread: it accepts a playwright's offer to dedicate his little men to insurrection.[5]

That drama can topple a king from his throne, or at least put an end to abuses of power, is the conviction uniting *Pearl*'s principal characters: Lord Grimscar, a nobleman whose politics may please the Puritans, but whose "patronage of players and poets" (32) does not; Tom Backhouse, a playwright who, as "guest at Grimscar Hall" (17), fulfills the lord's commissions; and Pearl herself, an envoy sent to England by Owen Roe O'Neill "to ask disaffected English Protestants to take up the cause of the Catholics in Ireland" (29). Of these three, it is Grimscar who first makes the effort to harness the theater's political potential. To this end, he mounts a production of Shakespeare's *Julius Caesar* expressly in order to demonstrate "that the worst despot in the world is yet vulnerable to the aroused outrage of honest men who love their country" (16). The Puritans assembled in the audience, however, disrupt the performance before its subversive intention comes clear. So much, then, for the notion that the theater can play politics. The idea dies a-borning—or would, were not Pearl in the audience. Instantly alert to the play's implications, Pearl sees how the theater, in theory, could inspire reform. As a consequence, her mission somewhat alters. Instead of seeking merely to win Grimscar to her cause, she seeks also to collaborate with Backhouse in converting a "dramatic entertainment" (39), which Lord Grimscar has commissioned, into a veritable call to revolution, glorious or otherwise. But the collaboration fails. The play that Backhouse writes with Pearl's assistance is laid waste by unscrupulous monarchists, who gut its key speeches in performance, then assault its two authors so sadistically that the one is left critically injured, the other grotesquely deformed.

Such is *Pearl* in broad outline, only barely reminiscent of *The Bagman*, if at all. But a closer inspection reveals some similarities too striking to ignore—as well as some critical differences. In particular, Pearl and Tom Backhouse so closely resemble the Young Woman and the Narrator as virtually to reincarnate them. This, though they moderate several key aspects of the earlier characters' nature and experience. What is more, Pearl and Backhouse disapprove of what passes for contemporary theater: precisely what passes for theater in *The Bagman*. This, though they venerate the stage as a worthy institution, rich with political and social potential. Finally, they recognize pervasive injustice in the world that they inhabit, so like to *The Bagman*'s in cruelty and severity. This, though they trust that such injustice can be mended—an article of faith that *Pearl* sanctions, if tepidly, in contrast to *The Bagman*, which scuttles all hope. The overall effect of these rough correspondences is to render *Pearl* a recapitulation of *The Bagman*, even while allowing for at least the possibility that *Pearl* may arrive at a better conclusion—one in which theater acquits itself well.

Consider, in this context, how much like *The Bagman*'s Young Woman Pearl is. Both characters, for instance, are half-castes, having concubines for mothers and, for fathers, outlandish men (or, in Pearl's case, the equivalent—an American Indian from the wilds of Virginia). Both contrive to be anonymous, the Young Woman bearing no name whatsoever, while Pearl answers only to aliases: "Pearl, Margery, whatever your name is" (46). Both are fervent revolutionaries who rely upon disguises to save them from detection. In particular, they masquerade as actresses and whores. Thus, we meet the Young Woman initially on stage, where she performs a lascivious dance; thereafter we find her in the Narrator's bedroom, where she offers herself (though she changes her mind) as a "small personal gratification appropriate to [the Narrator's] status" (B66). As for Pearl, she straightforwardly purports to trade in sex, attending *Julius Caesar* in the company and garb of Mother Bumroll's flock of courtesans. In addition, she expresses preconceptions about theater that reflect her past experience on stage: "Such actresses as I have known, as I have *been* indeed, actresses . . . little different from the very prostitutes among whom I am now huddled, were we memorable upon the stage for anything else but the hot smell of temptation?" (11). By their own example, then, the Young Woman and Pearl introduce a connection between theater and harlotry—a connection that their plays are at pains to repudiate.

At pains, because the task is sorely trying. Even in the 1640s, the hot smell of temptation that reeked in the theater did not emanate solely—or, for that matter, principally—from rampant sex for sale, but rather from the theater's inclination, as a highly public art form, to prostitute itself both to popular taste (in order to win an audience) and to political pressure (in order to avoid being censored or denounced). Now, to liberate the theater from this sort of prostitution is a complicated business, as *The Bagman* reveals. Only think of the Narrator's curious puppet shows: on the one hand, they operate free of all untoward influence; on the other hand, they act the whore instinctively, even if only in spite of themselves. So it is with the puppets' enacted insurrection. Here, beyond doubt, is a model of emancipated theater, beholden neither to the state nor to the populace—and not only emancipated, but emancipating, too, to judge from the way the performance affects the Young Woman in her dealings with the Narrator: "No, take away your fingers from where you are putting them or I will bite them off this minute . . . I was instructed to make love to you and I have suddenly turned today into a mood of rebellion. You know why? . . . Because of your little men . . ." (B70–71). Yet equally here, at the very same time, is a model of theater as the government's tool of repression. For see how the wily enormous Ambassador proposes to enlist the Narrator as a spy:

> I am going to regard you as a challenge and defy you to do your worst. In some sense it may be said that a challenge to us, in this place, is both desirable and requisite . . .
> (*In an undertone*) . . . at least a challenge that we are aware of—for it will attract to its publicity the other, occult, challenges of which at present we have no cognizance, only suspicion . . .
> SECRETARY: (*likewise in an undertone*). Rather more than suspicion in several cases, Excellence. I am compiling—as you told me—all these dossiers, and there will be certain surprises in the fullness of time—
> (B74–75)

Thus is the theater's subversion subverted; thus is its nature turned back on itself, so that whatever it is, it becomes its own opposite.

A similar blurring of distinctions mars the puppets' second effort, no less than their first, for all its apparent simplicity. In content, the performance is easily described: it is "nothing but extraordinary variations of erotic postures and intrigues, couplings and triplings and quadruplings, men and women together, men and men, women and women, women and men and women" (B78). But what, after all, is the point of the spectacle? Is it a thorough-going satire, as the audience's unfavorable response—they "had not liked it very much" (B78)—would seem to suggest? Or is it rather a naked attempt at titillation, patently designed to draw in the crowds—though in the pinch it goes too far and descends into pornography, leaving the Narrator "ashamed" (B78)? The answer is, at best, undetermined; at worst, indeterminable—and probably, in either case, beside the point. For what the audience desires is flattery. No wonder the Young Woman pleads with the Narrator to give up his bag when he joins her rebellion. In *The Bagman*'s cruel universe, the theater is not to be trusted: will it, nill it, it betrays what it espouses; and unless it aims to flatter, it offends.

This indictment of the theater, profound and disconcerting, is the legacy bequeathed by *The Bagman* to *Pearl*—a legacy acknowledged at the start of the play when Pearl speaks about acting and whoring as equivalent activities. The acknowledgment, however, does not signify acceptance. For *Pearl*/Pearl undertakes to vindicate theater: to release it from its old association with whoring and to equate it, instead, with the passionate expression of genuine principle. Pearl says as much, and more, when she repairs from *Julius Caesar* to Mother Bumroll's brothel, there to change her disguise from harlot to housekeeper, and to wait for Dr. Sowse to escort her to Lord Grimscar. While Sowse, a venal parson who had thought to ravish Pearl, relieves his "carnal need" (23) with an actual harlot, Pearl reflects upon the problem of her shifting identity and the shape of her own carnal longings.

I turn over and over one question: just who I am,
Who is the one who is thinking my thoughts,
Who is this woman who turns and turns at the mill of my brain?
And yet how unreasonably exalted would I find myself now had I
only been able to see the murder of Julius Caesar right through to
the end! Tantalus, ah Tantalus, and don't tell me, that beastly cler-
gyman, wouldn't he feel just the same about *me* . . . ? For each
several one of us, our immediate carnal need, perhaps today for the
first time I have truly discovered my own . . .
Who would have dreamed my brimstone blood would rage
At dance of so-called devils upon a stage,
Who performed no more than I have often done?
Yet never before did I so yearn and groan
In hope one day to set to them their tune—

(24)

Estranged from the person inside her own skin, Pearl here speculates that theater could restore her to herself. (For what else is exaltation but the ego self-possessed?) All that would be needed to secure this result would be for theater to espouse Pearl's republican politics, portraying on stage the rationale for revolution: "from this pit/There is a ladder out/And we must climb it, clamber, storm the bloodstained wall/And fight to death its keepers" (20).[6] Such a theater, as exemplified for Pearl in *Julius Caesar*, would cease to be a "bawdy-house" (19), no matter how "carnal" the need it fulfilled.[7] It would rather be a "trade" (36), a forthright occupation—and one "you [could] respect from the pit of your gut for the power and the discipline and the conviction of [its] craftsmanship" (11). This is the theater of which Pearl is moved to say, "Sure I have seen it and heard it, I will never give over—if only I can once find the way to begin" (37). And find a way she does, in the person of Tom Backhouse.

He complements her well. For if Pearl is *The Bagman*'s Young Woman made new—made receptive, that is, to the theater as politics—then Backhouse is *The Bagman*'s Narrator made shrewd—made judicious, discerning . . . in a word, made political. That the men have essentially the same personality is established at *Pearl*'s start in the Dramatis Personae, where Backhouse is revealed to regard "himself as the best in his line since Aristophanes: but would be astonished if anyone were to share his opinion." As the comment foretells, Backhouse duplicates the Narrator's fundamental make-up, mixing pride with an utterly paralyzing diffidence. Thus, despite his self-assurance and evident intelligence, Backhouse finally initiates nothing in *Pearl*. Rather Pearl and Lord Grimscar take charge of events, while Backhouse submits to their superior will. The very play that Backhouse writes for Lord Grimscar's private party is acknowledged by Backhouse himself to be Pearl's: "I sit still and write/And write the words of your desire" (49). As for his "own gold statue of desire, body and bone" (49), that is also of Pearl's making; for she not only rouses his sexual passion, but also contrives to control it, refusing to sleep with him "until the whole long tale of our bold daughter/Esther the Queen of Persia was all but made/Upon the pages as we wanted it" (50). In such deference to others, intellectually and sexually, Backhouse calls to mind the Narrator, a figure ever loath to assert himself.

Nonetheless, there is this difference: that where the Narrator was every inch a novice as a playwright—so much so that he thought of his puppets as free agents, entirely beyond his control—Backhouse, by contrast, is master of all revels. His practical experience, for one thing, is vast: he has worked the English stage for a quarter of a century—"and don't tell me I haven't worked well" (45–46). What is more, he is versed in the theory of theater. Witness how he answers the Puritans' objection to a "round-eyed boy parading his false bosom under the title of Calpurnia" (14): with a learned, if dull, philosophical lecture on the "frank and open pretense" (18) of theatrical performance. More pertinent still, he accepts the "art of Roscius" as being "more than pastime" (17). For by whom, if not Backhouse, has Grimscar been instructed that "religion and justice and liberty *and* true poetry can all of them be one and the same thing"

(28)? As Grimscar reveals, "Mr Backhouse is an old friend: his opinion is cardinal in all my affairs" (25). And rightly so, if we judge from the wisdom Backhouse shows in "mistrust[ing] Dr Sowse" (30) as a political confidant. (Would that Grimscar had done without Sowse altogether.) For all, then, that Backhouse resembles the Narrator, he nonetheless corrects for the Narrator's shortcomings insofar as the stage and the state are concerned.

It follows that Backhouse is ideally positioned to revisit the question at the heart of *The Bagman*: whether theater can instigate political reform. He is neither so different in nature from the Narrator as to change the theater's fortunes by dint of personality, nor so like to the Narrator in general inexperience as to make the theater's failure a foregone conclusion. He merely moderates those of the Narrator's traits that would have served to impede a fair test of the theater, had the Young Woman let such a test be conducted. Just as Pearl counteracts the Young Woman's refusal, so Backhouse counteracts the Narrator's ineptness. Together, then, Backhouse and Pearl forge a link between *Pearl* and *The Bagman*, even while distancing *Pearl* from *The Bagman*'s defeatism. So telling, moreover, are this link and this distinction that both are repeated elsewhere in *Pearl*, each in its own separate context: the link, in the play's thumbnail sketch of the theater's recent history, which fully accords with the little men's exploits in *The Bagman*; the distinction, in the play's invocation of a Christian theology grounded in hope, where *The Bagman* saw only despair.

With respect to the theater, consider how Backhouse describes it to Pearl. The description, though brief, is powerfully indicting, charging theater with the crime of having narrowed its audience and trivialized its mission. As Backhouse laments, whereas once the stage spoke to the public at large, "to the whole people," now it is "capable of holding only the attention of the court-harlots and their embroidered stallions" (46). The theater, in short, has withdrawn from public discourse, "run[ning] like a rabbit from all mention of public affairs" (37). What is worse, were affairs to develop as Backhouse would wish—that is, were England to become a parliamentary republic—the theater would presumably vanish altogether, since there "are those in the Parliament have said openly they'd close down every playhouse if they once attained full power" (46). What Backhouse here offers is a virtual redaction of the little men's behavior in *The Bagman*. They perform, at the first, in a public arena, enacting politically volatile scenes that promote revolution while warning of its risks—surely an embracement of public affairs for the whole people's benefit. Yet no sooner have they thus laid a claim to authority (political and, arguably, moral as well) than they move from

the public arena to court, where they aimlessly parody upper-class intrigues—this, to the "courteous but unenthusiastic applause" (B78) of
such court harlots and embroidered stallions as consent to pay attention
to the spectacle. At the last, then, the puppets are objects of contempt,
spurned by those committed to the coming revolution—a response that
corresponds to the Parliament's threat to close down every playhouse in
the country.

Manifestly, *Pearl*'s view of the theater directly derives from *The Bagman*. If the same were the case with *Pearl*'s view of the world—if *Pearl*
equally shared in *The Bagman*'s unqualified pessimism—the implications
for Pearl and for Backhouse would be vast. In particular, their efforts to
rescue the theater from opprobrium would be doomed by definition,
since *The Bagman* admits of no outcome to human endeavor but failure.
Yet *Pearl* would appear to transpire under more forgiving circumstances.
For where *The Bagman* is shackled to the fearsome *Pilgrim's Progress*,
affirming its threats while ignoring its promises, *Pearl* takes for its guide
the consolatory Pearl-poem, a medieval elegy on the death of a child,
Margaret or Margery, who confirms for her mourning poet-father the
truth of salvation. Admittedly, it is only through Pearl's aliases—"Pearl,
Margery, whatever your name is" (46)—that the connection between
*Pearl* and the Pearl-poem is drawn. Thus, the promise of salvation that
glimmers in *Pearl* may be quite as insubstantial as Pearl's own identity.
Admittedly, too, the Pearl-poem itself is so variously interpreted as to
leave its theology in question, with heresy itself a distinct possibility.[8]
Nonetheless, in allowing that grace may exist, however remotely, *Pearl*
goes far to distinguish itself from *The Bagman*.

The distinction, moreover, is confirmed by the temperate behavior in
*Pearl* of one Gideon Grip, spokesman for the "Children of God" (14).
A carpenter, as "was Our Saviour at His trade in Nazareth" (15), Grip
may well be more severe than the Christ he invokes; but he is moderate,
indeed, by comparison to *The Bagman*'s grim Park-Keeper, who anticipates Grip in his rigidly literal reading of the law and even, perhaps, in
his carpenter's pencil, but not in the use to which that pencil is put:
namely, to load a huge Bible-like tome "to the endpapers with the names
and addresses of all those who were accursed" (B42). Where the Park-
Keeper knows no forgiveness for those that "lived in fornication" or
"moved their neighbour's landmark" (B42) or otherwise transgressed,
Gideon Grip has a sense of proportion. Thus, when his fellow Sectarians
put a stop to *Julius Caesar* and further propose to "strip the whores [in
the gallery] and whip their backs for 'em," Grip objects on the grounds
that "this is not the Lord's work," but rather "a debauch no less contemptible than that which I brought you all here to upbraid" (19). Grip's

intent is not to punish all sinners alike nor to bar the gates of Eden to those who would pass through. It is rather to establish an Eden on earth—or what would seem to be an Eden to those who are oppressed: a "free Republic of the English Commonwealth" (45) secured through the full restoration of Parliament.

Grip, then, betters the Park-Keeper as all of *Pearl* betters *The Bagman*—by evidencing hope of improving the world and by envisioning a means of effecting that improvement. In Grip's own terminology, such vision is "soul"; and he excoriates Backhouse for lacking it:

> If you make claim
> That mutual intercourse is all your aim
> To show folk how they live, I tell you—well:
> Present to them a picture of their own living hell
> And they will wallow in it, deep. Why not?
> It being beyond the reach of your pale soul
> To know that from this pit
> There is a ladder out.
>
> (20)

But what is Parliament to Backhouse, if not precisely such a ladder? And what is the play that Backhouse writes about Esther, if not an open invitation for the commonfolk of England to mount the ladder's rungs and ascend from the hell in which they wallow? Grip's lacerating comment may apply to *The Bagman*, where the puppets serve merely to "mirror" (B58) the audience, while the Narrator weakly laments that "all I can do is to look at what I see" (B88). But Backhouse has political ideals no less than Grip; and he means to promote those ideals in his play. What is more, he anticipates near perfect conditions for staging that play: a private venue, presumably safe from interference by censors or other officials of government; and a hand-picked audience—"Gideon in person and all his flock" (45)—predisposed to accept the play's challenge. The result, as Pearl thinks, should be drama "so powerful and unprecedented that any Puritan"—not to mention, any skeptic— "who sees it will immediately reverse his whole attitude to the English theatre" (52).

A fine forecast, if only it proved true. But in the event, no reversal takes place, however assiduously *Pearl* has prepared for one. Instead, "Esther," when staged, is "treacherously undone" (71) by the sadistic Captain Catso, a mercenary appointed by Grimscar's rich mistress to construct "Esther's" scenery and ensure, in the process, that the play does not discommode the monarchists. What Catso produces in fulfilling his charge, aside from confirmation of his own moral squalor, is theater as flawed as that depicted in *The Bagman*—indeed, more so. Was the Narrator's lack of conviction reflected in *The Bagman*'s several puppet shows? Inevitably so. Still, the puppets were provocative, though their meaning was oblique; and their performances were tolerated, though the state might have easily silenced them. In "Esther," by contrast, through Catso's machinations, key speeches are cut or obscured by stage business (bursts of music, creaking scenery), so that the playwright's convictions, though firm, are yet compromised. As for *The Bagman*'s second puppet show, was it sexually explicit? Apparently it was—but not outright obscene. In "Esther," by contrast, at Catso's direction, the effrontery is brazen: "bare-breasted women [appear in] every episode" (72); and the closing tableau features Catso himself in a flagrant display of perversion:

> He was dressed as the lowest type of grotesque priapic clown, on his head he wore the mask of a goggle-eyed demon, he had Pearl's right arm twisted cruelly behind her shoulderblades, he had caught her, God in Heaven, at the very middle of her costume change, her garments fell down around her loins, she was totally and shamefully exposed in the glare of the candles. Her mouth was wide open with shock, and it looked as though she laughed at us, as though on fire with blasphemous mockery.
>
> (73)

One need hardly be Gideon Grip to object to this spectacle, which is all the more appalling when fully understood. For the scene is not acted, but actual torture. At its finish, Pearl is permanently blinded and mutilated, while Backhouse lies bleeding from wounds meant to kill him. Thus is the theater reconceived as a literal battleground—with just the results that *The Bagman*'s puppets feared: "fracture and breakage that we cannot repair" (B86). And irony of ironies, the damage is for nothing; for no sooner have Backhouse and Pearl been disabled than news is received that the "King's army has been defeated by the Scotch Presbyterians!" (74). While "Esther" has been failing at politics on stage, political gains have been made on the field.

Were the stage, then, to be judged by the fortunes of "Esther," *The Bagman*'s grim verdict would evidently stand. Theater would be branded as a nullity in politics or, worse, a liability. But since "Esther" in performance is thoroughly bastardized—reauthored illegitimately, not to mention maliciously—it is open to question if we ought to disparage all drama on this one play's account. If we do, we join Pearl, metaphorically speaking, in dreaming the nightmare that rises "like vomit" (50) at the dawn after "Esther's" completion. Awake but entranced, Pearl envisions "a terrible tall gaunt woman with the head of a kingfisher" (50) emerging from the sea and proceeding toward "a sort of temple, ruined and roofless, with a heavy leather curtain hung upon brass rings between the pillars" (51). In this open-air theater (for so it appears), the woman raises an arquebus, takes aim at the curtain, and shoots. Her shot fells an armor-clad figure, whose helmet encloses a "dead skull. Dead and rotten five hundred years. And the skull went on screaming, and [Pearl] knew whose it was. . . !" (51): "Tom, it was *your* dead face in the helmet— yours—!" (51). The figure thus emerges as a pre-incarnation, so to speak, of Tom Backhouse; and as such it has compelling implications. It suggests, for example, that the temple of activist theater is abandoned; that its goddess has murdered the playwright-as-warrior; and that only a trace of the playwright remains—a scream in a moldering corpse.[9] But what truth is there, if any, in this agonizing vision? If more than we might hope, to judge from *Pearl*'s action, which justifies treating the vision as prophecy, still less than we might fear, to judge from *Pearl*'s subtext, which justifies treating the prophecy as false. Or, at any rate, vexed.

At issue in the subtext is the work of four playwrights, canonical all, whom Arden brings to our attention in connection with Backhouse's "Esther." Two of these playwrights, the Bard and Ben Jonson, are explicitly offered as models for Backhouse in fulfilling his commission from Grimscar—or, more precisely, Grimscar's mistress, Belladonna. In particular, he can choose to create a high tragedy on a political theme, in the manner of Shakespeare's *Julius Caesar*; or he can follow the example of Jonson's many court masques and produce "a dramatic entertainment" (39) of the sort that his patrons expect: "They want nymphs in it with round bare legs, Bacchanalians, a pair of lovers who turn out to be brother and sister, and at the end a bloody great rainbow and Diana coming down in a cloud. The like of what they kept Ben Jonson fooling around with thirty years ago" (45). The remaining two playwrights, Jean Racine and Friedrich Schiller, emerge by innuendo: the one, from "Esther's" subject and conditions of production; the other, from Catso's credentials for serving as "Esther's" designer. Racine partakes in "Esther" by virtue of the fact that he, too, based a play on this book of the Bible and did so, moreover, under circumstances similar to Backhouse's— namely, in response to a commission from the mistress of his patron (in Racine's case, Madame de Maintenon, the Sun King's morganatic wife) for a work to be "presented in a private house" (61) and not a public theater. As for Schiller, he is conjured by Catso's tall talk of having staged General Wallenstein's triumphal march through Prague, with the result that for "one entire afternoon, under command of *my* pageantry, that man became Caesar" (57). But just for one afternoon? Why, for well on two centuries, the General has been Caesar by command of Schiller's trilogy on Wallenstein's political ambitions and consequent assassination in the midst of the Thirty Years War. Schiller, Racine, Jonson, and Shakespeare: here, so to speak, is the backup for Backhouse—the company of playwrights who can vindicate drama despite its disgrace in the matter of "Esther." Let any of these playwrights confer upon theater the slightest political value consistent with curbing abuses of power, and Pearl's pagan nightmare must pale, reinstating the ethos of the Pearl-poem, which represents salvation as attainable. This is the challenge that *Pearl* sets the playwrights of the subtext. And, however imperfectly, they rise to the occasion.[10]

Take Shakespeare for example, and *Julius Caesar* in particular.[11] What the play recommends as a right response to tyranny is admittedly a matter of dispute. Many critics, maybe most, find the play to be conservative, reflecting its author's purported conviction that "no matter how bad the king, rebellion can never be excused" (William and Barbara Rosen, 110). Even one critic whose leanings are Marxist has argued that "Caesar is representative of the monarchical principle necessary for the well-being of Rome" (Siegel, 97). But a competing view of Shakespeare finds him somewhat left of center.[12] As Alvin Kernan puts the case, Shakespeare's "better plays were never finally homilies on obedience, and looking back from the present it is possible to see many of the greatest plays as covertly, and sometimes openly, revolutionary in effect if not in intent" (90)—a statement that easily embraces *Julius Caesar*, even as the question of Shakespeare's intentions must remind us of *The Bagman*, where the puppets' insurrection is so radically ambiguous that the ministers of state disagree about its meaning:

> UNPOPULAR MINISTER: And precisely *what* did he intend? Subversive encouragement to insurrection and revolution. Setting up the cause of the outlandish men against the citizens. . . .
> . . . . . . . . . . . .
> I ask you: is that politic?
> I tell you, no, it makes me sick.
> POPULAR MINISTER: Not altogether as stupid as you would make me out to be. The story concluded after all with the complete failure of the rebellion to consolidate its achievement.
> UNPOPULAR MINISTER: I did not consider it a logical development of the plot. And if I did not think so there are likely to be others who would share my opinion.
>
> (B63–64)

Is Shakespeare, then, hoist on the very petard that explodes at *The Bagman*'s conclusion? That is, are his politics so subtle or unsettled as to frustrate definition, with the stinging result that the state has no fear of him and reformers (recall the Young Woman) no need of him?

It might seem so. And yet reformers throughout history have recognized Shakespeare as one of their own and have exploited his plays, *Julius Caesar* among them, for decidedly political ends. As a salient example, the American revolutionaries in their war for independence looked to *Julius Caesar* for "the growing spirit of liberty it breathes."[13] And in 1937, when Orson Welles sought to comment on the rising fascist menace in Europe, he did so in a startling production of the play subtitled "The Death of the Dictator" and "viciously hacked to underline the political motif" (Ripley, 222). On such occasions as these has Shakespeare acquired political consequence,[14] even if only through the pointed intervention of politically minded directors and actors—a condition that in no way begs the question, since theater is above all a collaborative enterprise, as Grimscar and Backhouse are reminded to their sorrow. Perhaps Shakespeare cannot boast, any more than John Arden, that, "like Cicero . . . [he] had saved the state,/Nor yet, like Cataline, that [he] had tried/[His] fiercest best to have it all destroyed" (B37). But he nevertheless gives the lie to Pearl's disconcerting image of the activist playwright as dead and unreclaimable. For, as Grimscar intuits, such playwrights survive to be claimed and reclaimed in many "a great play . . . exceeding well-seasoned" (17).

Also, perhaps, in some plays that are not so well-seasoned nor, given their provenance, likely to deviate much, if at all, from political orthodoxy: plays like Ben Jonson's masques, which were commissioned expressly to flatter King James and his court. Here is drama of the sort that Backhouse openly mocks as a form of "fooling around" (45)—precisely the charge Arden fears may apply to drama in general. (In this fear, as it happens, Arden is joined by the playwrights he conjures: most notably Jonson, but also Shakespeare and Racine, all three of whom persistently questioned the value of their art.)[15] No doubt Backhouse does well to reject Jonson's masques as a model for "Esther," which contemplates sedition, like the plays of Jonson's youth,[16] not collusion in things as they are, like his masques. Nonetheless, it must be granted that Jonson had the wit to turn his regal commissions to aesthetic, and even political, account. In particular, he not only found the means "to treat [his] masques as significant didactic poetry" (Orgel, 106)—thanks largely to his development of the antimasque, through which he imported topical satire into a traditionally encomiastic genre—but he actually amassed political capital, acquiring influence valuable at court. Thus was Jonson instrumental, for example, in mollifying King James when the monarch grew incensed with John Selden over the publication of his

*History of Tithes.* "For a mere poet to intervene, and prevail, in a matter of such consequence," observes David Riggs, Jonson's recent biographer, "was an extraordinary coup" (262)—one wholly incidental to the masques in themselves, yet born of them nevertheless.[17] And therein lies a lesson of some urgency for *Pearl.* For if political authority, no matter how modest, can accrue to a playwright from precisely such drama as Backhouse thinks to scorn—that is, from drama made to order for aristocrats, solely for the purpose of proclaiming their privilege—then the potential for activism must inhere in all theater, notwithstanding Pearl's dream to the contrary.

But how to harness such potential: that is the question, more readily answered in theory than practice, as Racine's case and Schiller's thereafter attest. The essential conditions for politicizing theater are obvious enough. The playwright must have the opportunity, and furthermore the will, to be outspoken. In addition, his audience must consent to hear him out, and hear him true, though he dismay them with his candor. Not an easy combination to secure. The opportunity alone, as Backhouse discovers, may appear to be at hand when it is not. But even when the chance to speak is genuine, the playwright may prove reticent or the audience immune to his instruction. So it seems to have been with Racine, when Madame de Maintenon arranged for him to write first *Esther*, then *Athaliah*, two biblical pageants to be performed before the Sun King by the schoolgirls from St. Cyr. Here was an occasion for Racine, long retired from the stage and installed with Boileau as Historiographer-Royal, to turn to writing plays again and, what is more, to do so for the very king's amusement. Why, then, not also for his edification? Either no such idea occurred to Racine in the course of writing *Esther*, or he set the thought aside as ill-advised. At any rate, *Esther* is politically inert. But not so *Athaliah*. For into this play about the ascension of Jehoash to the kingship of Judah, whose throne Athaliah had usurped, Racine insinuates a speech at once so candid and persuasive that it well might cause a monarch to moderate his power—if not to fly into a rage at the playwright's presumption, should he think himself reflected in the passage.

The speech that thus plays politics in *Athaliah* is delivered by the High Priest Jehoiada as a warning to Jehoash when the boy is informed of his secret identity as the rightful king of Judah. Cautioning Jehoash against the selfsame excesses to which history confirms that he later fell prey, Jehoiada pronounces a stirring indictment of regal prerogatives:

> Nurtured far from the throne, you do not know
> How fatal is this honour's poisonous spell.
> You do not know the wine of absolute power,
> Nor the seductive voice of flatterers.

They will soon tell you that the holiest laws
Bind subjects, but must bend before their kings;
The only brake a king has is his will;
And to his greatness must all immolate.
His people are condemned to tears and toil,
And want a rod of iron ruling them;
That if they're not oppressed, they will oppress.
And thus from trap to trap, from chasm to chasm,
Corrupting the pure sweetness of your soul,
They'll end by making you detest the truth
And painting virtue in a hideous guise.
Alas! They led astray our wisest king.

(IV, iii, 1387–1402)

Whether Racine here intended to lecture the Sun King—a possibility that scholars have raised and dismissed[18]—is finally immaterial, since essentially he did so, whatever his intent. In the context of a monarchy, these uncompromising lines cannot but spell a challenge to the government's integrity. Yet if the king felt affronted, he gave no indication by word or by deed. Though this speech of Jehoiada's may have set off a salvo, the shots were not heard, or at least not acknowledged. Not for almost a century. Only on the eve of the French Revolution did this "famous passage, with its condemnation of absolutism, and its reminder of the people's rights, [acquire] . . . a revolutionary force," as evidenced by the fact that it "was thunderously applauded whenever an actor spoke it during the last years of the Old Régime" (Brereton, 275). So it is that *Athaliah*, by dint of the responses that it drew from its audiences, took decades to become what in truth it always was: politically radical in despite of its origins.

But what bearing, if any, has Racine upon *Pearl*? Much, if we recognize that Backhouse's "Esther" (at least what we know of it) duplicates the politics, though not the reception, of Racine's *Esther* on the one hand and of *Athaliah* on the other—a flat contradiction that proves to be possible only because "Esther" by Backhouse exists in two versions. Take the expurgated version that Backhouse delivers to Barnabas for rehearsal by his company of actors. Here is a play that is specifically designed to be politically neutral: a play, then, that is comparable to *Esther* by Racine. And yet Barnabas complains of its audacity in any case, insisting that "if this were going on in the public theatre, I am morally certain that the royal censor would object to it" (61). Accordingly, Barnabas sets about shifting "the balancing-point of the whole play" (59) by changing its title from "The Brave Deeds of Godly Queen Esther for the Salvation of her People Israel" (47) to "The Tragedy of Haman and his Contentious

Rebellion against the Commands of the King of Persia" (59), by tampering with "the emphasis of the production" (59), and by contemplating "certain loppings and prunings [in the text] the better to consolidate it" (59). In light of this reaction, it is hardly any wonder that Barnabas has no qualms about silencing "Esther" in its unabridged version, which Backhouse and Pearl are inopportunely discovered to be rehearsing in secret. This unabridged "Esther," in the manner of *Athaliah*, "takes its whole tone" (66) from a single politically fractious set speech reminiscent of Jehoiada's, although far more confrontational—that is, from an epilogue that presumes to name names and arrive at appropriate penalties for "those whom you well know have tried—/And failed—to fix upon this realm the chain/Of bondage everlasting" (66–67). Given the climate in which Backhouse must operate—one, as Barnabas shows, in which even a decorous play can arouse some suspicion—such effrontery is wholly insupportable. Thus, "Esther" sparks the self-destructive mayhem predicted in Pearl's dream. But there are other climates, too, as Racine's better fortune proves: climates in which politically engaged theater can survive against the odds (à la *Athaliah* in the court of the Louis XIV) or can actually flourish (à la *Athaliah* in the last days of Louis XVI). The pity is that climates are resistant to control (hence Backhouse's predicament) and that, even when ostensibly hospitable, they yet may be malign.

Let Pearl dream of the apocalypse, it still is the case that what activist playwrights for the most part must fear is not annihilation, and not even rejection, but rather acceptance in a political climate that turns their work against their own allegiances. Racine may himself have encountered such a climate with respect to *Athaliah*. For no one can know if he would have approved of the French Revolution or have wished for his play to be implicated in it. Maybe so; maybe not. But if not, then the cheers of delighted anti-monarchists in the late eighteenth century can only have served to hijack the play, just as "Esther" is hijacked by Catso when he reconceives its epilogue as a pornographic orgy. To be sure, Catso acts out of malice aforethought; and in order to effect his evil purpose, he wreaks havoc on the play that he traduces—indignities Racine was spared, if in fact he was traduced at all. But neither malice toward a playwright nor disruption of his plays is prerequisite to misrepresenting him. Naive admiration can produce the same result, as Catso's allusion to Schiller (through *Wallenstein*) is suited to remind us. What Schiller's plays bespeak—as has generally been recognized outside his native land[19]—is their author's mature understanding of the moral complexities implicit in history and politics. Yet in German-speaking countries for a hundred fifty years this subtle, cosmopolitan playwright was lauded as a spokesman for sentimental patriotism—a misreading that led, in the fullness of time, to the Nazis' identification of Schiller as spiritually one with the Reich.[20]

The violence done to Schiller by this misappropriation falls nothing short of that endured by Backhouse at the hands of Captain Catso. Both playwrights are compromised, intellectually and morally, even if for wholly different reasons: outright textual sabotage in Backhouse's case; in Schiller's, a wholesale distortion of meaning achieved by the placing of improper emphasis on lines that, in context, speak half-truths at best. Moreover, once injured, the playwrights' reputations can never be redeemed, at least among some of their spectators. As Grimscar observes about Catso's production of "Esther": "For the Roundheads in that audience the blasphemy was absolute. Whatever I said to them I could never persuade them now that Tom Backhouse and myself had nothing to do with this abomination of desolation" (74). Schiller likewise has suffered lasting damage with his countrymen, to judge from the example of Hansgünther Heyme, the West German "director who has worked most consistently on Schiller productions since the 1960s" (Sharpe, 330).

In an arresting analysis of Heyme's perspective, the scholar Lesley Sharpe suggests that Heyme has confronted his audiences

> with the terrible usability of Schillerian texts for political propaganda, particularly in the Third Reich. In his 1966 and 1983 productions of *Wilhelm Tell* the audience saw not only their revered poet's potentially sinister sentiments but also their own past willingness to tolerate a regime which traded on nationalist fervour. The 1983 production was set in 1923 in the French-occupied Rhineland with the French in the position of the Austrians. Ultimately it was impossible to tell from the production whether Heyme saw Schiller as guilty of the kind of banner-waving nationalism portrayed in the play or whether he regarded the play as inseparable from the uses that have been made of it at certain times.
>
> (330)

Of the two views of Schiller here attributed to Heyme, the first of them (the image of the playwright as a banner-waving nationalist) can no more be dispelled, among those who would believe it, than can the Roundheads' impression of Backhouse as complicit with the monarchists. What Wallenstein says of himself when suspected of treason is what Schiller and Backhouse must equally say:

> Guilty I stand, and I can not shake off
> This guilt no matter how I try. The mere
> Ambiguousness of life accuses me,

And even pure deeds from a blameless source
Will be misread and poisoned by suspicion.[21]

(Schiller, 142)

As for the second view of Schiller (that his drama is inseparable from
what others have made of it), this suggestion bears only too heavily on
*Pearl*. For if the action of history can alone corrupt a play, through no
fault of the playwright's, then plays are forever at risk of corruption as
long as their names are remembered, and no playwright can ever rest
quiet in the grave, lest the work that today brings him honor disgrace
him tomorrow. A noisome idea—and one that returns us forthwith to
Pearl's nightmare, from which we had thought to awaken by means of
*Pearl*'s subtext. The dream may no longer impress us as describing the
fate of every playwright unconditionally. But it does describe the fate of
some, as Schiller makes apparent. What is more, the nightmare threatens
even playwrights who have gone unscathed for decades or for centuries,
since their plays may be misused—and their reputations murdered—at
any time, in any place, though they be "dead and rotten" (as Pearl would
have it) "five hundred years" (51).

We see, then, where our tour of *Pearl*'s text and its subtext has led
us: from an engagement with characters very like those in *The Bagman*
(Pearl is the Young Woman's double; Backhouse, the Narrator's), to
indications that *Pearl* will attempt to reverse *The Bagman*'s pessimism
(the theater emerges in *Pearl* as an instrument of change, and society
as capable of change for the better), to the utter collapse, in the course
of *Pearl*'s action, of the theater's pretensions to do good, or even well
(the subversion of "Esther" confirms *The Bagman*'s doubts about
drama's utility), to a renewal of faith in the theater's potential (*Pearl*'s
subtext reminds us, through canonical playwrights, that drama has
proven its political value), to a final apprehension of the theater's
limitations as an agent of politics (gross misreadings of Schiller show
that plays can be subverted rather easily and perhaps irretrievably). In
short, we have nearly come full circle, from *The Bagman*'s nightmare-
vision of all human institutions, the theater included, to Pearl's own
nightmare-vision of the theater in particular. That the circle does not
close is due to this concession only, emergent from *Pearl*'s subtext: that
some very few playwrights may have profited society on some very few
occasions—a slender affirmation remarkably hard won. Why, then,
should we credit it? Precisely because it is tendered in a play, a medium
that powerfully validates the message. And precisely because the playwright is Arden, who had five years beforehand renounced the English
theater from a platform no less lofty, or conspicuous, than the stage
of the Royal Shakespeare Company.

On the occasion in question, in December 1972, an audience was gathered at the RSC in London for a performance of *The Island of the Mighty*, an Arthurian epic first written by Arden as a trilogy for television (it was never produced in this solely authored version), then substantially revised by Arden and his wife, Margaretta D'Arcy, partly to suit the demands of the theater, and partly to reflect the couple's politics-in-progress.[22] Now radically shortened to the space of one evening, *The Island* was being rehearsed at the Aldwych, while the Ardens were marching with pickets at the stagedoor in a rancorous dispute with the director, David Jones.[23] According to the Ardens, Jones's staging, setting, and music for *The Island* had had the effect of imbalancing the play, so that its anti-imperialism was fatally compromised, indeed contradicted. Jones, for his part, was assuring reporters that the matters in dispute had been approved in rehearsal by Arden himself; that the objections originated with Margaretta D'Arcy, who had attended no more than *The Island*'s first run-through; and that fundamental changes could not be introduced so late in the process of mounting the play. Come the preview, come the crisis. A member of the audience halted the show by calling for the authors to make an appearance. The rest is theater history. D'Arcy leapt to the stage and tore at the scenery, while Arden tried to speak and was roundly shouted down.

> A chorus from the audience shrieked: "Get out, get out."
> [Arden] walked to the center of the stage and faced the audience. "Look, are you actually saying to me that you wish me to leave this theater?"
> The audience roared: "Yes!"
> "In that case," he said, "I will leave this theater and never write one word for you again."
>
> (Weinraub, 52)

And thereupon Arden fell silent.

Or virtually so, until *Pearl*.[24] That *Pearl* speaks to these events is unmistakable. Transparently, "Esther" is *The Island of the Mighty*, a coauthored play that was forced in performance to testify falsely against its own politics. As for Backhouse and Pearl, they are Arden and D'Arcy, the mild-mannered playwright and the political firebrand joined in a mutual improvident effort to rescue the theater from its social irrelevance. How such disparate spirits can have looked to each other to collaborate in drama is no enigma in *Pearl* any more than in life. Backhouse/Arden discovers in Pearl/D'Arcy an adamantine resolve to regenerate the theater, irrespective of all obstacles. In return, Pearl/D'Arcy gains a vibrant, articulate voice through her playwright, as well as a passport to the legitimate stage, otherwise closed to her in England. As Pearl says of herself (being Irish and an actress) in a comment that equally pertains to D'Arcy (also Irish and an actress): "Of course it would be not good sense to have [my name] put upon an English play. In your country in public I do not exist. Except I should change my shape to the pretended shape of someone else" (48). When Arden, then, chose to defy all "good sense" by featuring D'Arcy as *The Island*'s second author and to do so, moreover, while working with a company in "no way inclined to [the Ardens'] point of view" (52), the reason was likely the same that Backhouse offers for entrusting his "Esther" to Barnabas: "I tell you I know him, I can handle him. . . . he *respects* me, don't you see?" (53). Alas, Pearl's rejoinder—"He has no reason to respect *me*. And I am part-author of the text" (53)—is the more acute assessment in connection with *The Island*, given how D'Arcy was rebuffed at the run-through.

Indeed, the RSC's refusal to accede to D'Arcy in the slightest particular, when she made her critique of Jones's production, can be taken as the principal cause for the scandal that quickly enveloped *The Island*. To those (and there are many) who believe that D'Arcy was herself the true culprit, doing Arden incalculable damage with her singular intransigence, not to mention her bald importation of leftist ideology into Arden's more traditional notion of theater,[25] Arden breathes not a word of denial in *Pearl*. Rather, he concedes the charge so readily, so movingly, as to shame the critics crass enough to raise it. Thus, Backhouse to Pearl at their secret rehearsal of "Esther":

> We can present this goddamned play, girl, see it through to the finish
> and curdle the blood with it . . .
> One moment, before we continue, there is one thing to be said:
> Too true, with your bereft craziness, you have well curdled *my* thin
>     blood,
> Too true, I may well in the upshot receive my ruin—
> If so, I walked into it blithe and alive to all it might mean:
> Pearl upon a bright new brooch shining out at my withered throat,
> Pearl like a descended star full aflame in the pit of my bed,
> Pearl every word hitherto unheard of all the poetry that works in
>     my head—
> Flood-tide in the wide sea:
> It is you that have made it, not me . . .
>
>                                                                      (67)

As the last words that pass between Backhouse and Pearl in this play about *The Island* (and so much else besides), these verses stand as Arden's public tribute to D'Arcy, uncontroverted by the ruinous spectacle that does, in fact, follow apace.

So patently does Backhouse act as Arden's loyal spokesman, insofar
as Margaretta D'Arcy is concerned, that we look to him also to frame
a defense of Arden himself as *The Island*'s injured author. Yet here we
find Backhouse entirely inept. Only see how he handles his differences
with Barnabas over the staging of "Esther's" "damned dumbshows" (60)
and the delivery of its "jingle-jangle rim-ram-ruff . . . rhymed couplets"
(61): namely, by grandstanding rather than appealing to reason or aesthetics. "I know my business," says Backhouse to Barnabas; "I wrote
what I wrote and I'm expecting you to do it" (61). Such a representation
is hardly persuasive as an answer to the criticism Barnabas raises (presumably on David Jones's behalf) with respect to certain episodes in
"Esther"/*The Island*, which "as they are written [Barnabas] cannot believe any audience of today will be prepared to take . . . seriously" (60).
Similarly, there is little force of feeling apparent in Backhouse's offer (the
same one the Ardens extended to Jones) to "work with the actors alone"
(61) on the scenes in dispute. For the offer is neither repeated nor
defended when Barnabas rejects it (as Jones did before him) on the
predictable grounds that "You will have pulled out and unravelled every
stitch in the goddamned knitting from top to bottom of three weeks'
work! Tom, I will not permit it! I am master of this company or I am
nothing, Tom" (61). Even Barnabas's proposal to cut the role of Esther
(the inverse of Jones's decision to stress Arthur's role in *The Island of
the Mighty*) evokes only bluster from Backhouse: "Both the part and the
casting are *correct*: I stand fast by them: I will *prove* them correct, by
God I will prove it in your teeth!" (62). But how can he prove it, except
in performance? And what performance can succeed without an adequate
production?

Aye, there's the rub. In truth, nothing Backhouse says, or could
conceivably say, can answer to the questions that *The Island* provokes
and that Catso so rudely expresses: "Why, what ails our severe playwright all of a sudden, Camarado—? Can it be he has come to realise
that this his new strange work doth betoken some diminution of his
erstwhile unquestioned genius . . . ?" (62). Let a playwright so affronted
turn to "reasoned disputation" (17) in his own self-defense—as when
Backhouse tries to justify boy-actors to the Puritans—and he instantly
becomes what he denies himself to be: "the dullest tame poet . . . ever
heard of in the world" (18). A playwright proves his prowess in his
drama, nowhere else. Thus, had Arden kept the vow that he made at
the Aldwych, never to write for the theater again, his silence would have
meant for him professionally what Backhouse's silence meant for him
personally: that he "never recovered of his wounds" (76). Moreover,
once the vow is broken (*Pearl* having been written), the test of recovery

can only reside with the play in its entirety, not with Backhouse (or any other character) in particular.

If we look, then, to *Pearl* not merely to vindicate Arden as a dramatist, but also to restore him to the practice of his art, what we find is altogether encouraging. For one thing, the play was a critical success, receiving favorable reviews and a coveted Giles Cooper Award—unimpeachable defenses of the playwright's skill and artistry. Equally important, as the public expression of a private change of heart, *Pearl* signals Arden's reconciliation with the theater. But not with the theater as the West End conceives it: not as spectacle "dressed and decorated according to [its patrons'] most improvident taste, equipped with new music and moveable scenes" (38), all paid for by poisonous Belladonnas and their "cormorant companions, . . . demanding nothing from their poets but to make a scarecrow out of honest men" (36). For theaters like these, in fact, Arden has written not a solitary word since *The Island of the Mighty*. His singly authored plays have been written for the radio exclusively.[26] And it is well that it is so, given what Arden demands for his drama: namely, conditions of production hospitable to plays that articulate ideas in estimable scripts. Such conditions, as it happens, are relatively rare on the contemporary stage, but come naturally to radio, the modern equivalent—in several key respects that are definitive for Arden—of those theaters that nurtured Shakespeare and Jonson, Racine and Schiller, the venerable playwrights of the subtext.

If, when *Pearl* opens, it is not as *Pearl* at all, but as "*actors performing 'Julius Caesar' in an echoing hall*" (9), we are thereby forewarned: Arden will have no compunction in *Pearl* about using the radio to accommodate drama that is fundamentally, conventionally, theatrical. In fact, *Pearl* was itself mildly criticized, at the time of its original broadcast, for being "essentially a stage picture in radio terms" (Trussler, 16)—a perfectly reasonable appraisal of a play that handles sightlessness deftly, but that neither exploits the condition philosophically nor turns it to technical advantage. Not that *Pearl* could repair to the stage without change. The ending, in particular, would likely require substantial revision, since it operates principally as narrative. If it seems to be dramatic, look to Arden's virtuosity: to his skill in dividing the story of Backhouse's ruin among multiple voices (Grimscar, Belladonna, Backhouse, and Pearl), and to his cleverness in cutting from the story to bona fide theater (the performance of "Esther" in Belladonna's mansion). Such are the means by which Arden conveys the impression of movement in *Pearl*'s final scenes, though the ending is actually static, as a production on a stage would disclose. Manifestly, *Pearl*'s conclusion is constructed for radio, even to the image of Catso as a "grotesque priapic clown" (73) flinging Pearl to the floor "like a rag of wet linen" (74)—an action that the radio likely enhances, since imagination works to intensify the horror. And yet, for all of it—for all of the ways in which Arden assures that *Pearl* melds to its medium—the play could no doubt have been fashioned for theater (as Arden, in fact, may have originally intended)[27] with little, if any, conceptual loss. *Pearl* indeed is a "stage picture" shown on the radio, and not only in the sense that it could have been staged, but also in the sense that it evaluates theaters, and even represents them in its action. The implication is that radio can double for a stage—perhaps even supersede one. But how can Arden dare to suggest so?

The idea is not only counterintuitive, but virtually heretical as a perspective on radio drama. After all, from the early 1920s, when plays first appeared on the radio in Britain—with scenes, no less, from *Julius Caesar*,[28] which thus opened an era before it came to open *Pearl*—the single, inexorable challenge for radio has been to free itself from theater and to forge a new genre, consisting of plays that belong on the airwaves. Are we now to be told that the radio has properly been, all along, but a substitute stage, whatever else it is besides? In a manner of speaking, we know as much already from the fact that the radio has long served in Britain as a national theater for airing the classics. Indeed, the playwrights of *Pearl*'s subtext—Shakespeare and Jonson, Racine, and Schiller, too[29]—have been heard on the radio. But always as a service to the nation, not their plays, which have a visual dimension that radio neglects. Radio-as-theater is theater manqué, as everyone knows. Everyone, that is, except Arden, whose decision to "stage" his own *Pearl* on the radio provides an unexpected outlook on the medium—one best apprehended in the context of "Playwrights and Play-Writers," a lecture that Arden delivered at several universities in 1975 (three years before *Pearl* was first broadcast), then published in 1977 as the last of the essays in his volume *To Present the Pretence; Essays on the Theatre and Its Public*.[30]

Arden's argument in "Playwrights" is that contemporary theater subordinates language to spectacle, and hence playwrights to directors. Inevitably, such theater only dallies with ideas, since visual images, as Arden suggests, are inherently ambiguous, and directors rarely hesitate to temper lines that might offend. To the extent, then, that contemporary theater provokes any controversy, Arden finds that it does so through nudity, violence, and generalized sentiments, not through forthright engagement with particular issues rendered in vigorous dialogue. Yet it was not always so. As Arden reminds us, directors were unheard of before the late eighteenth century, when the Duke of Saxe-Meiningen first took such a role; and even then, the Duke intended not to rein in feisty playwrights or to sanitize their scripts, but to restore intellectual and dramatic integrity to the performance of plays, such as Shakespeare's, that had devolved into vehicles for bombastic declamation by star actors. Accordingly, the Duke replaced leading performers with a company trained to perform as an ensemble—the very kind of acting that prevailed in Shakespeare's day, when there "were no 'original creative ideas' except the play itself—but there was a group of well-practised professionals who had at their fingertips every technique needed to make the play work" (PP184).

If Shakespeare's theater so described sounds curiously similar to radio drama, Arden himself does not mention the likeness. In fact, he never so much as alludes to the radio in "Playwrights and Play-Writers." Still, the fit is hand to glove between what Arden admires in Shakespearean theater and what radio drama is by necessity. Arden notes, for example, that the Elizabethan actor, having only two weeks to rehearse a production, would have chiefly endeavored "to make himself word-perfect, and then to establish the correct verbal interpretation of his role with his colleagues, and—in the case of a new play—with the *Author* at hand to explain the required shades of meaning" (PP180). A better description of the cast's general aims and behavior in a radio studio would be difficult to come by. On the airwaves, word-perfection is regarded as the norm, since scripts are read, not memorized. Interpretation forcibly addresses words alone, since nothing else is taped, except for sound effects. And an author, when present (as is common with new drama), retains unparalleled authority, since no one—not even the director—has time to supplant him in the four to five days that are normally allotted for rehearsing and recording a two-hour play. By contrast, a full-length contemporary stage play will undergo four to eight weeks of rehearsals, involving elaborate costuming, set design, lighting, choreography, musical background, and special effects, all of which entail countless choices and compromises that can substantially alter the playwright's conception, even when everyone wishes to please him. (Possibly, such was the case with *The Island*.) How much simpler were conditions in Elizabethan theaters, where "blocking and stage-business" were largely "traditional" (PP184), so that actors and crew members all could be "taught from the beginning of their careers the standard craftsman's response to standard situations" (PP182–83). Because everyone who worked on such a stage "must have known without having to be told exactly what to do in any given situation that was likely to arise" (PP180), plays could be mounted with very little risk that the playwright would be startled, much less galled or overwhelmed, by the staging of his play. (Here the masque is the exception, as the legendary struggles between Jonson and Inigo Jones can attest.) In its craft, as entirely distinct from its language, the Elizabethan stage was self-assured, but self-effacing—exactly like the radio, which depends upon highly accomplished technicians and versatile actors to employ the apparatus of a radio studio not for its own sake, but rather for the sake of the words on display.

Now though Arden himself invokes none of these parallels between Shakespearean theater and radio drama, his silence in the matter is far from conclusive. For chronology speaks with some force on his behalf. First comes "Playwrights and Play-writers," in which Arden espouses, as his standard in drama, the "verbal intensity" (PP178) of "European classical theatre" from Shakespeare and Jonson to Ibsen and Shaw (PP175)—an allegiance that sets him at odds with "the 'high-art' theatre of the present time" (PP176), in which spectacle is all.[31] Soon thereafter comes *Pearl*, verbally intense by any measure whatsoever, written for the stage and yet never performed there (see note 27), entrusted instead to the radio. What could Arden be suggesting, by this sequence of events, but that radio outstrips the contemporary theater as a showcase for *Pearl*—and if for *Pearl*, then for all of *Pearl's* predecessors, too, right back to *Julius Caesar*? The caveat is clear: under current conditions, such playwrights as are poets (in the broad sense of the word) can produce a play on radio and lose spectacle entirely, or can insist on having spectacle and thereby lose the play. These being the choices, Arden chooses as he must—that is, he casts his lot with radio. But the question still arises how the radio can suit him, given not just his genius for creating thrilling stage effects (only think of the skeleton in *Serjeant Musgrave's Dance*), but also his acknowledgment that drama has a "*dual structure*" (PP185), arising first from its dialogue, second from its "stagecraft" (PP185).

It is stagecraft, in fact, that in Arden's opinion differentiates the playwright in all his creativity from the so-called play-writer, altogether less accomplished. As Arden explains,

A Play-writer is simply a person who puts pen to paper and sets down dramatic dialogue. But the Playwright pursues an ancient and complex craft analogous to the crafts of the Cartwright, the Millwright, the Shipwright, or—in old Scots—the Wright, pure and simple. The origin of the word is Old English *Wyrht* = a work, or *Wyrcan* = to work. The Playwright *works* drama just as the Millwright *works* mill-gear. And working or making a play includes what are now thought to be the activities of the Director *as well as* those of the Script-writer. Such an artist requires a wider workshop than the keyboard of a typewriter. He/she must see him/herself as a person capable of presenting a complete artistic vision upon the

stage—not as a semi-skilled sub-contractor to the theatre, who requires someone else actually to produce the play once its text is
completed.

(PP210–11)

What is troublesome here, with regard to the radio, is the seeming
implication that, absent a physical stage on which craft can be exercised,
a dramatist can be only a writer, not a wright. If so, then the radio can
hardly serve to remedy the failings of the theater, by Arden's own criterion. And yet surely all depends upon what Arden means by stagecraft.
Insofar as the term denotes visual motifs, imposed upon the dialogue and
not to be deduced from it, stagecraft and radio are no doubt incompatible. Insofar as the term denotes a pattern of ideas, separate from the
dialogue yet integral to it, radio should readily accommodate craft. Let
us see, then, how Arden takes the measure of the term.

To illustrate stagecraft in its visual dimension, Arden analyzes *Hamlet*:
in particular, the Ghost and the scene in the graveyard. Of the Ghost,
Arden argues that his vestment of armor, a most peculiar costume for a
spirit, provides a "vivid indication" that the play is "about the revenge
of an heir to the throne *in a nation on a war-footing*" (PP194). With
respect to the graveyard scene, it is Arden's contention that when Clau-
dius enters with the mourners for Ophelia, the audience should observe
him to lock eyes with Hamlet and to register at first "a recognition—not
of Hamlet as such," but of a young man dressed in black and "holding
a Skull" (PP190). This "stage-picture" would function, according to
Arden, to establish the Prince for exactly what he is "from the King's
point of view": namely, "a revenant, a man come back from the dead"
(PP190). Arden further contends that "to produce the correct hieratic
effect of such images, the Actors would have . . . to avoid all attempt at
naturalism, and adopt some formal posture like those of the Kings,
Queens and Jacks in a pack of cards with their swords and other prop-
erties" (PP190–91). If Arden is right about the staging of this scene, he
has identified an insuperable problem for radio, since the medium is
helpless to display formal postures, exchanges of glances, or even un-
remarked entrances. (To be known to have entered, a character in radio
must speak or else be spoken to, or at least be spoken of.) So much for
silent action as well as tableaux: being absent from the dialogue, they
must be absent, too, from radio. As for the Ghost's suit of armor, though
we see it from the moment that Horatio says, "Such was the very armour
he had on/When he th'ambitious Norway combated" (I, i, 60–61), the
comment is not offered till the Ghost has come and gone at the outset
of the play. On the radio, then, as in theater productions where the Ghost
is represented as a disembodied voice, the armor is an afterimage (rather

like an afterthought), considerably less "vivid" than Arden recommends. These examples being typical, we are forced to this conclusion: that visual stagecraft is tricky for radio, and sometimes entirely impossible.

By contrast, consider the conceptual stagecraft that Arden associates with *Henry V*. Arden's argument here is that Shakespeare "regularly sets up a certain atmosphere of noble enterprise by means of evocative blank verse speeches, and without comment, deflates it through an alternation of scenes showing something very near the opposite" (PP202). In Act I, scene ii, for instance, the King is represented as seeking advice about whether to enter into conflict with France, when the matter, in fact, is already decided—or so Arden argues on the grounds that French envoys at the end of the scene bring the Dauphin's responses to a list of ultimata that Henry must have issued considerably beforehand. Similarly, at the start of Act II, a Chorus announces that all England's youth are on fire to fight, although nothing in the play serves to justify the comment—an omission, as Arden believes, that "can only be by deliberate choice," since Shakespeare could have easily "given at least one picture of honest enthusiastic volunteers setting forth to achieve the Kings' Right" (PP202). Still again, by attending to the order of the scenes that are set at the Battle of Agincourt, Arden draws the conclusion that Henry is "a murderer of surrendered men" (PP205)—an indictment that is nowhere expressed in the dialogue. Finally, from "the sandwiching of [Kate's and Henry's] duologue between two full court-scenes," Arden infers that "Kate knows, and Henry knows, that the marriage must take place" (PP207)—an understanding left unspoken between the two principals. All in all, Arden finds that in *Henry V* "there is a remarkable and consistent disparity between what is said to be done and what is seen to be done" (PP195)—a subtle form of stagecraft that requires the spectator "to look at the complete structure of [the] play before and behind the scene actually on stage" (PP207).

Without question, this is stagecraft that radio can handle. Indeed, the medium may handle it better than the theater, since the absence of a stage provides us an incentive for looking beyond scenes, and not merely at them. Arguably, radio enjoys an advantage where conceptual stagecraft matters more than the visual, as may well be the case in a good deal of Shakespeare, if *Hamlet* and *Henry V* are representative. For in *Hamlet*, as Arden acknowledges in passing, the visual stagecraft is largely superfluous: that is, it "amplifies [and] fulfils" but "does not contradict its verbal counterpoint" (PP195). But in *Henry V*, the conceptual stagecraft is deeply subversive, supplementing the "overt text" (PP199), in which Henry is celebrated, with "a secret play in parallel" (PP199), in which Henry is dispraised. If radio can help us apprehend this secret play (and

such others as may figure elsewhere in drama), its invisible stage surely
rivals a real one for the production of drama conceived for the theater.
So, too, where the radio evokes inner vision that would benefit drama
even on stage. After all, when the Chorus in *Henry V* complains that the
stage is an "unworthy scaffold," inadequate to "hold/the vasty fields of
France" or to contain "the very casques/That did affright the air at
Agincourt" (I, Pro., 10–14), it speaks to the theater's universal limitation:
no matter how well accoutered, no stage can come close to reproducing
reality. Only the cinema can rise to this achievement, and it does so at
the price of diverting us from dialogue, engaging us, instead, with mostly
visual imagery. A playwright, then, who wants to keep words in the
foreground, yet nevertheless have a "kingdom for a stage," must do as
Shakespeare does, relying upon our "imaginary forces" (I, Pro., 18) to
see what is not shown, to "piece out [the theater's] imperfections with
[our] thoughts" (I, Pro. 23), to "eke out [a] performance with [our]
mind" (III, Cho., 35)—the very responses that radio fosters. Radio may
thus be the theater of choice for plays that transpire outside of locales
(mainly, drawing rooms) that a stage can portray realistically, as well as
for drama that spurns mere reality: particularly those numerous Elizabethan plays, *The Tempest* chief among them, that have been said to aspire
to "some pure theater of the imagination, free of the limitations of real
actors, stages, and audiences" (Kernan, 135). For whatever the radio's
own imperfections, it comes closer to such purity than any other medium.
    Whether Arden perceived this advantage in radio at the time of *Pearl*'s
broadcast can only be conjectured, since nothing in *Pearl* confirms that
he did. Indeed, nothing in *Pearl* can be taken to establish that he would
not have preferred a conventional stage, had a suitable one been available.
Yet if we look ahead four years to a piece that Arden wrote for the London
*Sunday Times* (22 August 1982), we will find there a generous endorse-
ment of radio assessed in connection with the theater.[32] That Arden
recognizes radio as hospitable to stage plays emerges from his memory of
a 1950s broadcast, on the BBC Third Programme, of *Wallenstein* in
Coleridge's translation. Far from regretting the absence of spectacle, Arden
actually contends that his engagement in the "quiet, monotonous, non-
verbal task" of preparing architectural drawings while he listened "fix[ed]
his] mind upon [his] ear, as the latter fill[ed] up with the play's dialogue."
The result, as he reveals, is that, some thirty years after, he could "still
run off yards" of Schiller's "bombastic blank verse crammed with rhetorical inversion." No wonder that *Wallenstein* figures in *Pearl*: through the
agency of radio, it had acquired a place in Arden's personal canon. How
better could the stage have served the interests of the play?
    Or the interests of the playwright? If a dramatist's goal is to deliver

his audience to a world of his own individual making, where characters live by his efforts alone, then the stage by its nature is distinctly inconvenient. As Arden observes,

> In a stage play [actors] are three-dimensional human beings in motion, with all their inconsequential individuality, their unexpected characteristics (which are often disconcertingly at odds with the writer's original notion of the fictional people in the play). . . .
> On the radio they are reduced to voices, still individual, still unpredictable, and of course unavoidably their own responsibility; but they are no longer *images* (made by God, not by the playwright). . . .
> Skilled radio actors can project personalities that have absolutely no resemblance to their own size and shape.

Here Arden's description of radio accords with the "pure theater of the imagination" referred to above—a theater in which "the limitations of real actors, stages, and audiences" cease to exist, so that a play can be all that its playwright intended. To quote Arden's conclusion to the *Sunday Times* essay:

> For the writer [a radio production] is a strangely private experience. . . .
> The play comes straight back into your head (from which it originally emerged) and—barring serious misunderstandings and misinterpretations—it comes back more or less as you always hoped that it would. For all the physical distance between yourself and your public, you seem so very much nearer to them than is ever possible in the theater.

These are poignant reflections from the author of *The Bagman, The Island,* and *Pearl,* all of which bear upon Arden's concern that the contemporary theater has carelessly estranged him not only from his audience, but even from his plays in their fundamental social and political import. What Arden then regains through the medium of radio is the unimpeded voice that a playwright requires in order to disseminate provocative ideas. And by his own demonstration, he recovers that voice without sacrificing stagecraft in its crucial dimensions.

The radio, as Arden goes far to make plain, is a stage not much hampered by being invisible—indeed, a stage that often profits from its insubstantiality. That being the case, let the theater beware. For if the radio is suitable for Shakespeare and Schiller, and better than the theater for a play like Arden's *Pearl,* its lure to other playwrights who live by the word will not be diminished by its absence of spectacle.

# Afterword

THROUGHOUT the foregoing chapters, radio drama has been represented in a host of different guises. In *Scenes from an Execution*, it
has been shown to wield a painter's brush; in *Artist Descending a
Staircase*, to produce optical effects that Escher might have envied. The
genre's affinity to music (what Pater would have called its aspiration to
the condition of music) has been discovered in *Transfigured Night*, and
then again in Beckett. It has been treated as a mind in action: *Wings*
and *A Slight Ache*. As a world arrayed against an individual: *Cries from
Casement*. As a theater in spite of its immateriality: *The Bagman* and
*Pearl*. But nowhere in the book has the genre been treated as poetry,
although radio easily accommodates verse drama (as, for instance, in
*The Bagman*), with the consequence that poets, including such masters
as Louis MacNeice and Dylan Thomas, have long been ranked among
its best practitioners. How, then, this omission? It has contrary sources.
In part, I have given poetry short shrift on the grounds that the verse
in verse drama is merely instrumental in the making of meaning, not
meaningful in and of itself. In part, I have taken poetry for granted on
the grounds that all radio plays, whether in prose or in verse, are
inherently poetic. All partake of modern poetry as defined by Wallace
Stevens: "The poem of the mind in the act of finding / What will suffice."

To be sure, "Of Modern Poetry," from which this definition comes,
was not written about radio. But Stevens's sense of modern poetry as a
theater obliged to "construct a new stage" readily encompasses radio
drama. Every radio play, after all, must construct a stage different in
nature from the physical space in which other plays unfold. What is
more, every radio play must

> be on that stage
> And, like an insatiable actor, slowly and
> With meditation, speak words that in the ear
> In the delicatest ear of the mind, repeat,
> Exactly, that which it wants to hear, at the sound
> Of which, an invisible audience listens,
> Not to the play, but to itself, expressed
> In an emotion as of two people, as of two
> Emotions becoming one.

Here is as cogent a characterization of radio drama as the genre is likely to command. From the delicatest ear in the mind of a playwright, a radio play repeats words as that ear wants to hear them: articulated, inflected, hence powerfully animated, yet safe from eclipse by theatrical apparatus. And at the sound of these words, an invisible audience listens intently, not only to the play, but also to itself as expressed in the play's events and gestures, which perforce bear the stamp of whoever envisions them. Thus do the audience and the playwright become one, united in their effort to realize a work that, existing as a mutual "act of the mind," is what Stevens denominates poetry.

As for the mind that, in acting, produces this poetry, Stevens names it in a metaphor: it is a "metaphysician in the dark." The image embodies the very quintessence of radio drama, a genre that approximates pure metaphysics by creating whole universes out of ideas. No matter that the broadcast of radio plays depends upon technically sophisticated machinery: upon state-of-the-art recording studios, vast transmission networks, and myriad receivers to pick up the signals. In performance, the machinery simply evaporates. In its place appear worlds, fully operative, fully populated, although nary a molecule sustains them. From the dark, from the void that this darkness bespeaks, arise phantoms that reproduce life in its boundless variety. Arguably, then, it is radio drama that is consummately the "poem of the mind in the act of finding / What will suffice"; for whatever suffices, regardless of scale, a radio play has the breadth to contain.

Of course, the purported connection between radio drama and Stevens's "Of Modern Poetry" is merely serendipitous; and my appeal to the poem in defense of the genre is just a sleight of hand. But I would hope to be forgiven my legerdemain, if for no other reason than that the survival of radio drama in contemporary society is by no means assured. Ours, after all, is a culture that far prefers seeing to hearing. Even music, at least of the popular variety, has come to be pictorialized (and rather cryptically at that) on MTV. In such circumstances, aural art is at a disadvantage; and radio plays will remain at special risk so long as those few that are widely esteemed are read as books, or staged as theater, but rarely ever heard in their proper form as sound. Should their alienation from their source become complete, radio will cease to be attractive to playwrights; and our art will have lost a mature and subtle genre that speaks to us—literally speaks to us—with such intimacy and immediacy that it gives the impression of having originated spontaneously inside our own heads. Insofar as is possible, my book is meant to stem that loss. So it is that I have shown, for every play that I discuss, the measure of meaning that radio alone has the power to release. If, in the process, I have seemed to prove my claim, made with help from Wallace Stevens, that radio drama at its best is really poetry, that is all to the good; but it is none of my doing. The plays have worked that magic for themselves.

# Notes

## Preface

1. The volumes in the series are entitled *Best Radio Plays of 19—*; and all of them have been published by Methuen in association with BBC Publications. With respect to the statement here quoted, it bears mention that the word "writing" ceased to be italicized in 1984. Otherwise, the statement has remained unchanged, except in 1981, when the following variant appeared: "The deciding factor throughout was the quality of the writing, for which this award is made, and not the part played in the final broadcast by acting or production."

## Chapter One: *Scenes from an Execution*

1. All quotations from *Scenes from an Execution* are cited from *The Castle; Scenes from an Execution*. The play's first broadcast was on BBC Radio 3 on 14 October 1984.
   This particular bit of dialogue, although it appears in the printed text of the play, is not in the BBC broadcast. Perhaps it was a late addition, interpolated when *Scenes* was prepared for publication. Or perhaps it appeared in the original text, only to be cut during recording or editing, in the interests of holding the performance to a 90-minute running time.
   Wherever the printed text of the play is more expansive than the broadcast, I have treated the text as authoritative. For the reader's information, however, I have identified dialogue not included in the BBC production by adding "pto," for printed text only, to the relevant page references.
   2. Barker typically declines to make reductive statements in his plays. What he "want[s] to see in drama" are ideas that are "complex, interesting, contradictory" (Donesky, 340). As for telling audiences what they already know, he chooses not to. Thus his observation that "I wouldn't want to put much of my energies into proving that newspaper chiefs told lies: it seems self-evident" (Donesky, 339).
   3. "I cannot let myself be splintered like this, can I? I cannot!" appears in the printed text only.
   4. "Can't you just crush me in the night?" appears in the printed text only.
   5. To judge from the deeply unsettling nature of his plays, as well as from his public statements, Barker shares Galactia's sense of art as socially disruptive. As recently as 1990, he identified himself with the "Theatre of Catastrophe," which tries, in his words, to "unpick morality" (Longwell, 29). Elsewhere he has said that "what I'm interested in doing in drama is to subvert preconceived notions—to worry away at people's conviction, if they have any conviction" (Donesky,

336). Thus, in the issue of *Gambit* devoted entirely to Barker, the introductory "Editorial" (presumably written by the issue editor, Dunn) observes that "any audience for a Barker play will pass an evening seeing itself flayed alive on stage" (3). Nevertheless, Barker, like Galactia, stops short of inviting literal riot and ruin, even if such is the logical result of his ideas. As he candidly observed in 1975 while discussing *Stripwell*, his sole (and half-hearted) attempt at producing "bourgeois domestic drama" (Dunn, "Interview," 43): "In a way it's a very despairing play because if you are not going to accept the Labour Party morality anymore then you have to vote for the opposite, which is to vote for a violent class war. And that's something I'm not prepared to do, because it's going to be—violent" (Grant, 39).

   6. One is put in mind of Barker's play *The Castle*, which in fact has twice been published in the same volume as *Scenes from an Execution*. For Barker, the castle is "a twin symbol—both of protection and of oppression. Where does one pass into the other?" (Dunn, "Interview," 34). Urgentino has the same duality.

   7. In the BBC broadcast, Rivera speaks of "*our* cause."

   8. The printed edition of *Scenes* assigns these words to Carpeta. But the context alone would suggest that they are spoken by the Doge, as indeed is the case in the BBC production of the play.

   9. It is tempting, perhaps, to see the struggle between Carpeta and Galactia as fundamentally social in origin—a proof of Barker's contention, as expressed in a 1981 interview, that "any potentially vivid sexual relationship is distorted by a social relationship which frustrates or murders it" (Hay and Trussler, 6). But by 1984, when *Scenes from an Execution* was in progress, Barker had begun to modify this bleak perspective. In particular, in an interview with Dunn, he announced his intention of writing a play that would "involve sexual love and its redemptive power" ("Interview," 33). Apparently, he was speaking of *The Castle*. As he observed at the time, sexual love "has always been one element in everything I've written. It has existed, as a refuge or a despair, never tenderly or profoundly. It has seemed spoiled to me by the violence of the world we live in. But that is wrong. Sexual love is regenerative. Absolutely so" (Dunn, "Interview," 36). *Scenes from an Execution* appears to hover between the old dispensation and the new. Thus, Carpeta's marriage and his assumption of the Lepanto commission distort his affair with Galactia, but far less than one might have expected. And though Galactia remains barren, even after recovering her fertility in jail, she does respond to imprisonment by yearning to litter like a badger. Still, on balance, sex appears to strike her less as a profundity than as a refuge from annihilation: "It's funny but a funeral is calculated to make me want to fuck" (64).

   10. The line in question is from scene 12: "I think you are—I hate to say this—you are a little mad" (75, pto). Prodo, too, questions Galactia's sanity: "Don't trust you, got a mad eye—" (50).

   11. Here the play would seem to speak for Barker. In a 1981 interview with Hay and Trussler, he commented as follows on the actions of a character who, like Galactia, seeks to locate responsibility: "What Bela does in the stage version of the play [*All Bleeding*] is to insist on blame—and the worst aspect of humanism is its rejection of blame, the idea we are all guilty. A wicked, paralyzing posture" (10).

12. Although *Scenes* all but invites a feminist interpretation, it is well to heed Barker's own warning: "I wouldn't describe myself as a feminist. I have no theory to refer to, and my plays will not be feminist plays any more than they are socialist plays. . . . I will follow the demands of my own imagination before I consider my responsibility to any movement. Any contradictions that arise from this I rejoice in" (Dunn, "Interview," 39).

13. In the BBC broadcast, the dialogue cuts directly from Galactia's question "What sort of face have you got?" to the Man's bewildered response, "I haven't seen my face for seven years." In the printed text, however, the following exchange intervenes between question and answer.

| GALACTIA: | You sound like you have a big nose. |
|---|---|
| MAN IN THE NEXT CELL: | I have a big nose. |
| GALACTIA: | Fancy that! |

(81)

Although the interpolation may indicate that the Man does, in fact, know his own face, Galactia's surprise when he confirms her guess as accurate suggests otherwise. In particular, we may suspect the Man to be so thoroughly a stranger to himself that he simply succumbs to Galactia's suggestion in the absence of any other information about his own appearance.

14. Should there be any doubt about the moral worth of the Man in the Next Cell in relation to Galactia, we may refer to a comment of Howard Barker's quoted by Itzin: "The argument that's put against all kinds of political activity in the west [is] that you're being tolerated, that you're being turned into the conscience of the bourgeoisie, that your freedom is a product of their repression. I don't accept that argument because I don't want to. The alternative is simply to shut up" (257). "SHUT UP," we may remember, is what the Man in the Next Cell first says to Galactia when she is ushered into prison. Although she comes to thank him for that advice, she never follows it. Instead, she occupies herself by speaking out in pictures, drawing "a man, in granite, with granite" (84) on the prison wall.

15. In an interview with Dunn conducted while *Scenes from an Execution* was in progress, Barker observed that "Struggle, and endurance, are what I celebrate" (42). The comment would seem to embrace Carpeta, particularly in light of Barker's later remarks about *Victory*: "You can live through reaction. You can hide in the cracks during reaction, but you're not actually touched by it even though you perform endlessly and acquiesce. You can *perform* acquiescence" (Donesky, 342, my emphasis). Carpeta, I would argue, performs capitulation— and is thus morally superior to the Man in the Next Cell, who capitulates through absolute passivity.

16. Rabey, in *Howard Barker*, describes the goal and the outcome of the painting somewhat differently from me. He sees Galactia's project as an effort at "single-handedly effecting the mass rising of the proletariat" (99)—an interpretation that owes less to the particular details of *Scenes* than to the general drift of Barker's other plays. As for "the effectiveness of the canvas," he contends that after Galactia's "accord with the State . . . the work of art lives its own subsequent

life (demonstrated by its effect upon the Young Sailor and the weeping peasant) as a truth-teller unreduced by the compromises—perhaps even personal corruption—of Galactia herself" (99). This assertion, reaching as it does beyond the events of the play, claims more for the painting than may actually be justified. Nonetheless, the claim begs our assent, if only because the play approves Galactia, despite her faults and her excesses. What Rabey says of *No End of Blame* applies equally to *Scenes*: it "manages to be inspirational without sentimentality" (*British and Irish Political Drama*, 161).

17. Although the ending of *That Good Between Us* may be taken as ironic, Barker appears to have intended otherwise. Thus, Itzin quotes him as follows: "The only person who is actually fully connected to his ideals is McPhee and McPhee is betrayed through his simplicity and honesty. Taken at face value, that is pessimistic. On the other hand McPhee is the sole survivor, and his last words are an affirmation of the spirit of survival, of coming through" (255). Except that Galactia is betrayed by the state, as well as by her own personality, Barker's statement applies equally to *Scenes from an Execution*.

18. The Sketchbook opens the play in the printed text only, and not in the BBC broadcast.

19. Everything from "a dramatic diagonal" on appears in the printed text only.

20. For a lucid, non-technical discussion of the power and the limitations of the human imagination, see the chapter on "Imagining" in Taylor. Also of interest is a discussion with George Mandler in Miller, particularly pages 147 and 152.

21. As one of several examples of the kind of drama peculiarly suited to radio, Arnheim cites "a radio version of Meyrink's *Golem*," the story of a giant out of Hebrew folklore. The playwright, says Arnheim, "related that he had in his mind as basic theme of his sound-drama a heavy stumbling Golem-motif." Arnheim goes on the comment that "it is no such simple matter as the naturalistic sound of the Golem's voice or the Golem's footsteps, but, far more generally, simply the sound-expression of the figure of the Golem, which can be manifested in an accompaniment of sounds or music" (44).

22. This example, drawn from Wittgenstein, is cited by Jerome Fodor in a conversation recorded in Miller (89). The thousand-sided figure, which is drawn from Descartes, and the man not scratching his nose are also examples from Fodor. In context, they are intended to illustrate why contemporary psychologists have rejected the theory that the language of thought consists of mental images analogous to photographs. As Fodor explains, "whatever mental representations are like . . . they've at least got to be the right kinds of symbols to express the kinds of things you can believe, because the underlying picture is that believing is in some way entertaining these mental representations. Now, it's certainly possible to *believe* that something is *not* the case. But try to imagine drawing a picture of something not being the case. It's easy enough to draw a picture of a man scratching his nose, but it's very hard to draw a picture of a man *not* scratching his nose. And yet a man not scratching his nose is a perfectly reasonable object of thought. . . . One problem about imagery is that its, as it were, 'expressive capacity' is extremely limited in comparison with, say, discursive symbols" (86).

23. In the discussion that follows, I address the two stage performances of

*Scenes* that I have attended. Because I did not myself see the production by Juha Malmivaara that Barker describes in *Arguments for a Theatre* (63–65), I do not comment on it. (Barker's description does not, in any case, bear upon the questions at issue in my analysis.) But in Barker's opinion, the production "was so bold in its effects I could scarcely say anything was forfeited" in the transfer from radio to the stage (letter to me from Barker dated 25 November 1991).

## Chapter Two: *Artist Descending a Staircase*

1. For a play specifically designed to exploit this idiosyncrasy of radio, see Olwyn Wymark's *The Child*.

2. All quotations from *Artist Descending a Staircase* are cited from Stoppard's *Four Plays for Radio*. The play's first broadcast was on BBC Radio 3 on 14 November 1972.

3. In fact, since snoring and buzzing have far less in common than Stoppard imagined, the drone in the BBC production was produced—as the producer, John Tydeman, admits—by a radiophonically treated recording of an actor blowing on a comb wrapped in tissue paper. In an intriguing explanation for Stoppard's mistaken notion that snoring and buzzing sound alike, Tydeman speculates that Stoppard was misled by the convention, in comic strips, of representing both these sounds by a string of z's, as follows: zzzzzzzzzzzzzzz.

4. The artists may also embody, to a lesser degree, the three Duchamp brothers: the painter Jacques Villon; the sculptor Raymond Duchamp-Villon; and, of course, Marcel Duchamp, the youngest and most daring of the three. Duchamp-Villon, who died at the front in 1918 of typhoid fever, posthumously achieved recognition as one of the finest cubist sculptors. As for Villon, he became commercially successful only in old age. Although Villon "never said a word against Marcel in public," Pierre Cabanne speculates that he "probably suffered secretly from Duchamp's rather paradoxical reputation, for [Marcel] had lampooned and condemned everything Villon held dear, and all he lived for—painting and pictures" (*Brothers*, 194).

5. Compare Duchamp's contention that he wanted "to put painting once again at the service of the mind" (quoted in Schwarz, 21) or his observation that "every picture has to exist before it is put on canvas and it always loses something when it is turned into paint. I prefer to see my pictures without that muddying" (quoted in Golding, 86). In an interesting comment on Duchamp's predisposition to "devalue art as craft in favor of art as idea," Paz proposes that "in its turn the idea constantly sees itself negated by irony" (*Marcel*, 153).

6. See, for example, *Rrose Sélavy & Co.*, Duchamp's book of puns published in Paris in 1939. (An English translation is included in *Salt Seller*). Throughout Duchamp's notes, which are voluminous, wordplay runs rampant; and puns are fundamental even to much of his visual art. Hence Paul Matisse writes of "the extraordinary dimensions that Marcel put into his work through the use of puns. . . . He chose his key words with the greatest care, and as a result very few of them can be translated into English without losing all of their secondary French dimensions."

7. As Kelly remarks about *Artist*, "Stoppard's work [seems allied] with the very avant-garde concerns he is bent on ridiculing" (198). Duchamp may be said to have displayed a similarly equivocal attitude toward the avant-garde and modern art. Paz argues cogently that "Duchamp is at one and the same time the artist who carries avant-garde trends to their final consequences, and the artist who, in consummating them, turns them back on themselves and so inverts them. . . . Duchamp's art undertakes the criticism of modernity, and exchanges nods of recognition with the art of the past" ("*Water,"147–48). If Paz is right, then Duchamp fulfills what Jenkins considers the "implications of *Artist Descending*—that the artist's responsibilities are ultimately to his own sense of truth and to the standards of historic tradition" (115).

8. With respect to World War I, note that Stoppard—by playing on the name of Edith Sitwell—seems to joke about the fact that the dada-ists spent the war *well sit*uated in Zurich, where (Switzerland being neutral) they were free from the obligation to fight. "Edith was never in Switzerland," Donner rightly observes to Beauchamp, who thinks he remembers her there (26). No doubt part of the joke depends on our knowing that Duchamp, too, was never in Zurich, though he managed, in both the world wars, to avoid any military service.

9. That Sophie's given name means "wisdom" strikes Oscar Mandel as a key to Stoppard's play. In Mandel's interpretation, Sophie is seen to exhibit "inner wisdom, like that of Teiresias and others." As a result, Mandel gives full credit not only to Sophie's "sincerity and depth of character" (she is admirable because she is "capable of loving"), but also to her aesthetic opinions. Mandel thus "read[s] the play as a half-funny, half-sad attack on avant-gardism by a conservative who accredits himself by showing that he is no fusty traditionalist but is as peppy an experimenter as they come" (125).

My own sense of the matter is that the halves of Sophie's name, in contradicting each other, cast into doubt her appearance of sagacity. (See my comments, on page 36 above, about the surname Farthingale.) As the most vulnerable character in *Artist*, Sophie surely wins our sympathies. What is more, she confirms, by her example, the enduring need for love in human relationships. (Hence the propriety of Stoppard's naming her for wisdom.) But in her utter rejection of the avant-garde in modern art, Sophie contravenes Stoppard's evident respect, if not unstinting approval, for the work of Duchamp.

Still, Mandel is right that Stoppard, however peppy an experimenter, is finally artistically conservative. So it is that *Artist* is traditional in form. And to the extent that the form of the play is a part of Stoppard's argument (how could it not be?), Stoppard may be said to side with Sophie (i.e., traditionalism), not with Donner and company (i.e., avant-gardism). Mandel's interpretation in concert with my own thus promotes a conception of *Artist* as an optical illusion, gaily oscillating between mutually exclusive meanings right before our eyes.

10. Stoppard thus disproves McShine's contention that Duchamp's work is "unparaphrasable and untranslatable." Of course, McShine was really thinking of expository prose, for which it probably is true that "Duchamp's oeuvre . . .can be contemplated, described, theorized upon, but not explained" (129).

11. For a discussion of Cage's radio "circus," *Roaratorio*, see Chapter Three, pages 95–98.

12. In New York, the play opened at the Helen Hayes Theater on 30 November 1989. Previously, it had run in London, opening at the King's Head Theatre on 2 August 1988, then transferring to the Duke of York's Theatre on 2 December 1988.

13. In the New York production, Donner left the stage midway through Sophie's monologue. So, too, in London, as the stagescript reveals (French ed. 29).

14. Note that the stage cannot duplicate this magic. In the theater, we see from the start that the horse is a fiction, created by Beauchamp's juvenile penchant for horsing around with coconut shells.

## Chapter Three: *Transfigured Night*

1. All quotations from *Transfigured Night* are cited from *Best Radio Plays of 1984*. The play's first broadcast was on BBC Radio 3 on 28 October 1984.

2. For a detailed and inclusive discussion of the varied interactions between music and literature from classical Greece through the twentieth-century, see Winn.

3. Bettmann shows how Bach "utilized a core of proven rhetorical convictions to make sure that what he had to say would reach its mark" (118). As for the rise of "autonomous"—that is, purely instrumental—music even in the course of Bach's lifetime, see Neubauer.

4. Browning had training in musical theory—so much training, in fact, that he was able to consider composing an opera. (See Irvine and Honan, 8). If Browning seems, in his poetry, to play fast and loose with musical terminology, the reason is presumably not ignorance, but the pressure of creating a smooth poetic line. Moreover, the errors that musicians have noted in his verse may be merely ostensible. Thus, Cooke justifies Browning's reference to "lesser thirds" and "sixths diminished" in "On a Toccata of Galuppi's" (71). We may suppose that in "Abt Vogler" Browning sought to describe not the objective nature of music, but its subjective effect upon listeners.

5. For the poles of the debate, see Cooke, *The Language of Music*, and Kramer, *Music as Cultural Practice, 1800–1900*.

Cooke, a musicologist probably best known for having reconstructed Mahler's Tenth Symphony, argues that "music cannot express concepts; . . . [it] can only express feelings" (xii). Moreover, he attempts to establish that the feelings it expresses are quite specific and unambiguous. His method involves examining compositions, primarily song and opera to see what musical intervals and idioms have traditionally been associated with particular emotions: the major third, for example, with pleasure; the minor sixth with anguish; rising pitch with outgoing emotion; falling pitch with an inrush of emotion. This manner of interpreting music would seem to bear affinities to the eighteenth-century notion that music conjured specific feelings among listeners by imitating speech rhythms supposedly reflective of those feelings.

Kramer, by contrast, argues that "works of music have discursive meanings" (1). While conceding that music cannot make truth claims—that "it never makes propositions" (5)—he cites J. L. Austin's theory of speech acts as authority for the contention that truth is not the sole objective of expression: "Constative utterances make truth claims, and are accordingly evaluated as true or false. Performatives attempt to achieve something, and are accordingly evaluated as successful or unsuccessful" (7). Proposing that "musical processes" are "expressive acts" performative in nature, Kramer suggests that "if we can learn to recognize them as such, to concretize the illocutionary forces of music as we concretize its harmonic, rhythmic, linear, and formal strategies, we can then go on to interpret musical meaning" (9). The kinds of questions Kramer raises about music are reflected in his chapter on "Liszt, Goethe, and Gender," where he asks "how the defense of the feminine ideal against its contrary is articulated by the *Faust* Symphony" (124). In general, his method of answering such questions involves explicating the form of a musical composition, then extrapolating to the cultural implications of that form. Thus, in discussing Chopin's A-Minor Prelude, he observes: "Given the expressive polarity that divides the melody from the accompaniment, it is tempting to hear the vacillation between the two as a musical analogue to the psychological defense mechanism known as doing and undoing—the classical manifestation of unacknowledged ambivalence" (76–77). To follow Kramer's arguments in detail requires training in music theory.

6. For an extended example of a program, consider Vivaldi's *Four Seasons*, which purports to depict peasants dancing, storms raging, shepherds sleeping, and all manner of country activities. Without reliance on program notes, the portraits are virtually unidentifiable. Moreover, such reliance soon proves a monumental distraction from the music.

7. From Schoenberg's album notes for the recording. Cited in Bailey, 31.

8. Brigid Brophy's witticism, cited in Winn, rightly captures the difficulty of depicting concrete objects—and, by extension, plot and action—in musical terms: "Almost the only thing music can represent unambiguously is the cuckoo—and that it can't differentiate from a cuckoo-clock" (232).

9. The quotations come from Payne, 20. As for the contention that chromaticism is painful, see Cooke, xiii: "Since the new language [of atonality] is unrelievedly chromatic by nature, it must be restricted to expressing what chromaticism always was restricted to expressing—what indeed we feel even the very earliest chromaticism of the sixteenth-century Italians still to this day expresses—emotions of the most painful type (though a wide variety of expression can naturally be achieved by presenting these emotions in diverse ways—gently, fiercely, satirically, grotesquely, even jestingly)."

10. Charles Rosen, 39. Rosen goes on to compliment Schoenberg, remarking that *Erwartung*'s ostensible free form has made it "a well-attested miracle, inexplicable and incontrovertible."

11. Kramer, *Music and Poetry*, 10. By an "intelligible pair," Kramer means

"a poem and a composition [that] converge on a structural rhythm . . . a shared pattern of unfolding [that] can act as an interpretive framework for the explicit dimension of both works" (10). An example would be Wordsworth's "The Thorn," and Beethoven's Appassionata Sonata, both of which exhibit what Kramer calls "Romantic repetition—the 'unnecessary' repetition of a phrase, a gesture, a narrative unit, a sectional unit, or the like," giving the impression of "a mental stammer, a sign that the normal operations of consciousness have been thwarted" (27). Kramer's argument extends from instrumental music to song, and encompasses "Schoenberg's first fully atonal work, *Das Buch der hängenden Gärten (The Book of the Hanging Gardens)*, to texts by Stefan George" (161). In this song cycle, as in Schoenberg's "other expressionist vocal works, *Erwartung, Die glückliche Hand*, and *Pierrot lunaire*," Kramer finds a "relentlessly tragic view of sexuality" (166). The same, of course, can be said of *Transfigured Night*.

12. The precise reasons for Schoenberg's difficulties in producing large forms during his atonal period is differently described by different musicologists. Thus, Charles Rosen posits that "as long as no substitute had been found for the absolute final consonance of tonal music, the creation of large forms would remain a problem: absolute consonance is a final demarcation of form. With it, the limits of the form are indicated: and they can be approached at the pace determined by the composer" (55–56). Payne, by contrast, proposes that "one of Schoenberg's main problems, as a naturally expansive artist, was to see how a large form was both technically and, more important, aesthetically possible when his increasing polyphonic elaboration and formal compression were continually reducing the ratio of time to density of experience" (19). As for Glenn Gould, he maintains that during 1911–1912, when Schoenberg confined himself to "writing tiny pieces for the piano," his circumscribed activity bespoke the desperation he must have felt at the prospect of "committing himself to a language which he did not know—a language which he had no means to govern except through his innate musicality" (115).

13. See also Dahlhaus, who proposes, in an essay on "Schoenberg's Aesthetic Theology," that "however implausible the idea may seem, . . . in the period of early atonality the text was merely a means of building large-scale forms without the support of tonality" (85). Later, in another context, Dahlhaus observes that "in the atonal works of the pre-dodecaphonic period the music either shrank to extreme brevity or had to rely on a text as its primary form-building principle" (146).

14. See also Dahlhaus, 77, in an essay entitled "Schoenberg's Poetics of Music."

15. Whether *Words and Music* is Beckett's third, fourth, or fifth play for radio depends upon whether one chooses to count two unfinished sketches ("Rough for Radio I" and "Rough for Radio II") and, if so, how one chooses to date them. Although most of Beckett's critics ignore the "Roughs" entirely, my own decision has been to count them. After all, Beckett not only published the "Roughs" (although more than a decade after they were composed), but even permitted "II" to be produced. As for dating the sketches I have treated them as falling between *Embers* and *Words and Music*, as follows:

*All That Fall* (1956)
*Embers* (1959)
"Rough for Radio I" (late 1961)
"Rough for Radio II" (early 1960)
*Words and Music* (late 1961)
*Cascando* (1962)

This is the order and the dating of the plays adopted in the Grove Weidenfeld edition of Beckett's *Collected Shorter Plays*; and it is an arrangement that has served me well in the development of my argument about the nature and meaning of Beckett's experiments with words-as-music in his radio drama.

In dating "Rough II" before "Rough I," Grove follows common practice. But its dates for both plays are earlier than those adopted by Esslin, who quotes Beckett as assigning "Rough I" to "vers 1962–63?" and "Rough II" to "années 60?" ("Beckett," 142). If Beckett is right, one or both of the "Roughs" may be taken to come after *Cascando*. Zilliacus, however, regards Beckett as mistaken about the dating of "I." On the basis of a holograph draft of the play in the original French, where its title was *Esquisse*, Zilliacus assigns "I" to November/December 1961 (119–20). Thus, he situates the play "halfway between *Words and Music* and *Cascando*, chronologically as well as in other respects" (122). As for "Rough II," Zilliacus is silent, no doubt because his seminal work on *Beckett and Broadcasting* was completed before the publication and production of "II" in 1976. According to Fletcher et al., however, Beckett's "années 60?" indicates a date of composition "perhaps *ca.* 1962" (166), which again might place it later than *Cascando*.

Given this dissension, I have regarded a definitive dating as essentially unachievable, and have accepted the order that best suits my purposes—namely, Grove's. But I believe that my argument stands, whether or not the "Roughs" actually preceded *Words and Music* and/or *Cascando* in their dates of composition.

16. Although *Eh Joe*, which Beckett wrote for television, is also called a "piece," it bears an obvious affinity to a radio play. Its only speaking character, after all, is a woman who remains invisible throughout. The woman's monologue, moreover, is reminiscent of Beckett's radio pieces (especially *Embers*) in its use of a fragmented narrative, which, as I argue below, has musical implications for Beckett.

17. All quotations from Beckett's plays are cited from *The Collected Shorter Plays of Samuel Beckett*.

18. Although Krapp remains sexually active, Beckett regarded him as displaying an "ascetic ethics, particularly abstinence from sexual enjoyment. Sexual desire, marriage forbidden." This comment, from Beckett's notebook for the German production of *Krapp's Last Tape*, is quoted in Morrison, footnote 9, page 59.

19. Morrison's analysis of Beckett's radio plays is characteristically perceptive. But because she is specifically interested in Beckett's use of narrative, and because she assumes that "radio dramas are, by their very form, akin to narrative: they are 'told' not seen" (74), she misses Beckett's efforts, in his radio writing, to

transcend the very stories that he tells. Her approach to Beckett's radio drama thus works best for *All That Fall* and *Embers*, where the engagement with music is relatively subtle. But it visibly falters with *Words and Music* and *Cascando* (she does not treat the "Roughs"), if only because she makes no sense whatever of the role that Music plays in either piece. Of *Words and Music*, Morrison observes that "Words's and Music's own interaction (sometimes mutually helpful, sometimes hostile) gives that play interest and variety but no climax" (94)—a contention that my argument below refutes. As for *Cascando*, Morrison disregards Music entirely, arguing that the "drama of the play is in the phenomenon of narration itself" (119). Admittedly, both *Words and Music* and *Cascando* present interpretive difficulties for literary critics, who are accustomed to dealing only with words. But to ignore Music's function *as a character* in these pieces is to miss a large part of their meaning.

20. For a reading of Beckett's radio plays that stresses the element of time, see Cleveland, who contends that Beckett on radio "exploits the power of the voice to evoke a transitory presence in a temporal universe antagonistic to that presence" (269). Cleveland maintains that the "drama [of the plays] is in the struggle of the voice to mark time, whether time is silent or filled with competing rhythms and sounds" (269).

As the phrase "competing rhythms" might suggest, Cleveland perceives a musical impulse at work in the plays. Thus, she observes that the three-part structure of *All That Fall* is analogous, in music, to "repetition in retrograde" (271) and that Henry's voice in *Embers* establishes a kind of counterpoint with the rhythm of the sea. As for *Words and Music* and *Cascando*, Cleveland proposes that "Beckett has based the structure of the first on tonal distinction and the structure of the second on the problem of rhythm and continuity" (280). Nonetheless, the claim that Cleveland makes for the plays is not that they aspire to the condition of music, but rather that they "create in sound analogies for perceptual struggles" (270).

21. Note that Beckett spoke of *Endgame*, written just a year later, as "a string quartet" (Zilliacus, 103).

22. See McWhinnie, 133–51. In Maddy Rooney's footsteps to and from the station, McWhinnie identified a "four-in-a-bar metre" (133) that he sought to reproduce throughout the play. Thus, he treated the rural sounds with which the play opens as "a strict rhythmic composition . . . correspond[ing] exactly to the . . . metre of Mrs. Rooney's walk"—an effect made possible by his decision to have "human beings . . . impersonate the exact sound required" (133). Later, after Maddy's encounter with Christy, McWhinnie chose to "replace her footsteps by brush-strokes on a drum; bearing in mind the four-beat time of the opening, we do this quite formally: four pairs of footsteps followed by four pairs of drum-strokes, then Mrs. Rooney soliloquizes in the same rhythm. From now on we have established a relationship between reality and a musical shorthand expression of it; it will be possible, later, to intensify the expressive qualities of this basic device" (138–39). McWhinnie's general approach was to use "the symbolic footsteps as a purely musical device, and sometimes simply for the sake of their own musical effect" (148), as when the footsteps are heard with the wind

and the rain that assault Maddy and her husband on the road home. In this way, McWhinnie hoped to endow the "sound-pattern" of his production with "a kind of musical texture of its own" (149). All in all, McWhinnie may be said to have orchestrated the play in the course of directing it.

23. In one draft of the play, Beckett had Dan specify the sex of the child: "A little girl" (Zilliacus, 133).

24. Mercier suggests that "in music . . . [Beckett's] taste seems to have remained essentially traditional" (113); and Zilliacus quotes Beckett as telling his nephew, the composer John Beckett, that "Schubert's music seems to me to be more nearly pure spirit than that of any other composer" (38). Nevertheless, it was Beckett who "suggested Morton Feldman as the composer" for Everett Frost's recent American production of Words and Music (Frost, 372), and Beckett who suggested Humphrey Searle for Katharine Worth's earlier productions of both Words and Music and Cascando. Both of these choices surely indicate respect for modern music, from which pleasure would seem likely to have followed. I have thus treated Beckett's musical taste as an open question.

25. Beckett's dissatisfaction with this "Rough" may be gauged from his refusal to grant permission for its production, even in the recent Beckett Festival of Radio Plays, directed and produced by Everett C. Frost. As Frost recalls: "In 1985 Beckett described [Rough I] as 'unfinished and now unfinishable' and requested that we not include it" (Frost, 361, footnote 2).

Tapes from the Beckett Festival, which are indispensable to a full appreciation of the plays, are available from the Pacifica Program Service, P.O. Box 8092, Universal City, CA 91608, 1–800–735–0230.

26. In a television broadcast about Samuel Beckett, Theodor Adorno represented Words and Music as "a kind of parody of the old question whether music or poetry comes closer to Truth." He then proposed to have it on Beckett's own authority that the play "clearly ends with the victory of Music." The full quotation from Adorno, as given in Zilliacus (114), is as follows: "Es gibt von ihm ja dieses Hörspiel Words and Music, das eine Art Parodie der alten Frage ist, ob die Musik oder die Dichtung mehr dans le vrai ist, und das wird von ihm auf eine sozusagen satanische Weise zugunsten der Musik entschieden, aber deshalb, weil es zu der nihilistischen Mystik von Samuel Beckett dazugehört, dass es das Wort nicht leisten kann. Er entscheidet sich sozusagen für die Musik gegen sich selber. ( . . .) Ich darf mich hier—ich möchte wirklich nicht auf persönliche Dinge rekurrieren—ich darf mich hier auf etwas beziehen, das er mir vor wenigen Tagen gesagt hat: dass es eindeutig mit dem Sieg der Musik endet." My own interpretation of Words and Music accords with Adorno's but stresses, instead of the victory of Music, the fortunes of Words in defeat.

27. Beckett himself says as much in a letter quoted by Zilliacus (118). After calling Cascando "an unimportant work, but the best I have to offer," Beckett remarks that "It does I suppose show in a way what passes for my mind and what passes for its work."

28. According to Marcel Mihalovici, the composer for Cascando in its first (French) production, Beckett did, in fact, provide the impulse or stimulus (les impulsions musicales) for the original score. In a letter to Zilliacus (131),

Mihalovici maintained that "Beckett . . . avait dirigé tout le travail. . . . Il assista même à toutes les répétitions et aux enregistrements de ma musique . . . Oui, c'est Beckett qui donna toutes les impulsions musicales de Cascando. . . ." But the same is not true of subsequent productions: namely, Katharine Worth's, with the composer Humphrey Searle; and Everett Frost's, with the composer William Kraft. Worth observes, in particular, that the "character of Music is indeed something of a mystery. There are no clues such as the 'Love and soul music' of *Words and Music*; only a dotted line to stand for the musical entries into the narrative. In our production we have assumed that Music is telling in his own language the same story told by Voice, for they have no difficulty in keeping pace at whatever point they are 'opened,' whether separately or together" (211). Whatever the extent of Beckett's collaboration with Mihalovici, the script's silence with respect to the character of Music would appear to suggest that Beckett, like the Opener, regarded himself as essentially powerless to prescribe the behavior of Music.

29. See Zilliacus (128), who follows the genesis of Voice through numerous drafts of *Cascando* (originally written in French; hence Voix): "Voix's delivery is rapid, panting: *débit rapide, haletant* says an initial direction in C2+4. The speed aimed at by the author becomes clear from C7, which contains holograph indications for the Voix exposures. We find, for instance, that the two longest exposures of Voix, *I* and *III*, are supposed to run for 1' and 40", respectively. It would require an almost superhuman effort to obey these instructions. In the BBC production, for example, Patrick Magee needed 1'52" for *I* and 1'45" for *III*. Much of the text would necessarily be lost if delivered at the speed demanded by the author. To Beckett, this is hardly an objection. Toneless, rapid, at beginning and end of play largely unintelligible voices are specifically called for in his next dramatic work, *Play*."

30. The technique of having several people speak at once, for the most part unintelligibly, was a favorite device of Glenn Gould's in the radio documentaries that he developed for the Canadian Broadcasting Corporation. Gould's first use of the technique, which he called "contrapuntal radio" (376), was in "The Idea of North" in 1967; and he defended it by analogy to music:

> The point about these scenes [in "The Idea of North"], I think, is that they test, in a sense, the degree to which one can listen simultaneously to more than one conversation or vocal impression. It's perfectly true that in that dining-car scene not every word is going to be audible, but then by no means every syllable in the final fugue from Verdi's *Falstaff* is, either, when it comes to that. Yet few opera composers have been deterred from utilizing trios, quartets, or quintets by the knowledge that only a portion of the words they set to music will be accessible to the listener—most composers being concerned primarily about the totality of the structure, the play of consonance and dissonance between the voices—and, quite apart from the fact that I do believe most of us are capable of a much more substantial information intake than we give ourselves credit for, I would like to think that these scenes can be listened to in very much the same way that you'd attend the *Falstaff* fugue (Gould, 393).

For Gould's extended discussion of his radio documentaries, see "Radio as Music: Glenn Gould in Conversation with John Jessop" (Gould, 374–88).

31. In an essay on "The Music in Samuel Beckett's *Play*," Gaburo contends that "*Play* either performs as a composition performs, with fluid motion, and without indulgence, caprice, para-sentiments, or does nothing. If one pauses, even for an instant, to meditate on a transmitted expression, a very large number of others will have passed by unnoticed. It is in the kind of attempt to fix meaning, or fix on meaning, as *Play* unfolds, which will cause it to forever be unintelligible (incomprehensible). But, if one lets go, *Play* is abundantly rich in sonority and alive with human expression and circumstance" (83).

As an interesting sidenote, it bears mention that Gaburo's essay, like *Play* itself, has roots in both music and narrative. On the one hand, his paper grew out of "a 6 month rehearsal and subsequent performance of *Play* (5.10.73) by the New Music Choral Ensemble IV" (83). On the other hand, it was published not in a journal of music, but in *The Review of Contemporary Fiction*.

32. The quotation, which is from Cage himself, comes from a conversation between Cage and *Roaratorio*'s director, Klaus Schöning. A transcript of the conversation, entitled "Laughtears," appears in the volume, *Roaratorio*, that Athenaeum published in conjunction with a cassette of the radio production. The volume and cassette were distributed together in a boxed set. For the quotation, see page 107.

33. I have quoted the words "intention" and "ideas" from the following statement by Cage: "Norman Brown said—after telling me of that book [the *Shorter Finnegans Wake*], which I haven't read—he thought that these mesostics [Cage's excerpts from the novel] were actually the best shortened version. Because there is no intention in them. They are freer. They are freer of ideas" (Cage, 83). Although citing Cage's words out of context, I trust that I have not misrepresented him.

34. Note Beckett's assessment of *Finnegans Wake*, as quoted in Kennedy, 11–12: "Here form *is* content, content *is* form. You complain that this stuff is not written in English. It is not written at all. It is not to be read—or rather it is not only to be read. It is to be looked at and listened to. His writing is not *about* something; *it is that something itself*." The comment "Here form *is* content, content *is* form" recalls Pater's observation that "It is the art of music which most completely realises this artistic ideal, this perfect identification of matter and form" (Pater, 138–39).

35. See Cory for a detailed discussion of the development of German radio drama (*Hörspiel*) from an art form with a significant visual dimension to one that is exclusively acoustical, at least at its most experimental. Cory's monograph encompasses plays, like Paul Pörtner's *Schallspielstudie I*, that "emancipat[e] sound effects from semantic domination" (26). Such plays frequently have their origins in electronic music and thus are not "capable of transmission through verbal forms" (37). As Cory explains, "the focus on the process of listening, as opposed to the mere content of what is heard, is basic to the new direction of the genre" (62).

In considering whether purely acoustical *Hörspiel* should be treated differently from those plays that exhibit "literariness," Cory reflects that to make a distinction "is a reasonable and attractive approach, for otherwise the boundary between literature and music may dissolve completely. Yet the very appeal of a clearly defined boundary may pose a substantial threat to a better understanding of both literature and music, and consequently of the *Hörspiel*" (37).

Until recently, German radio drama—experimental or otherwise—has been all but unavailable to the English-speaking public. But in 1991–92, the SoundPlay/Hörspiel series from Voices International, co-produced by Everett C. Frost and Faith Wilding, brought English translations of 19 *Hörspiele* to public radio stations throughout the United States. Five were specifically designated as experimental: *Ursonate*, by Kurt Schwitters; *Ophelia and the Words*, by Gerhard Rühm; *Five Man Humanity*, by Ernst Jandl and Friederike Mayröcker; *Radio*, by Ferdinand Kriwet; and *Wind and Sea*, by Peter Handke. And indeed, none of the five can be satisfactorily reduced to print any more than can *Roaratorio*, which was also broadcast in the series, having been commissioned by the West German Radio (WDR, Cologne) and co-produced in 1979 with the South German Radio (SDR, Stuttgart) and Dutch Catholic Radio (KDR, Hilversum).

Among those *Hörspiele* that are traditional enough to be printed as texts, seven have been published in *German Radio Plays*, ed. Frost and Herzfeld-Sander. For a discussion of this volume, see my review in the *ABR*. Also see Siegfried Mandel (145–63) for a general consideration of radio drama's significance in post-war Germany.

36. See Cage, pp. 173 and 175, for all unannotated quotations in this paragraph and the next one.

37. Note, however, that Beckett was adamant about withholding approval for a theatrical production of *All That Fall*, easily the most stage-worthy of his radio plays. In a letter quoted by Zilliacus, Beckett writes: *"All That Fall* is specifically a radio play, or rather radio text, for voices, not bodies. I have already refused to have it 'staged' and I cannot think of it in such terms. A perfectly straight reading before an audience seems to me just barely legitimate, though even on this score, I have my doubts. But I am absolutely opposed to any form of adaptation with a view to its conversion into 'theatre.' It is no more theatre than *End-Game* is radio and to 'act' it is to kill it. Even the reduced visual dimension it will receive from the simplest and most static of readings . . . will be destructive of whatever quality it may have and which depends on the whole thing's coming out of the dark . . ."* (Zilliacus, frontispiece). Given the fragility of the music made by words in *All That Fall*, Beckett was probably right to suggest that to act the play would be to kill it. For acting would necessarily emphasize the narrative, to the destruction of the music.

## Chapter Four: *Wings* and *A Slight Ache*

1. All quotations from *Wings* are cited from the published text of the stage play. I have used the fifth printing, which differs slightly from the first in pagination. Kopit's prefatory material, his stage directions, and his interpretive comments are quoted verbatim, although I have not always followed the text's use

of capital letters and italics. As for citations from the dialogue, they have been emended to correspond with the Earplay broadcast of *Wings* as a radio play. (See note 2 below for information on that broadcast.)

With respect to individual speeches, the differences between the stage play and the radio play tend to be slight. But in transferring *Wings* from the radio to the stage, Kopit added some material (most of pages 29 through 33, for instance), omitted some (see, for instance, notes 10, 12 and 13 below) and reorganized some (principally, pages 35 through 45). Overall, then, the published text of *Wings* is only roughly faithful to the radio version. Still, to read the play as published is to approximate the radio play if one is careful to discount patently inapplicable stage directions.

For a summary and discussion of the textual differences between *Wings* on the radio and *Wings* on the stage, see Edgerton, whose essay includes extensive quotations from an interview with John Madden, director of both productions.

2. According to the Preface, Kopit received his commission from Earplay in the fall of 1976. *Wings* was then released for broadcast—that is, vinyl disks of the play were distributed to stations affiliated with National Public Radio—in August or September of 1977. Since the affiliated stations were free to broadcast *Wings* (or not, as they chose) at any time during the 1977–78 Earplay season, no date of original broadcast for the radio play can be ascertained.

It would appear, however, that some stations put *Wings* on the air very soon after receiving it. At any rate, again according to the Preface, Robert Brustein (then Dean of the Yale School of Drama) had heard the radio play by November of 1977, when he invited Kopit to transfer *Wings* to the stage (Preface, xvi). The transfer was accomplished so expeditiously that when *Wings* was first performed at the Yale Repertory Theatre on 3 March 1978, it had not yet been broadcast on WGBH in Boston, where the Earplay season had been put off until May (personal communication).

Popular with audiences, *Wings*-the-stage-play has been performed around the world, with notable runs in New York and in London. It has even been reconceived as a musical (book and lyrics by Arthur Perlman; music by Jeffrey Lunden; original production by the Goodman Theatre, Chicago, Illinois, October 1992). But whatever the virtues of *Wings* on the stage, only the radio version, as I argue below, enables the audience fully to participate in Emily's experience and hence to appreciate the questions *Wings* poses about the nature of both knowledge and perception.

3. The opening of *Wings* on the radio may be regarded as a veritable Rorschach test in sound, evoking from first-time listeners an astonishing range of responses. As a measure of how far these responses can stray from the true import of the scene, consider one listener's suggestion that the sounds represent a woman having intercourse, or possibly masturbating. Only in retrospect—that is, only on second hearing—does this interpretation seem necessarily bizarre.

4. In this context, see Kelley, who interprets *Wings* as a play about the limitations of language, a work that "prompt[s] us to question how the difficulties with communication and information acquisition and dissemination inherent to our society and literature might be related to illness, personal autonomy and external restraints" (385). Confining her interpretation solely to *Wings* as per-

formed on a stage, Kelley understands Emily to reject "ordered discourse" (387), but not—as I argue with respect to the radio play—empirical reality itself.

So strongly does the stage in *Wings* reinforce our faith in both the world and our ability to know it empirically that, according to Auerbach, Emily is not "cut off from the world" (104) by her aphasia. And yet Auerbach also quotes Kopit's observation that "'Language is more than a form of communication; it's one of the ways of knowing'" (106). If Emily, then, loses language, must she not also lose one way of knowing the world that she inhabits? Though Auerbach pointedly glosses Kopit's comment as follows—"Like the philosopher Wittgenstein, Kopit knows that only by understanding the structure and limits of language will we learn the structure and limits of thought" (106)—still she does not use this insight in interpreting *Wings*, no doubt because thought has little to do with *Wings*-on-the-stage, though it matters immensely to *Wings*-on-the-radio.

5. As Kopit makes clear in his Notes on *Wings*' production, disembodiment is exactly the effect he intended, even on stage: "It is posited by this play that the woman we see in the center of the void is the intact inner self of Mrs. Stilson. This inner self does not need to move physically when her external body (which we cannot see) moves. Thus, we infer movement from the context; from whatever clues we can obtain" (3). Much depends, then, in a stage performance on the audience's willingness to regard what is seen as inaccessible to sight—an awkward endeavor at best, maybe even impossible. Only look to Rich's review of the musical as performed in New York, with Linda Stephens in the starring role: "Ms. Stephens does not have the diaphanous, aged quality that made Constance Cummings so memorable in the play. . . . The conceit of 'Wings' is that the audience never sees the patient as the world sees her, as a wheelchair-bound invalid. But is Ms. Stephens such a big-boned musical-theater presence that we too often forget that Emily the patient exists?" (4). Perhaps. Yet the fault may as easily lie not so much with Ms. Stephens's particular presence as with the tendency of any presence (even Ms. Cummings's) to insist upon itself for its own sake, rather than the sake of a metaphor. If Emily's body is meant to be invisible, she is best apprehended on radio, where she literally cannot be seen.

6. Both on stage and on radio, *Wings* is meant to be played without any interruption. Hence its divisions in the printed text—Prelude, Catastrophe, Awakening, and Explorations—are imperceptible in performance, except insofar as they may influence an actress's interpretation of Emily as a role.

7. For a good overview of those features of early aviation that figure in *Wings*, see Roseberry—in particular, chapter 4, "The Rollicking Barnstormers," and chapter 33, "Sisters of the Blue Yonder."

8. Consider, for example, this haunting sentence from the first chapter, "The Craft": "And yet we have all known flights when of a sudden, each for himself, it has seemed to us that we have crossed the border of the world of reality; when, only a couple of hours from port, we have felt ourselves more distant from it than we should feel if we were in India; when there has come a premonition of an incursion into a forbidden world whence it was going to be infinitely difficult to return" (25). It seems likely that *Wind, Sand and Stars* constituted a source for Kopit in his depiction of Emily. There are apparent

appeals to the memoir, for instance, not only in Emily's amazement that she weathered terrifying flight conditions without fear (see note 9 below), but also in her references to a crash in the desert (23–24) and to a "cyclone [that] must've blown in on the Andes from the sea" (58)—precisely the conditions Saint Exupéry describes in his chapters "Prisoner of the Sand" and "The Elements." Moreover, the ending of *Wings* is especially reminiscent of Saint Exupéry: in particular, Emily's reluctance, in flying at night, to stop circling a small town that beckons from below—"I just can't give it up, . . . just can't bring myself to give it up" (76)—and her subsequent joy in the act of breaking free. These emotions are similar to those expressed in the following passage from "Prisoner of the Sand," where Saint Exupéry confesses to "know nothing, nothing in the world, equal to the wonder of nightfall in the air": "I, too, in this flight, am renouncing things. I am giving up the broad golden surfaces that would befriend me if my engines were to fail. I am giving up the landmarks by which I might be taking my bearings. I am giving up the profiles of mountains against the sky that would warn me of pitfalls. I am plunging into the night. I am navigating. I have on my side only the stars" (184).

9. Compare Saint Exupéry: "And this spectacle [of a four-hour flight through tornadoes] was so overwhelming that only after he had gotten through the Black Hole did Mermoz awaken to the fact that he had not been afraid" (26).

10. This information emerges on radio in a speech that Kopit omitted from the stage play. The full text of the speech, which continues on from "The room that I've been put in this time" (31), is as follows: "The room that I've been put in this time is quite large square, what does large mean? . . . Two reasons why it's hard for me to turn. One, I'm missing half my arms and legs, yes it's true, very weird I know. Two, they've strapped me down. Three, the tubes get in the way, something wrong there. Four reasons why it's hard for me to . . ." The monologue then picks up on page 33 at "This is not a hospital of course."

11. What Rich observes in his review of the musical is true, though to a lesser extent, of the play: "As Emily improves a bit, 'Wings' sinks into the shopworn language, predictable narrative and mechanical uplift of a television disease-of-the-week movie" (4).

It is the banality of the stage play's realistic scenes that accounts, I think, for Carol Rosen's criticism of *Wings* as "overwhelmingly literal" in its "social setting" (79) and hence incapable of "achiev[ing] a transition from the particular to the general, . . . [incapable of] transforming societal facts into conceits, [of] reacting to grueling, patterned life as if it were a song" (80). However valid these criticisms may be for *Wings*-the-stage-play, they have little bearing on *Wings*-the-radio-play, where the social setting is firmly subordinated to the conceit, the song, of Emily's flight.

12. The quotation, which comes from the radio broadcast and not the printed text, is part of Emily's "Stop hold cut stop" monologue (26). The relevant passage on radio goes as follows: "Something under way about to see I think I hope would expect so going slowly just a knife slit opening of light but getting bigger getting larger I can almost see the place I'm in and oh my God oh my God now I see now I understand they've got me oh my God."

13. In the stage version of *Wings*, the words in question appear only once, near the end of the play, where their effect is benign. In the radio version, by contrast, they open the play as well as end it. And when heard early on (namely, in the Catastrophe section among the "Sounds outside herself"), the words are unsettling, even menacing—all the more so for being unclear: "[something incomprehensible] how you changed your mind." On radio, then, the words serve not only to announce *Wings*' theme, but also its shape—that is, its movement from fear and confusion to clarity and peace.

14. All quotations from *A Slight Ache* are cited from *A Slight Ache and Other Plays*. The play's first broadcast was on the BBC Third Programme on 29 July 1959.

15. Among critics of *A Slight Ache*, opinion is divided on the extent to which the play embraces Flora's perspective on the matchseller or reveals much of moment about Flora herself. Powlick is persuaded that "the play speaks to us from Edward's point of view" (27) so completely that Flora "is not an objective character, but only a projection of Edward's awareness" (30). This bias, to my mind, mars an otherwise sensitive reading of the play by forcing Powlick to interpret Flora's meeting with the matchseller solely through Edward's eyes, even though Edward is not present to observe it. Still, Powlick's response to *A Slight Ache* is reminiscent of Trussler's opinion that "the play's crucial weakness may well lie in [the] under-development of Flora" (*Pinter*, 61), as well as Burkman's contention that "the drama is conceived as an *agon* between the two men. A ritual reading of the play suggests not that the matchseller is Edward's projection but that he is another aspect of Edward, who in one sense plays both roles" (49). Even Diamond, while opining that Flora is "no mere pawn," remarks that she is "nevertheless used by the playwright to support the situation developed in the Edward-Matchseller interviews" (39). For critics like these, Flora's role in the play is supportive or peripheral rather than central.

As might be expected, Flora looms somewhat larger for Sakellaridou and Cahn, who address *A Slight Ache* in the context of gender issues in Pinter. But even critics with no special interest in gender have accorded Flora equal weight with Edward. Thus, Sykes proposes that "*A Slight Ache* is only in part about Edward's self-destruction; the play as a whole shows how two people react in totally different ways to the same deliberately negative force or being (like Ionesco's Killer, possibly he does not exist at all?) and under pressure of his presence, reveal themselves, and the nature of their relationship" (45–46). As for Esslin, he observes that "the Matchseller is a product of the *two characters'* fevered imaginations rather than a real person and that the play is an extended and complex poetic metaphor, a *concertized* image of the feelings and emotions of a middle-aged married couple in the face of the actual, imagined, or longed-for death of the male partner" ("Harold Pinter's Work for Radio," 50, my emphasis).

My own reading of the play, though related to Powlick's in stressing perception, yet rests on the premise that Edward and Flora are each of them observers, fully independent and equally matched.

16. See Ooi for a cogent reading of *A Slight Ache* based on the premise that "Edward has, in the common phrase, made nothing of himself, and he will come

to nothing. The black joke of Pinter's play is that Nothing, the Matchseller, *Le Néant*, his Nemesis comes for him and he comes to be *Le Néant*" (133).

17. Because literary critics, in assessing *A Slight Ache*, have largely attended to the play in its stage version, they have generally overlooked the play's adamant refusal to verify even so much as the matchseller's physical existence. Thus, Trussler argues that "since the Matchseller is undeniably, physically *there* in any stage production, for his movements are clearly indicated in the directions—his solidity, if not his reality, must necessarily be accepted" (*Pinter*, 59). Similarly, Gale proposes that "Questioning [the matchseller's] existence is unjustified for two reasons: first, the matchseller is included as a character in the stage directions of the stage version, so he exists by definition; second, and more important, the other two characters act as though he exists" (80). In his second reason, Gale echoes Hayman, who seems almost critical of radio for putting "the reality of the matchseller . . . in doubt": "Obviously he isn't a fantasy because Edward and Flora both see him and speak to him and Flora feels him" (44). Just so. But it is radio's genius, not its defect, to be able to convey the idea that one character's responses to another are not alone sufficient to make the second character's existence either necessary or obvious.

Significantly, those critics who have given extended attention to *A Slight Ache* on radio have recognized the matchseller's existence as impossible to verify—or, for that matter, disprove. Esslin, for example, observes that "one of the main sources of the impact of the play on radio is the element of uncertainty as to whether the Matchseller actually exists in the flesh. . . . The mystery surrounding that question is an essential element in the play. We are meant to wonder about it, to remain uncertain" ("Harold Pinter's Work on Radio," 50–51). For Esslin, however, the ambiguity inherent in the matchseller's existence bears not on the nature of human perception, but on the "undefined dread waiting outside the enclosed, seemingly safe space of the characters' private world" (51). It is Wertheim who proposes that in *A Slight Ache* "Pinter has written a drama about seeing, about insight, and about vision" (69), with the result that we must ask ourselves: "Is *A Slight Ache* a Chinese box in which a radio audience mentally see characters they do not see physically, and these characters in turn mentally see a character they do not see physically? The question is a marvelously vexed one and one that goes to the heart of Pinter's dramaturgy" (70).

18. Originally conceived as a radio play, *Herr Biedermann und die Brandstifter* was first broadcast by Bayrische Rundfunk on 26 March 1953 (Butler, 80). As a stage play, it opened in Zurich on 29 March 1958. Thus, Pinter could well have known, or known of, *Biedermann* when he wrote *A Slight Ache*, which was commissioned in July 1958 and delivered to the BBC in October of that same year (see Esslin, "Harold Pinter's Work for Radio," 48). Still, it must be conceded that Pinter completed *A Slight Ache* before *Biedermann* had received English-language productions in London, first on BBC Radio (13 June 1961), then on stage at the Royal Court (21 December 1961). The connection that I posit between *A Slight Ache* and *Biedermann* may thus be coincidental.

If so, the coincidence is compounded by Heilman's positing of similarities between *Biedermann* and still another Pinter play of 1958—namely, *The Birthday*

*Party.* Note, too, that in an interview with Bensky ("Harold Pinter: An Interview," 29), Pinter related this curious anecdote about *The Caretaker,* first staged in 1960:

> I had a terrible dream, after I'd written *The Caretaker,* about the two brothers. My house burned down in the dream, and I tried to find out who was responsible. I was led through all sorts of alleys and cafés and eventually I arrived at an inner room somewhere and there were the two brothers from the play. And I said, so you burned down my house. They said don't be too worried about it, and I said I've got everything in there, everything, you don't realize what you've done, and they said it's all right, we'll compensate you for it, we'll look after you all right—the younger brother was talking— and thereupon I wrote them out a check for fifty quid . . . *I* gave *them* a check for fifty quid!

Here again are shades of *Biedermann,* a play in which Schmitz is all but rewarded for the devastation that he threatens and eventually commits.

19. All quotations from *Biedermann and the Firebugs* are cited from Bullock's translation, which uses the British title *The Fire Raisers.* Page numbers are cited in the text and preceded, as here, by the letter B.

20. Pinter, "Writing for the Theatre," 576. In a subsequent paragraph, again relevant to *A Slight Ache,* Pinter notes that "We will all interpret a common experience quite differently, though we prefer to subscribe to the view that there's a shared common ground, a known ground. I think there's a shared common ground all right, but that it's more like a quicksand. Because 'reality' is quite a strong firm word we tend to think, or to hope, that the state to which it refers is equally firm, settled and unequivocal. It doesn't seem to be, and in my opinion, it's no worse or better for that" (576–77).

## Chapter Five: *Cries from Casement*

1. All quotations to *Cries from Casement* are cited from the BBC edition of the play—the only version ever published, and now out of print. The play's first broadcast was on BBC Radio 3 on 4 February 1973.

2. The quotation is from "The Chameleon & the Kilt," 72. All further quotations from the essay will be indicated in the text by a page number preceded by "Kilt."

3. For Rudkin's assessment of the diaries, see "Postface to 'Casement'."

4. See "The Chameleon & the Kilt," 71. Rudkin takes pains in this essay not only to argue the validity of his theory about Casement's homosexuality, but also to justify the liberties he has taken with historical fact. Thus, where Inglis contends that Rudkin's portrayal of Casement "as an out-and-out jingo at the play's start is historically imprecise," Rudkin responds that, as a dramatist, he has reason to de-emphasize Casement's early "Irish separatist streak." As Rudkin puts it, "unlike the subject of a biography, the hero of a play travels across an inner *evolutionary* distance; he cannot always be seen as humping contradictory baggages across the years" (72). Nonetheless, for all that Rudkin seeks a poetic

(rather than a factual) truth about Casement—a quest that sets him well apart from Inglis—he praises the biography as "excellent" and describes himself as "struck [by] how similar Mr. Inglis' consciousness seemed to mine . . . [in its] peculiarly Anglo-Irish passion" (71).

5. For Rudkin's assessment of the RSC production, see "Thoughts on Staging the Play," a brief essay appended to the published script of *Cries from Casement*. As Rudkin reports, significant changes, some of them structural, were required to make the play work on the stage. Because, for example, a "solemn and melancholy mood cannot be sustained [in the theater] for long" (82), the figures from the past who apologize to Casement as he lies in state in Dublin were entirely cut out, and the visitations from other figures were reduced. In addition the "Author's lecture in V was broken up, and parts of it transplanted" (82); "various aspects of Casement [were] shared out between different actors, so that his disparate personae [were] separately embodied" (83); and "the history sequence, VII . . . was divided up and interleaved throughout the play" (83). Although none of these changes can fairly be said to have desecrated the script, they certainly changed it considerably, in ways that Rudkin analyzes deftly in "Thoughts."

6. Reid remarks that "Casement's nature was divided to a depth just short of real pathology, of disastrous incoherence. Was he an Irishman or an Englishman; an Irish patriot or an English public servant; a countryman or a cityman; a man of the people or a gentleman; an Irish peasant or an Irish senator; an intellectual or an artist; an intellectual or a man of action; an idealist or a pragmatist; a sensualist or an anchorite; an African or a European; a Protestant or a Catholic; a man or a woman; a man or a boy? He did not know: he was all of them" (454).

7. This detail appears to come from the report of a spectator describing Casement in the dock: "His hand, white and thin, almost womanish, quivered" (MacColl, p. 187; quotation unattributed). By assigning the comment to Casement himself, Rudkin emphasizes the justice of using a feminine voice to speak for Casement the patriot.

8. Actually, the remark is made by Crippen, Casement's Pentonville gravemate, with respect to the exchange of words between the corpses. But so minimal is the dialogue between Casement and Crippen that the remark seems intended to apply to the play as a whole.

9. The remark, which is quoted in Inglis (384), is from the dedication to *Casement's Last Adventure*, Monteith's semi-autobiographical account of his (and Casement's) activities in Germany, on the high seas, and in Ireland in the months before the Easter Rising.

10. Or if not Casement, then Rudkin on Casement's behalf. For as Rudkin has observed, "I don't see why, *a priori*, a national hero has to be a 'pure' man" ("Postface," 171).

11. Rudkin's judicious editing may well make Casement seem a better rhetorician than he was in real life. None of Casement's biographers has much respect for Casement's writing; and Reid is particularly harsh. He maintains, for example, that "Casement's eloquence was rarely genuine, rarely subjected to reflection or reason. Commonly it was close to bombast: pretentious diction,

false heat and false color, a bludgeoning style that hid its loose thinking and loose feeling, its poverty of evidence and argument, under a noise of verbal forms" (163). In Reid's opinion, "one has to fight through Casement's writings to the finer man. He had a ready flux of words not really grounded in knowledge, hence he was verbal but not fundamentally articulate. He wrote in meretricious forms of true feelings" (34). Nevertheless, what we hear in the play is frequently Casement's own language, edited or not; and the effect, if only through Rudkin's art, is usually thrilling.

12. Of the gongstroke, and indeed the whole panorama, Rudkin has written as follows: "When I got to ' . . inly am' at the end of the Murlough Strand scene, I heard a massive gong-stroke in my head; and I think the oscillation-alternation rhythm of the history sequence was an evolution of the wave-rhythm in the preceding scene. The history lesson was inevitable: nothing and no one in Ireland makes sense, without reference to history; and that history begins at the beginning. Also, most people think that Ulster only 'began' to be a problem in 1922, or perhaps 1690. It needed saying that Ulster was a difficult part of Ireland from very ancient times. The intended effect of the sequence was of a massive gathering torrent of cruelty and suffering and blood, with the innocuous name of Casement suddenly bobbing up on the tide of it" (letter to me from Rudkin dated 10 November 1988).

13. See Rudkin, "Thoughts on Staging the Play," 83.

14. Rudkin writes that "Elgar is an ambiguous figure: he has one face and voice that address an Imperialist England; he also has a private, tragic, tortured self. This ambivalence was in the music all along; it has taken biographers a very long time to catch up with it" (letter to me from Rudkin dated 10 November 1988). Rudkin's sense of Elgar's complexity accords with his patently ironic use of the composer's most imperialistic music—the " 'Land of Hope and Glory' tune from Elgar Pomp and Circumstance March Number One, its grandest appearance"—as the background for the "Statistics of Dublin Rising" (42).

15. The statement is paraphrased from remarks that Rudkin made to me in conversation.

16. Quoted in Itzin, 185, from the edition of Ashes published by Pluto Press, London, 1978.

17. Several days after Cries was first broadcast, Rudkin published an essay conceding that his "conception of Casement was more contentious than any other I had seen proposed. With Ireland racked by old polarities and bitterness again, I felt it would be irresponsible to put forward such a disputatious view without forcibly reminding the audience that this was my Casement. I must find means, within the play, constantly to reassert my authoric responsibility for him, and, at a good juncture, present my justification" ("Postface," 171). Hence Rudkin introduced himself, as the Author, into Sequences III and V—a device that the radio nicely accommodates.

Some fifteen years later Rudkin reiterated the necessity of "put[ting him]self into the play," but added that in "the context of the time, this was a potentially suicidal thing for me to do—it was a time of terrible sectarian murders—and it was as much for superstitious reasons that [at the end of Sequence V] I dramatized violence to myself (to prevent it actually happening), as much as to remove myself from the play now that my work as this Casement's 'creator' was done" (letter to me from Rudkin dated 10 November 1988).

Was Rudkin right to fear reprisals? The question is moot. But to judge from the reflections of Etherton as late as 1989, *Cries from Casement* must have had a fair potential for striking the Irish the wrong way. As Etherton would have it, "the intersection of sexual and the political themes, in [Rudkin's] drama, is grounded in a philosophical view which is uniquely English: libertarian, pragmatic, non-ideological. It is the composure of a dominant, colonising culture" (31). In fact, Etherton could hardly be further from the mark, since Rudkin is thoroughly disdainful of dominant, colonising cultures. Yet Etherton's faulty conclusion has at least this one virtue: it shows how readily an unconventional view of the Irish question may lend itself to misinterpretation.

In this context, it seems only fair to mention that *Cries from Casement* gave promise of offending the British no less than the Irish, since the play is implicitly a criticism of England's relation to Ireland in the early 1970s. Perhaps from a reluctance to incur official wrath—or perhaps solely from the fear that Irish violence would ensue from a broadcast in which Casement was depicted as homosexual—the BBC held back *Cries from Casement* for some eighteen months after the play was recorded. Indeed, the length of the delay gave rise to suspicions that the Corporation intended to suppress the play entirely—a difficult decision to have taken, since the cast included prominent BBC figures who would no doubt have raised a storm of protest against censorship. (See the "Distribution of Parts" published at the end of the script, in which Rudkin indicates that the English and German Announceresses, the two World-at-One commentators, and the radio talk show host Joan Bakewell "were each played by themselves" [79].) In the end, however, the play was freely, if tardily, released by the BBC—without incident, and to critical acclaim.

## Chapter Six: *Pearl* and *The Bagman*

1. The words in quotation marks serve as *Pearl*'s subtitle in its published edition (Eyre Methuen). All quotations from the play are cited in the text by page number. *Pearl*'s first broadcast was on BBC Radio 4 on 3 July 1978.

2. When first broadcast in 1970, *The Bagman* was apparently thought to be benign, not only by reviewers, but even by its director, Martin Esslin, who is said to have regarded it as "Arden's farewell to political commitment" (Hunt, 150; see also Gray on Esslin, 67). Of these mistaken notions, Arden himself has since commented that "I was interpreted by some critics at the time as absolving the playwright from having anything to do in society. I don't believe that, and I didn't believe it then. The play is a satire, a self-satire; if I were writing it now I would try to make that clearer" (quoted in Page, *Arden on File*, 62; for similar sentiments, see also Arden's Preface to *Two Autobiographical Plays*, 17). Perhaps, roughly speaking, Arden does bear some responsibility for misconstructions of *The Bagman*, insofar as the fairy-tale atmosphere of the play may enamor its

listeners into thinking it lighthearted. But as I attempt to establish in the following analysis, the play's allusions to Bunyan provide strong internal evidence that *The Bagman* is satiric and that it engages what Page has aptly called Arden's "crises of conscience" (*John Arden*, 105).

3. All quotations from *The Bagman* are cited from Arden's *Two Autobiographical Plays*, with page numbers preceded, as here, by the letter B. The play's first broadcast was on BBC Radio 3 on 27 March 1970.

4. In his "Author's Note" to *Pearl*, Arden writes that "There is something finally futile, I suppose, about plays that are written from the premise: 'If only it had happened otherwise . . .' But so long as . . . [here follow examples of misguided behavior by the English toward Ireland] . . . then maybe there is still good reason for re-examining an earlier period of history when disastrous decisions were taken for the most plausible motives, when everyone was aware that the times were highly critical, and yet so few could divest themselves of their erroneous received ideas." The comment suggests that *Pearl* does, after all, raise the question of ends—as naturally it must, at least to the extent that, in writing the play, Arden wanted English audiences to learn from their history with Ireland rather than repeat it. (To this same extent, *Pearl* exemplifies the activism that Arden appeals for in drama.) But as the end that *Pearl* promotes is entirely straightforward, whereas its sense of how to reach that end is very deeply vexed, the question of means appears to be paramount.

For an essay that considers the relationship among theater, history, and politics in *Pearl*, see Bas, who remarks that *Pearl*'s true subject is the theater itself, even though the play also addresses the current Irish problem by making reference to the English Civil War: "cette pièce, . . . tout en évoquant la première révolution anglaise afin de proposer une solution mettant fin à la tragédie irlandaise, a peut-être pour vrai sujet le théâtre lui-même" (425). Bas contends that, through Backhouse, Arden criticizes bourgeois theater, which takes for its subject feelings rather than politics: "Il est évident qu'à travers ce collègue du dix-septième siècle, le néobrechtien qu'est Arden exprime sa condamnation d'une dramaturgie dont les éléments majeurs—*hamartia* du héros tragique, 'sympathie' ou pitié, *catharsis*—constituent les germes du théâtre 'bourgeois' dans lequel sévissent toujours la psychologie, l'émotion et le sentiment" (433). As for Ireland, Bas observes that *Pearl*'s solutions to the country's predicament are better suited to the twentieth century than to the seventeenth: "Il est clair qu'Arden pense davantage ici à une solution pour la fin du XXe siècle que pour la période pré-révolutionnaire qui est celle de *Pearl*" (429).

5. *Pearl* would seem to be the play that Arden forecasts in his "Author's Preface" to *Two Autobiographical Plays*, when he notes that "I considered rewriting the last part of [*The Bagman*] but I decided against this, because it does reflect fairly enough the state of my mind in the spring of 1969: and I thought it would be better to demonstrate my opinions of 1971 in a new play—which is not yet written" (16–17). *Pearl* was first broadcast on BBC Radio in July of 1978, some seven years after the publication of this preface in 1971.

6. Although the words are Grip's, the sentiments are shared by Pearl and hence may be attributed to her. That she does not restate Grip's formulation testifies

to the economy of *Pearl's* script. As the play had to fit a conventional two-hour time slot for BBC Radio, Arden had little latitude for repetition.

Even so, scenes 5 and 9 were substantially abridged for the BBC broadcast—and not only for reasons of length, according to Bas, but also from political considerations: "Les coupures substantielles effectuées ne furent point toutes dictées par la longueur excessive du texte originel: certaines choses ne pouvaient être dites sur les ondes de la BBC. Il faut donc croire qu'Arden accepta de s'auto-censurer" (footnote 7, page 428). Bas's speculation has the ring of truth, given that, by Arden's own report, the BBC had previously cut "a whole chunk of dialogue and a song referring to the Irish Rising of 1798" from a radio version of Arden's and D'Arcy's *The Hero Rises Up*. Moreover, the BBC had also declined Arden's proposal to write a radio play about "James Connolly, who was shot as a 'terrorist' in 1916 by the British Army. The very idea was rejected out of hand. It might, said Mr Esslin's shamefaced letter, 'inflame passions' in the North of Ireland" (untitled review by Arden in *Plays and Players*).

In any case, whatever the reasons for the BBC's foreshortening of scenes 5 and 9, *Pearl's* published text restores the cuts while indicating, in two appendices, what transpired on the air. The few other deviations from the published text that occurred in the broadcast are inconsequential.

7. Pearl's impression of the theater as constituting her own "immediate carnal need" (24) should probably be taken literally. For she becomes Backhouse's mistress only upon his completion of their play, as if the one consummation produces the other.

8. For a good overview of the numerous (and varied) critical controversies provoked by the Pearl-poem, see Conley, ed., *The Middle English Pearl; Critical Essays*. Of particular note in relation to Arden is Robertson's "The 'Heresy' of *The Pearl*," which attempts to refute the contention that the Pearl-poet's "interpretation of the Parable of the Vineyard includes the 'heresy of Jovinian,' to the effect that there is no differentiation in status in the celestial Jerusalem" (291). Given that Arden's own *Pearl* entertains severe doubts about the world's beneficence, there would seem to be a special propriety—or, at any rate, irony—in the play's appeal, for consolation, to a poem that has itself been accused (and only possibly acquitted) of proffering false hope.

9. Pearl, for her own part, understands her dream differently: namely, as an omen that the King's forces will overcome the Parliamentarians before the latter have so much as fired their first shot by producing Backhouse's "Esther." Such an interpretation, though reasonable in context, proves painfully naive by the end of the play.

10. Imperfection, in fact, is all but guaranteed, to judge from Arden's comment in an interview with Peck nearly twelve years before *Pearl's* first broadcast in July 1978: "Protest," Arden said, "is a sort of futile activity in the theater. I would be very doubtful that plays of protest succeed in doing anything very successful." Even so, Arden held that "it's very necessary that it should be done. . . . I think the only thing you can do is to keep on saying what you don't like about the society in which you live, so that even if the forces that one objects to . . . finally win . . . , one will at least be able to say, 'Well, I did get up and

say no before it was too late.'" These observations, offered by Arden apropos of *Serjeant Musgrave's Dance*, are surely relevant to *Pearl*, if only insofar as they provide us with a measure of exactly how much (or how little) the playwrights of the subtext may reasonably be expected to achieve.

11. In the following paragraphs, *Julius Caesar* is explored solely for what it can demonstrate about the value of drama as an instrument of politics. This approach, however, hardly exhausts the play's relationship to *Pearl*. The two plays, for example, have major themes in common. Thus, just as *Julius Caesar* depicts the efforts of conspirators "to control history" (Mack, 296), so too does *Pearl*. And just as *Julius Caesar* attributes the conspirators' failure to their having been "blinded . . . by the very idealism that impelled" them (Mack, 297), so again does *Pearl*.

12. Arden himself subscribes to this view, to judge from his comments on Shakespeare in "Playwrights and Play-writers." In particular, while seeking to establish that *Henry V* is covertly critical of Henry's war with France, Arden comments: "We must be careful not to attribute to a sixteenth-century writer any modish anti-imperialism; but conquest and bloodshed have been hated by true poets since the time of Homer, and I cannot believe that Shakespeare could have happily sat down to elevate them into a criterion of beneficent rule" (197). For more on *Henry V*, see pp. 187–88 above.

Interestingly, Arden's sense of Shakespeare's politics is borne out by Hamilton, who contends that Shakespeare shared to some extent "his patrons' ideologies" (xi) and thus would have sympathized with the likes of Leicester, Sidney, and Essex in their promotion of "certain agendas that sometimes were in conflict with official policy, agendas that sometimes were articulated by way of a rather fixed set of arguments that defended the liberties of the subject and that opposed absolutist hierarchical positions" (xii). While reticent to characterize Shakespeare as actually opposed to the monarchy, Hamilton yet maintains that he "can be identified ideologically as 'other' than simply a Tudor or Stuart apologist" (191). Thus, she describes him as "an artist who involved himself in taking positions that foster the liberties of the subject" (192)—an involvement that Arden would clearly approve.

13. The quotation, which is cited in Ripley, is from "'Theatricus,' one of the earliest American drama critics" (100). Ripley further reveals that Abigail Adams not only quoted lines from *Julius Caesar* in letters to her husband, but "sometimes . . . even signed herself 'Portia'"; and that "Thomas Jefferson's commonplace book . . . begins with six selections from *Caesar* on the life-honour-death theme" (100).

14. In "Playwrights and Play-writers," Arden reminds us of another such occasion: "Laurence Olivier's famous film [of *Henry V*], made during the Second World War as a patriotic clarion-call to a democracy fighting dictatorship" (199). The example is telling insofar as it shows Arden himself informing against the burden of *Pearl*'s nightmare.

15. For a particularly elegant investigation of Shakespeare's doubts about the theater (with occasional references to Jonson as well), see Kernan, who concludes that "Shakespeare was . . . suspended between a vision of his art as noble as the

highest Renaissance views on the subject, and questions about that art as it had to be practiced in the actual conditions of playing in the public theater" (152–53)—a conclusion that applies equally to Arden (see pp. 182–89 above).

16. *The Isle of Dogs*, "an exceedingly subversive play" on which Jonson collaborated with Thomas Nashe in 1597 (Riggs, 32), caused the Queen's Privy Council not only to close London's theaters, but also to imprison some players, Jonson among them. Eight years later, in the spring of 1605, Jonson was again imprisoned, this time for satirizing King James in *Eastward Ho*, a comedy on which he collaborated with John Marston and George Chapman (Riggs, 122–26). Of one of these scrapes with the censors, Arden has written that Jonson "went to prison for co-authorship of a seditious play: he could have got off (he had not written the offending lines), but he preferred to show his fellow-dramatists a degree of solidarity" ("Ben Jonson and the Plumb-Line," 34).

Also in "Ben Jonson and the Plumb-Line," Arden praises Jonson's learning and artistry, and furthermore seeks to acquit him of "treachery" in his activities as "an undercover informant" against fellow Catholics during the Gunpowder Plot (34). In addition, Arden reveals that "I determined [in the early 1950s] that if I were to write social comedy, Jonson was the man to follow" (33). And follow he did, as even a cursory glance at Arden's earliest stage plays, *The Waters of Babylon* and *Live Like Pigs*, makes plain. Whatever Backhouse's (really, Arden's) reservations about Jonson's masques, there is no question that Arden approves of Jonson the satirist.

17. Chute, an earlier biographer of Jonson, claims considerably less for Jonson's role in this affair. Noting that Selden had not yet met the King when he was summoned to an interview, Chute remarks only that Selden "took Ben Jonson along to make the proper introductions" (303). Still, even this limited role is not negligible. Jonson must have enjoyed a fair status at court for Selden to have trusted him to set the right tone.

On the larger issue of Jonson's "work for a stupid, self-indulgent and greedy Court," Chute observes that Jonson wrote—coincidentally, in verses to Selden—that "he had sometimes 'praised some names too much,/But 'twas with purpose to have made them such'" (278). Here Jonson frames, in his own self-defense, a justification of his court poetry as morally activist, if not politically so. In this respect, then, as in others, Jonson was a man after Arden's own heart.

18. Brereton, for example, asks: "Are we to suppose that Racine deliberately stepped outside the limits of his story to deliver a lecture on the obligations of kingship either to Louis XIV or to his young grandson?" (275). His answer, only slightly hedged, is negative: "That [Racine] held liberal views in political matters might perhaps be assumed on general grounds, although the assumption rests on nothing more concrete than the passages under consideration. . . . But let us suppose, in the absence of conclusive evidence in either direction, that he felt strongly on the subject. It is still very difficult to see him, on his own initiative, affirming his opinion in a play commissioned by those nearest to Louis and in such a form that it could hardly fail to strike the ear of the King. Racine was no *lâche flatteur*, but he had enough common prudence not to give gratuitous and premeditated offence" (276).

See also Turnell: "It strikes us at once as a remarkably bold speech; an outright condemnation of Athalie and her entourage and to later generations at all events a very outspoken criticism of the policies of Louis XIV. On the last point there must be certain reservations. It cannot be assumed that Racine was deliberately attacking his king" (319).

19. In the final chapter of *Schiller*, Sharpe explores Schiller's reputation in France, Russia, and England, noting that Schiller was "safe outside Germany from the nationalistic distortions" (324) visited upon him at home.

20. See Sharpe, 317–18: "One of the most notorious products of the attempts of the Nazi faithful to claim the classical writers for their own appeared at the end of the Weimar Republic: Hans Fabricius' *Schiller als Kampfgenosse Hitlers (Schiller, Hitler's Comrade in Arms)*. . . . Yet though the popular image of Schiller as the noble German patriot and spokesman of high ideals remained during the Third Reich, the poet was not in fact as easy to integrate as the authorities might have wished. The liberal sentiments of *Don Carlos* acquired a new resonance in the days of state control of information and the media. *Wilhelm Tell*, in the early days of the regime, a particularly favoured play, was banned by express order of the Führer himself in 1941. Goethe and Schiller emerged relatively unscathed from the Nazi period, whereas Romanticism, with its associations of nationalism and irrationalism, had a more tarnished image."

21. For those who regard Schiller's drama as "pure deeds from a blameless source," this speech must seem particularly poignant in light of Heyme's "adaptation of *Wallenstein*, staged in Cologne in 1969 . . . , as a response to the Vietnam War" (Sharpe, 331). From Heyme's cuts in the text and from the nature of his staging, Sharpe concludes that "not only does Heyme seem to be condemning the brutality of war and the delusion prevalent among those in power that they can control what happens, but he also seems to be suggesting that Schiller himself turned his back on these sordid realities in order to conform to a literary category, namely high tragedy. Tragedy itself is thus exposed as a deception practised on the audience by the dramatist" (332).

22. See D'Arcy: "When J.A. fell ill in India and the deadline for the Welsh National Theatre was rapidly approaching, he asked me to help him completely reconstruct his three TV scripts for the stage. I found that India had made me see both Ireland and Britain in an altogether new perspective. . . . The combination of these experiences and reflections made it possible for me to map out a strong line for the new version of the three plays, emphasizing the 'concrete phenomena' of eruptive social change, and relating the reactions and emotions of every character to this circumstance" (19–20).

D'Arcy's reference to the Welsh National Theatre alludes to a commission that eventually fell through. As for the RSC production of *The Island*, no mention whatsoever is made of it in the published version of the play. The Ardens do, however, speak to the matter in an essay first published in 1973 as "The *Island* Controversy at the Aldwych," then reprinted in *To Present the Pretence* as "Playwrights on Picket."

23. For contemporary journalistic accounts of these events, see Hobson, Weinraub, and Brustein. Hobson sketches both sides of the dispute between the

Ardens and the RSC without declaring an allegiance. Weinraub, whose coverage of events is fuller than Hobson's, weighs in against the Ardens. And Brustein, whose account is the most detailed of all, sharply ridicules the Ardens, as well as *The Island* in both its text and its production.

For a reasoned defense of the Ardens and the play, see "Postscript December 1972: The Island of the Mighty" in Hunt, 157–64.

24. From December 1972 through July 1978, when *Pearl* was first broadcast, the only new play to bear Arden's name was *The Non-Stop Connolly Show*. Co-authored with D'Arcy, the *Show* was produced twice—once in Dublin, March 1975; and again in London, May and June 1976—at unconventional theaters under the authors' direction.

25. In an interview published in *The Guardian* on 28 November 1972 just before *The Island* opened, Arden himself made the following comment about D'Arcy's effect on his work in the theater:

> I've never regarded myself as anything but a writer. I have never seen myself as a director or political agitator but I've never been satisfied that the writer's role should simply involve sitting behind a typewriter. I've always wanted to be involved with more practical activities without having to initiate them, and so, in that way, our collaboration has enabled me to do a kind of writing which otherwise I would never have done.
>
> The kind of theatre that we do together is very nerve wracking and involves a much closer relationship with the audience and the public at large than writing plays for theatres in London. I think this ought to be done, although I'm not very happy about having to do it. . . . Yet I do think this is a direction in which the theatre ought to go. I probably wouldn't have found myself involved in this kind of theatre if it had not been for Margaretta D'Arcy (quoted in Page, *Arden on File*, 89–90).

The tone here is markedly ambivalent, though the sentiment being expressed is strongly held. Compare, in this regard, Lambert's assessment of those of Arden's essays in *To Present the Pretence* that discuss the difficulties that Arden and D'Arcy have encountered in conventional theaters: "Even when, as I suspect in these cases, he has much right on his side, the sense is somehow given of a man striking, in support of causes in which he does believe, attitudes in which he does not believe" (253).

26. One of these plays, *The Old Man Sleeps Alone*, won a Giles Cooper Award in 1982.

27. Gray observes of *Pearl* that it "was performed in a medium for which it was not originally conceived, that of radio" (145), while Trussler observes that "it is to the shame of the British theatre and to the honour of [Alfred] Bradley [the play's director] and the BBC that this work found its first production on radio" (*Stage and Television*, 16). The implication is that *Pearl* was written for the theater, but failed to find a home there.

28. Gielgud notes that "there is some conflict of opinion as to when the first radio-dramatic transmission in Great Britain actually took place [whether 2 September 1922 or 16 February 1923]. . . . In any case, there seems to be

agreement that the dramatist was Shakespeare, and that scenes were chosen from *Julius Caesar* . . . from *King Henry VIII* . . . and from *Much Ado about Nothing*" (17).

29. Even Bunyan has had performances on radio. In addition to numerous straightforward readings, *The Pilgrim's Progress* has been dramatized by the BBC about once every decade since the early 1930s.

30. Quotations from this essay will be cited in the text, with page numbers preceded by the letters PP.

31. As Arden puts it in a roughly contemporaneous comment: "The *content* of new plays is obscured and neutralized by over-emphasis on aesthetic theatrical *form*" (quoted in Kitchin, 46).

32. All quotations to Arden from here through the end of the chapter are drawn from the *Sunday Times* essay, which is entitled "Plays in the Theatre of the Mind."

# Works Cited

Adcock, Craig E. *Marcel Duchamp's Notes from the* Large Glass: *An N-Dimensional Analysis*. Ann Arbor: UMI Research Press, 1983.

*The Almost Complete Works of Marcel Duchamp*. Intro. Richard Hamilton. Catalog of exhibition at the Tate Gallery, 18 June to 31 July 1966. London: Arts Council, 1966.

Antin, David. "Duchamp and Language." d'Harnoncourt and McShine 99–115.

Apollinaire, Guillaume. "Duchamp." *Marcel Duchamp in Perspective*. Ed. Joseph Masheck. Englewood Cliffs: Prentice-Hall, 1975. 25–26.

Arden, John. *The Bagman or The Impromptu of Muswell Hill. Two Autobiographical Plays* 35–88.

———. "Ben Jonson and the Plumb-Line." *To Present the Pretence* 25–36.

———. *Pearl: A Play about a Play within the Play*. London: Eyre Methuen, 1979.

———. "Plays in the Theatre of the Mind," *Sunday Times* 22 Aug. 82: 31.

———. "Playwrights and Play-Writers." *To Present the Pretence* 173–212.

———. "Playwrights on Picket (Written in Collaboration with Margaretta D'Arcy)." *To Present the Pretence* 159–72. (Originally published as "The *Island* Controversy at the Aldwych." *Performance* 2.1 (1973): 11–20.)

———. *To Present the Pretence: Essays on the Theatre and Its Public*. London: Eyre Methuen, 1977.

———. *Two Autobiographical Plays*. London: Methuen, 1971.

———. [untitled contribution to the journal's monthly review of radio drama] *Plays and Players* 19 (1971): 59.

Arnheim, Rudolf. *Radio*. London: Faber and Faber, 1936. History of Broadcasting: Radio to Television. New York: Arno Press and the New York Times, 1971.

Auerbach, Doris. *Sam Shepard, Arthur Kopit, and the Off Broadway Theater*. Boston: Twayne, 1982.

Bailey, Walter B. *Programmatic Elements in the Works of Schoenberg*. Studies in Musicology 74. Ann Arbor: UMI Research Press, 1984.

Barker, Howard. *Arguments for a Theatre*. London: John Calder; New York: Riverrun, 1989.

———. *The Castle; Scenes from an Execution*. London: John Calder; New York: Riverrun, 1985.

Bas, Georges. "Théâtre, histoire et politique dans une pièce radiophonique: *Pearl* (1978), de John Arden, et la question irlandaise." *Etudes Anglaises* 39.4 (1986): 424–37.

Beckett, Samuel. *The Collected Shorter Plays of Samuel Beckett*. New York: Grove Weidenfeld, 1984.

————. *Proust*. 1931. *The Collected Works of Samuel Beckett*. New York: Grove, 1970.

Bensky, Lawrence M. "Harold Pinter: An Interview." *Paris Review* 39 [1967]: 13–37. (Rpt. in *Writers at Work; The Paris Review Interviews*. 3rd series. New York: Viking, 1967. 347–68. Also rpt. in *Pinter: A Collection of Critical Essays*. Twentieth Century Views. Englewood Cliffs: Prentice-Hall, 1972. 19–33.)

Bentley, Eric. "The Science Fiction of Bertolt Brecht." Introduction. *Galileo*. By Bertolt Brecht. Trans. Charles Laughton. New York: Grove, 1966. 9–42.

Bettmann, Otto. "Bach the Rhetorician." *The American Scholar* 55.1 (1985/86): 113–18.

Brereton, Geoffrey. *Jean Racine: A Critical Biography*. London: Cassell, 1951.

Brustein, Robert. "Picketing His Own Play," *New York Times* 7 Jan. 73, sec. 2: 1, 5.

Bunyan, John. *The Pilgrim's Progress*. London: Penguin, 1987.

Burkman, Katherine H. *The Dramatic World of Harold Pinter: Its Basis in Ritual*. [Columbus]: Ohio State Univ. Press, 1971.

Butler, Michael. *The Plays of Max Frisch*. New York: St. Martin's, 1985.

Cabanne, Pierre. *The Brothers Duchamp: Jacques Villon, Raymond Duchamp-Villon, Marcel Duchamp*. Trans. Helga Harrison and Dinah Harrison. Boston: New York Graphic Soc., 1976.

————. *Dialogues with Marcel Duchamp*. Trans. Ron Padgett. New York: Viking, 1971.

Cage, John. *Roaratorio; Ein irischer Circus über Finnegans Wake; An Irish Circus on Finnegans Wake*. ed. Klaus Schöning. Königstein/Ts: Athenäum, 1982.

Cahn, Victor L. *Gender and Power in the Plays of Harold Pinter*. New York: St. Martin's, 1993.

Christ, William, et al. *Materials and Structure of Music*. 2nd ed. Vol. 2. Englewood Cliffs: Prentice-Hall, 1973. 2 vols.

Chute, Marchette. *Ben Jonson of Westminster*. 1953. New York: Dutton, 1960.

Cleveland, Louise O. "Trials in the Soundscape: The Radio Plays of Samuel Beckett." *Modern Drama* 11.3 (1968): 267–82.

Conley, John, ed. *The Middle English Pearl: Critical Essays*. Notre Dame: Univ. of Notre Dame Press, 1970.

Cooke, Deryck. *The Language of Music*. Oxford Univ. Press, 1959.

Cory, Mark Ensign. *The Emergence of an Acoustical Art Form: An Analysis of the German Experimental Hörspiel of the 1960's*. University of Nebraska Studies ns 45 (1974).

Dahlhaus, Carl. *Schoenberg and the New Music*. Trans. Derrick Puffett and Alfred Clayton. Cambridge: Cambridge Univ. Press, 1987.

D'Arcy, Margaretta. Author's Preface (2). *The Island of the Mighty*, by John Arden with Margaretta D'Arcy. London: Eyre Methuen, 1973 and 1974.

d'Harnoncourt, Anne. Introduction. d'Harnoncourt and McShine 34–45.

d'Harnoncourt, Anne, and Walter Hopps. Etant donnés: 1° la chute d'eau 2° le gaz d'éclairage: *Reflections on a New Work by Marcel Duchamp*. Philadelphia: Philadelphia Museum of Art, 1969.

d'Harnoncourt, Anne, and Kynaston McShine, eds. *Marcel Duchamp*. New York: The Museum of Modern Art and Philadelphia Museum of Art, 1973.

Diamond, Elin. *Pinter's Comic Play*. Lewisburg: Bucknell Univ. Press; London: Associated Univ. Presses, 1985.

Doane, Mary Ann. "Sound Editing and Mixing." *Film Sound: Theory and Practice*. Ed. Elisabeth Weis and John Belton. New York: Columbia Univ. Press, 1985. 54–62.

Donesky, Finlay. "Oppression, Resistance, and the Writer's Testament." *New Theatre Quarterly* 2.8 (1986): 336–44.

Drakakis, John, ed. *British Radio Drama*. Cambridge: Cambridge Univ. Press, 1981.

Duchamp, Marcel. *Salt Seller: The Writings of Marcel Duchamp (Marchand du Sel)*. Ed. Michel Sanouillet and Elmer Peterson. New York: Oxford Univ. Press, 1973.

Dunn, Tony. "Editorial." *Gambit; International Theatre Review* 11.41 (1984): 3–4.

———. "Interview with Howard Barker." *Gambit; International Theatre Review* 11.41 (1984): 33–44.

———. "Massacre of the Culpable." *Plays and Players* no. 372 (1984): 13–15.

Edgerton, Gary. "*Wings*: Radio Play Adapted to Experimental Stage." *Journal of Popular Culture* 16.4 (1983): 152–58.

Esslin, Martin. "Harold Pinter's Work for Radio." *Harold Pinter: Critical Approaches*. Ed. Steven H. Gale. Rutherford, NJ: Fairleigh Dickinson Univ. Press; London: Associated Univ. Presses, 1986. 47–63.

———. "Samuel Beckett and the Art of Broadcasting." *Mediations: Essays on Brecht, Beckett, and the Media*. 1980. London: Abacus, 1983. 125–54.

Etherton, Michael. *Contemporary Irish Dramatists*. Modern Dramatists. New York: St. Martin's, 1989.

Ferguson, Robert. *Transfigured Night*. Best Radio Plays of 1984. London: Methuen/BBC, 1985.

Fletcher, Beryl S., John Fletcher, Barry Smith, and Walter Bachem. *A Student's Guide to the Plays of Samuel Beckett*. London: Faber & Faber, 1978.

Frisch, Max. *The Fire Raisers*. Trans. Michael Bullock. London: Eyre Methuen, 1962.

Frisch, Walter. "Schoenberg and the Poetry of Richard Dehmel." *Journal of the Arnold Schoenberg Institute* 9.2 (1986): 137–79.

Frost, Everett C. "Fundamental Sounds: Recording Samuel Beckett's Radio Plays." *Theatre Journal* 43.3 (1991): 361–76.

Frost, Everett C., and Margaret Herzfeld-Sander, eds. *German Radio Plays*. New York: Continuum, 1991.

Gaburo, Kenneth. "The Music in Samuel Beckett's *Play*." *The Review of Contemporary Fiction* 7.2 (1987): 76–84.

Gale, Steven H. *Butter's Going Up: A Critical Analysis of Harold Pinter's Work*. Durham: Duke Univ. Press, 1977.

Gielgud, Val. *British Radio Drama, 1922–1956: A Survey*. London: George G. Harrap, 1957.

Golding, John. *Marcel Duchamp: The Bride Stripped Bare by Her Bachelors, Even.* New York: Viking, 1973.

Gombrich, E. H. *Art and Illusion: A Study in the Psychology of Pictorial Representation.* First Princeton/Bollingen paperback ed. Bollingen Series 35. Princeton: Princeton Univ. Press, 1969.

Gould, Glenn. *The Glenn Gould Reader.* ed. Tim Page. New York: Knopf, 1984.

Grant, Steve. "Barker's Bite." *Plays and Players* 23.3 (1975): 36–39.

Gray, Frances. *John Arden.* New York: Grove, 1983.

Guralnick, Elissa S. Rev. of *German Radio Plays,* ed. Everett C. Frost and Margaret Herzfeld-Sander. *American Book Review* 13.6 (1992): 11–12.

Haftmann, Werner. *Painting in the Twentieth Century.* Vol. I. New York: Frederick A. Praeger, 1965. 2 vols.

Hamilton, Donna B. *Shakespeare and the Politics of Protestant England.* Lexington: Univ. Press of Kentucky, 1992.

Hay, Malcolm, and Simon Trussler. "Energy—and the Small Discovery of Dignity." *Theatre Quarterly* 10.40 (1981): 3–14.

Hayman, Ronald. *Harold Pinter.* New York: Frederick Ungar, 1973.

Heilman, Robert. "Demonic Strategies: *The Birthday Party* and *The Firebugs.*" *Sense and Sensibility in Twentieth-Century Writing; A Gathering in Memory of William Van O'Connor.* Ed. Brom Weber. Carbondale: Southern Illinois Univ. Press; London: Feffer & Simons, 1970. 57–74.

Hobson, Harold. "Rough Waters for Arden, Osborne Plays," *Christian Science Monitor* 8 Dec. 1972: 4.

Hull, John M. *Touching the Rock: An Experience of Blindness.* New York: Pantheon, 1990.

Hunt, Albert. *Arden: A Study of His Plays.* London: Eyre Methuen, 1974.

Inglis, Brian. *Roger Casement.* London: Hodder and Stoughton, 1973.

Irvine, William and Park Honan. *The Book, The Ring, and the Poet.* New York: McGraw-Hill, 1974.

Itzin, Catherine. *Stages in the Revolution: Political Theatre in Britain since 1968.* London: Eyre Methuen, 1980.

Jenkins, Anthony. *The Theatre of Tom Stoppard.* Cambridge: Cambridge Univ. Press, 1987.

Kelley, Margot Anne. "Order within Fragmentation: Postmodernism and the Stroke Victim's World." *Modern Drama* 34.3 (1991): 383–91.

Kelly, Katherine E. "Tom Stoppard's *Artist Descending a Staircase*: Outdoing the 'Dada' Duchamp." *Comparative Drama* 20.3 (1986): 191–200.

Kennedy, Andrew K. *Samuel Beckett.* Cambridge Univ. Press, 1989.

Kernan, Alvin B. *The Playwright as Magician: Shakespeare's Image of the Poet in the English Public Theater.* New Haven: Yale Univ. Press, 1979.

Kitchin, Laurence. "Arden." *Contemporary Dramatists.* Ed. James Vinson. 2nd ed. London: St. James; New York: St. Martin's, 1977. 44–48.

Kopit, Arthur. *Wings.* New York: Hill and Wang, 1978. Fifth printing, 1984.

Kramer, Lawrence. *Music and Poetry: The Nineteenth Century and After.* Berkeley: Univ. of California Press, 1984.

———. *Music as Cultural Practice, 1800–1900.* Berkeley: Univ. of California Press, 1990.

Krenek, Ernst. "Anton von Webern: A Profile." *Anton von Webern: Perspectives.* Comp. Hans Moldenhauer. Ed. Demar Irvine. Seattle: Univ. of Washington Press, 1966. 3–14.

Lambert, J. W. "The Man in the Black-and-White Suit," *Times Literary Supplement* 3 March 1978: 253.

Lewis, Peter, ed. *Radio Drama.* London and New York: Longman, 1981.

Longwell, Ann. "Barker at the Double." *Evening Standard* 4 Jan. 1990: 29.

MacColl, René. *Roger Casement.* Hamish Hamilton, 1956. London: A Four Square Book, 1960.

Mack, Maynard. "'Julius Caesar,'" *Modern Shakespearean Criticism: Essays on Style, Dramaturgy, and the Major Plays.* Ed. Alvin B. Kernan. New York: Harcourt, Brace & World, 1970. 290–301.

Mandel, Oscar. Letter. *PMLA* 106.1 (1991): 124–25.

Mandel, Siegfried. *Group 47: The Reflected Intellect.* Carbondale: Southern Illinois Univ. Press; London: Feffer & Simons, 1973.

Marks, Laurence. "Off-Beat Track." *London Observer* 21 Feb. 1988: 24.

Marquis, Alice Goldfarb. *Marcel Duchamp: Eros, C'est la Vie: A Biography.* Troy: Whitston, 1981.

Matisse, Paul. Translator's Note. *Marcel Duchamp, Notes.* Arr. and trans. Paul Matisse. Boston: Hall, 1983. No pagination.

McShine, Kynaston. "La vie en Rrose." d'Harnoncourt and McShine, 125–34.

McWhinnie, Donald. *The Art of Radio.* London: Faber and Faber, 1959.

Mercier, Vivian. *Beckett/Beckett.* New York: Oxford Univ. Press, 1977.

Miller, Jonathan. *States of Mind.* New York: Pantheon Books, 1983.

Monteith, Robert. *Casement's Last Adventure.* First limited ed. Privately printed: Chicago, 1932. Rev. ed. Dublin: Michael F. Moynihan, 1953.

Morrison, Kristin. *Canters and Chronicles: The Use of Narrative in the Plays of Samuel Beckett and Harold Pinter.* Univ. of Chicago Press, 1983.

Neubauer, John. *The Emancipation of Music from Language: Departure from Mimesis in Eighteenth-Century Aesthetics.* New Haven: Yale Univ. Press, 1986.

Ooi, Vicki C. H. "Edward Agonistes or Anagonistes? Theme and Structure of *A Slight Ache* by Harold Pinter." *Theatre Research International* ns 3.2 (1978): 133–48.

Orgel, Stephen. *The Jonsonian Masque.* Cambridge: Harvard Univ. Press, 1965.

Page, Malcolm, comp. *Arden on File.* London: Methuen, 1985.

———. *John Arden.* Boston: Twayne, 1984.

Pater, Walter. *The Renaissance: Studies in Art and Poetry.* 1873. Library ed. London: Macmillan, 1914.

Payne, Anthony. *Schoenberg.* Oxford Studies of Composers 5. London: Oxford Univ. Press, 1968.

Paz, Octavio. *Marcel Duchamp: Appearance Stripped Bare.* Trans. Rachel Phillips and Donald Gardner. New York: Viking, 1978.

——. "*Water Writes Always In* Plural." d'Harnoncourt and McShine, 143–58.

Peck, Ira. "Art, Politics and John Arden," *New York Times* 10 Apr. 1966, sec. 2: 1, 3.

Pinter, Harold. *A Slight Ache and Other Plays.* London: Eyre Methuen, 1968.

——. "Writing for the Theatre." *The New British Drama.* Ed. Henry Popkin. New York: Grove, 1964. 574–80.

Powlick, Leonard. "A Phenomenological Approach to Harold Pinter's *A Slight Ache.*" *Quarterly Journal of Speech* 60.1 (1974): 25–32.

Rabey, Ian. *British and Irish Political Drama in the Twentieth Century: Implicating the Audience.* New York: St. Martin's, 1986.

——. *Howard Barker: Politics and Desire: An Expository Study of his Drama and Poetry, 1969–87.* New York: St. Martin's, 1989.

Racine, Jean. *Athaliah. Complete Plays.* Vol. 2. Trans. Samuel Solomon. 2 vols. New York: Random House, 1967. 371–459.

Reid, B. L. *The Lives of Roger Casement.* New Haven and London: Yale Univ. Press, 1976.

Rich, Frank. "Story of Stroke Made Into a Musical." *New York Times* 10 March 1993: B1, 4.

Riggs, David. *Ben Jonson: A Life.* Cambridge, Mass: Harvard Univ. Press, 1989.

Ripley, John. Julius Caesar *on Stage in England and America, 1599–1973.* Cambridge: Cambridge Univ. Press, 1980.

Robertson, D. W., Jr. "The Heresy of *The Pearl.*" *Modern Language Notes* 65 (1950): 152–55. Rpt. in Conley. 291–96.

Rodger, Ian. *Radio Drama.* London: Macmillan, 1982.

Roseberry, C. R. *The Challenging Skies: The Colorful Story of Aviation's Most Exciting Years, 1919–1939.* Garden City: Doubleday, 1966.

Rosen, Carol. *Plays of Impasse: Contemporary Drama Set in Confining Institutions.* Princeton: Princeton Univ. Press, 1983.

Rosen, Charles. *Arnold Schoenberg.* Modern Masters. New York: Viking, 1975.

Rosen, William and Barbara. "*Julius Caesar:* 'The Specialty of Rule.'" *Twentieth Century Interpretations of Julius Caesar.* Ed. Leonard F. Dean. Englewood Cliffs: Prentice-Hall, 1968. 109–15.

Rudkin, David. *Ashes.* New York: Samuel French, 1974.

——. "The Chameleon & the Kilt: The Complexities of Roger Casement." *Encounter,* 41.2 (1973): 70–77.

——. *Cries From Casement As His Bones Are Brought To Dublin.* London: BBC, 1974.

——. *Penda's Fen.* London: Davis Poynter, 1975.

——. "Postface to 'Casement'—David Rudkin's Thoughts on His Play about Roger Casement, Broadcast on Sunday on Radio 3." *The Listener* 89.2289 (8 February 1973): 171–72.

——. "Thoughts on Staging the Play." *Cries from Casement* 81–84.

Saint Exupéry, Antoine de. *Wind, Sand and Stars.* Trans. Lewis Galantière. [New York]: Harcourt, Brace, 1940.

Sakellaridou, Elizabeth. *Pinter's Female Portraits: A Study of Female Characters in the Plays of Harold Pinter.* Totowa: Barnes and Noble, 1988.

Schiller, Friedrich von. *Wallenstein: A Historical Drama in Three Parts.* Trans. Charles E. Passage. Rev. ed. New York: Ungar, 1960.

Schoenberg, Arnold. "The Relationship to the Text." *Style and Idea: Selected Writings of Arnold Schoenberg.* Trans. Leo Black. Ed. Leon Stein. New York: St. Martins, 1975. 141–45.

Schwarz, Arturo. *The Complete Works of Marcel Duchamp.* New York: Abrams, 1970.

Shakespeare, William. *Hamlet.*

———. *Henry V.*

Sharpe, Lesley. *Friedrich Schiller: Drama, Thought and Politics.* Cambridge: Cambridge Univ. Press, 1991.

Siegel, Paul N. *Shakespeare's English and Roman History Plays: A Marxist Approach.* Rutherford, N.J.: Fairleigh Dickinson Univ. Press; London: Associated Univ. Presses, 1986.

Stoppard, Tom. *Artist Descending a Staircase. Four Plays for Radio.* London: Faber, 1984. 19–58.

———. *Artist Descending a Staircase.* London: Samuel French, 1988.

Sykes, Alrene. *Harold Pinter.* St. Lucia: Univ. of Queensland Press; New York: Humanities Press, 1970.

Taylor, David A. *Mind.* New York: Simon and Schuster, 1982.

Thomas, Dylan. *Under Milk Wood: A Play for Voices.* New York: New Directions, 1954.

Tomkins, Calvin. *The Bride and the Bachelors: The Heretical Courtship in Modern Art.* New York: Viking, 1965.

Tomkins, Calvin, and the editors of Time-Life Books. *The World of Marcel Duchamp, 1887–.* New York: Time, 1966.

Trussler, Simon. *The Plays of Harold Pinter: An Assessment.* London: Victor Gollancz, 1973.

———. "Trying to Break the Bounds of Cups and Saucers Naturalism," *The Stage and Television Today* 13 July 1978: 16.

Turnell, Martin. *Jean Racine, Dramatist.* New York: New Directions, 1972.

Weinraub, Bernard. "London: Power Play for Center Stage," *New York Times* 18 Dec. 72: 52.

Weiss, Peter. Note. *The Investigation.* Trans. Jon Swan and Ulu Grosbard. 1966. New York: Atheneum, 1977.

Wertheim, Albert. "Tearing of Souls: Harold Pinter's *A Slight Ache* on Radio and Stage." *Harold Pinter: Critical Approaches.* Ed. Steven H. Gale. Rutherford, NJ: Fairleigh Dickinson Univ. Press; London: Associated Univ. Presses, 1986. 64–71.

Whitaker, Thomas R. *Tom Stoppard.* New York: Grove, 1983.

Whitehead, Kate. *The Third Programme: A Literary History.* Oxford English Monographs. Oxford: Clarendon Press, 1989.

Winn, James Anderson. *Unsuspected Eloquence: A History of the Relations between Poetry and Music.* New Haven: Yale Univ. Press, 1981.

Worth, Katharine. "Beckett and the Radio Medium." *British Radio Drama.* Ed. John Drakakis. Cambridge Univ. Press, 1981.

Wymark, Olwyn. *The Child. Best Radio Plays of 1979.* London: Eyre
Methuen/BBC, 1980.

Zilliacus, Clas. *Beckett and Broadcasting: A Study of the Works of Samuel
Beckett For and In Radio and Television. Acta Academiae Aboensis* ser. A,
Humaniora, 51: 2. Åbo: Åbo Akademi, 1976.

# Index